GW00992267

SEX, RACE AND

SAGE CONTEMPORARY CRIMINOLOGY

Series editors

John Lea ● Roger Matthews ● Geoffrey Pearson ● Jock Young
Centre for Criminology, Middlesex Polytechnic

Sage Contemporary Criminology draws on the best of current work in criminology and socio-legal studies, both in Britain and internationally, to provide lecturers, students and policy-makers with the latest research on the functioning of the criminal justice and legal systems. Individual titles will cover a wide span of issues such as new developments in informal justice; changing forms of policing and crime prevention; the impact of crime in the inner city; and the role of the legal system in relation to social divisions by gender and race. Throughout, the series will relate theoretical problems in the social analysis of deviancy and social control to the practical and policy-related issues in criminology and law.

SEX, RACE AND THE LAW

Legislating for Equality

Jeanne Gregory

⑤ SAGE Publications
London ● Newbury Park ● Beverly Hills ● New Delhi

SAGE Publications Ltd
28 Banner Street
London EC1Y 8QE

SAGE Publications India Pvt Ltd
C–236 Defence Colony
New Delhi 110 024

SAGE Publications Inc
2111 West Hillcrest Street
Newbury Park, California 9132

SAGE Publications Inc
275 South Beverly Drive
Beverly Hills, California

British Library Cataloguing in Publication Data

Gregory, Jeanne
  Sex, race and the law: legislating for
  equality. — (Contemporary criminology;
  vol. 1).
  1. Race discrimination — Law and legislation
  — Great Britain 2. Sex Discrimination —
  Law and legislation — Great Britain
  I. Title II. Series
  344.102'87   KD4095

ISBN 0-8039-8106-6
ISBN 0-8039-8107-4 Pbk

Library of Congress catalog card number 87-061622

Phototypeset by Fakenham Photosetting Ltd, Fakenham, Norfolk
Printed in Great Britain by J.W. Arrowsmith Ltd, Bristol.

Contents

Tables

Appendices

Acknowledgements

I should like to thank Paul Rock and Leonard Leigh who supervised the thesis which preceded this book for their advice, guidance and support and Rosemary Nixon and Nicola Harris at Sage for their constructive comments and encouragement. Without doubt, the most rewarding aspect of researching the material for this book has been the people I have met and the new friends I have made. I should like to thank all my friends, new and old, who have helped in a variety of ways, especially Christine Jackson, Sadie Robarts, Alice Leonard, Richard Kuper, Paddy Stamp, Corinne Sweet, Eric Robinson, Catherine Hoskyns, Elizabeth Meehan, Evelyn Ellis, Maureen Kingman, Victoria Greenwood, Shaista Faruqui and Jill Grainger.

Abbreviations used in case citations

AC	Appeal Court
All E R	All England Law Reports
Ch.	Chancery division
COIT	Central Office of Industrial Tribunals (unreported cases)
EAT	Employment Appeal Tribunal (unreported cases)
ICR	Industrial Cases Reports
IRLR	Industrial Relations Law Reports
KB	King's Bench
US	United States (Supreme Court decisions)
WLR	Weekly Law Reports

For Brian, Sue and Rick

Introduction

The purpose of this book is to bring together the experience and knowledge of practitioners and researchers working in the field of discrimination law in order to assess its achievements and limitations. Most discussions of discrimination law focus on either sex or race, with an occasional glance at developments in the other jurisdiction. There is much to be gained from attempting a systematic comparison between the two, in order to provide a more complete account of the strengths and weaknesses of the legislation. As the Labour government considered it appropriate to construct an almost identical statutory framework for combating race and sex discrimination, the case law developments in the two areas are inextricably linked. However, the decision to look at both sex and race discrimination law does not imply that the two forms of discrimination are identical. Indeed, as the case law unfolds, it becomes increasingly apparent that the structures of disadvantage are very different for the two groups.

Legislating for equality

The post-war campaign for sex equality focused initially on the most obvious manifestation of inequality: the existence of separate rates of pay for men and women doing the same work.[1] Resolutions in support of equal pay were passed regularly at annual conferences of the Trades Union Congress (TUC) from 1888 onwards, although in practice many unions were hostile or ambivalent towards the idea. A campaign on equal pay did not fit well with wage negotiations based on the ideal of the 'family wage': a wage adequate for maintaining a family and giving the wife the 'right' to stay at home. As an increasing number of married women entered the labour market during and after the Second World War, some trade unions began to adopt a more positive view of equal pay.

A Royal Commission on Equal Pay, set up in 1944 in response to wartime pressures, produced an unsympathetic and indecisive report. Its positive recommendations were confined to the area of non-manual employment in the public sector and it was in these areas (the civil service, local government, nationalized industries, the national health service and teaching) that the first equal pay campaigns were successfully fought. Women in the private sector were less well organized, more likely to be casual workers or subjected to job segregation. However, a number of women workers in industry began expressing resentment and were increasingly prepared to take action to rectify the inequalities. The best publicized of the 'equal pay' strikes was the one at Ford, discussed below. In 1961, the TUC asked the government to comply with the International Labour Organization's (ILO) Convention on equal pay for work of equal value and also pointed out that if Britain were to join the European Economic Community (EEC), Article 119 of the Treaty of Rome required 'equal pay for equal work'.[2]

The employers' association, the Confederation of British Industry (CBI), was less enthusiastic. When consulted by the government on the content of the legislation, they argued for a narrow definition of equal pay using the formula 'equal pay for the same work' and asked that industry be given seven years to implement the changes. The TUC had considered that two years would be sufficient. Barbara Castle, Minister at the Department of Employment (Ministry of Labour), compromised on both issues. She argued that the ILO definition was too abstract to embody in legislation; entitlement to equal pay was therefore restricted to women employed on like work or broadly similar work with a man in the same employment, or on work rated as equivalent under a job evaluation scheme.[3] On the question of implementation, she felt that five and a half years would give even those employers most affected by the legislation sufficient time to adapt (Parliamentary Debates, House of Commons, Vol. 795, cols. 914–29). Passed in 1970, the Equal Pay Act was to take effect in 1975. In 1973 Britain signed the Treaty of Rome and the scene was set for a clash between the British government and the European Commission over conflicting definitions of equal pay.

In the mid-1970s, the Labour government confirmed its commitment to equality by introducing two further measures on equal rights: the Sex Discrimination Act 1975 (which included the Equal Pay Act 1970 as a separate schedule and came into force on the same day) and the Race Relations Act 1976. Like the equal pay legislation, the anti-discrimination laws were the product of years of campaigning, both inside and outside parliament.[4] For women, the measures which took effect in 1975 were the first major legislative developments on sex equality since the period immediately following the end of the First World War, when they had won the right to vote and to hold public office (see below, Ch. 1). For men and women from racial minority groups, the 1976 Act was the third attempt in just over a decade to provide them with an effective form of redress against racial discrimination; two earlier Acts, passed in 1965 and 1968, had proved ineffectual.

The sex and race equality campaigns cannot fully be understood in isolation from each other. The relatively sophisticated measures on sex equality were a direct result of its association in legal minds with the need to strengthen the law on racial equality. The introduction of the Sex Discrimination Act in 1975 provided an ideal opportunity to test the climate of opinion and rehearse the arguments before introducing an almost identical set of measures on racial discrimination the following year.

These two parallel pieces of legislation have remained the backbone of British civil rights law for more than a decade.[5] Apart from the changes required to bring us into line with EEC law, the government has not considered it necessary to amend the legislation, despite a growing body of evidence that the laws are not working as effectively as expected. The Commissions responsible for enforcing and monitoring the legislation have drawn attention to these difficulties and suggested some amendments; so far, the government has not responded.[6]

Discrimination in employment
The 1970s equality laws are not exclusively concerned with employment discrimination: they also encompass discrimination in education and in the provision of goods, facilities and services. It is, however, the employment provisions that provide the central focus for this book. Although most of the legal and administrative activity has occurred in the area of employment, there are few signs that this concentration of effort is about to bear fruit. The evidence for such an assertion can be found in the government's own statistics.

As far as women's employment is concerned, the majority of women workers are to be found in a small number of occupations. They tend to be employed in the catering or service industries; they work as cleaners, hairdressers, shop assistants or clerical workers, or they are involved in repetitive assembly or packaging work. They are also over-represented within the education, welfare and health occupations. Within each occupation, they are heavily concentrated in the lower grades. Consequently, women's average hourly earnings are less than three-quarters of those of male workers, a situation that has changed very little during the last decade (see Ch. 1, Table 1.2). When translated into cash, this means that women in full-time work now receive on average £1 an hour less than full-time male workers. The proportion of women in part-time work has risen steadily over the years, so that 46 percent of the female labour force is now employed on a part-time basis.[7]

Black workers have fared no better and are evidently bearing the brunt of the recession, with an unemployment rate almost twice that of the white workforce. According to the Labour Force Survey, in 1984 the unemployment rate stood at 11½ percent for white males, at 29 percent for men of West Indian origin and at 34 percent for men who classified themselves as of Pakistani or Bangladeshi origin. For women, the contrast is even more striking, with unemployment rates for the three ethnic groups running at 10 percent, 17 percent and 40 percent respectively (*Employment Gazette*, December 1985: 467). A similar pattern of unemployment was revealed in a survey undertaken by the Policy Studies Institute (PSI). The author of the study explains the very high rate of unemployment of Asian women in terms of their concentration in manufacturing industry, particularly textile and clothing, where the effects of the economic recession have been particularly severe. The same survey showed that black people who were unemployed had been without jobs for a longer period of time than white unemployed workers; the high proportion of Asian and West Indian women who had never succeeded in obtaining a job was particularly striking (Brown, 1984: 154–6).

Those racial minority workers who do find jobs are mostly trapped in low-paid, low-status work and are rarely employed in a supervisory capacity. The men are to be found in manufacturing, distribution, transport and communications, rather than in public administration, financial services, or professional and scientific occupations. The pattern for women is similar, except for the large numbers of West Indian women employed by the National Health Service (Brown, 1984: 159–60). There is no evidence that this pattern of segregation is beginning to shift; on the contrary, it is becoming entrenched and self-perpetuating. Undeterred by the legislation, employers continue to discriminate against black job applicants as frequently as ever. A research study conducted in 1984 involved white, Asian and West Indian people who, carefully matched for qualifications, age, and sex, posed as job applicants. Comparing their results with earlier studies conducted along similar lines, the researchers found that there had been no reduction in levels of racial discrimination since 1974 and that at least one-third of the employers included in the study discriminated against black job applicants. They concluded that on a 'conservative estimate', there must be 'tens of thousands of acts of racial discrimination in job recruitment every year' (Brown and Gay, 1985: 31).

A possible response to this information would be to campaign for the repeal of the Sex Discrimination Act 1975 and the Race Relations Act 1976, on the grounds that their only function is to create the illusion that the problem of discrimination is in hand, thereby stifling effective action. A more constructive response, the one to be adopted in this book, involves taking a closer look at how the laws are operating in practice, so that we can discover precisely why they are so ineffective. Armed with this information, it should become possible to develop a strategy for tackling all forms of discrimination, working both inside and outside the legislation.

Evaluating the equality laws
The first task is to examine the concept of equality enshrined within discrimination law and to consider the ways in which its application to women and to racial minorities differs. There are two different strategies for achieving equality. The first insists on formal equality, so that the disadvantages of sex and race are ignored and everyone is treated in an identical fashion. The concept of formal equality is both sex blind and colour blind and so simply reinforces the substantive (i.e. material) inequalities that exist in reality. The second approach recognizes this limitation and seeks to overcome it by compensating for the social disadvantages suffered by certain groups. The search for substantive equality unearths a new set of problems by focusing on the material reality of people's lives; as different groups compete for the recognition of substantive differences, the concept is potentially divisive and in direct conflict with the idea of formal equality.

In the first three chapters, these ideas are explored on the basis of a comparison between British and American experiences with equality legislation, partly because the issues are brought sharply into focus in the context of American history and case law, and partly because the British legislation was quite explicitly drafted on the basis of developments in American case law. The central argument of Chapter 1 is that although the battle for formal equality has been relatively successful, the structures of disadvantage remain intact. Most of the historical and legislative material used to demonstrate the limits of formal equality is drawn from the campaign for sex equality. Yet it is precisely the irrelevance of this campaign when viewed from the perspective of black people that serves to underline its limitations. Employment segregation on the basis of race and sex persists. In the case of women it is acknowledged and partially controlled through equal pay legislation; for black workers it is condemned but then largely ignored.

Chapters 2 and 3 look at two different experiments with substantive equality embodied in the British equality laws, both of which have their origins in the United States. The first is the concept of indirect discrimination, which goes some way towards recognizing the existence of institutionalized discrimination. Unfortunately, it does not go far enough. It is contradicted by the dominant ideology of the legislation, which depends on the identification of an individual victim and an individual discriminator: an ideology with which the judiciary is much more at home. The second experiment with substantive equality is equally tentative: the positive action provisions operate within carefully prescribed limits and contain no element of compulsion. Ostensibly aimed at dismantling the barriers which prevent women and black workers from moving into the full range of jobs in proportion to their numbers in the workforce, positive action programmes as presently conceived in Britain can do little more than chip away at the edges of the problem. Although formal equality remains the dominant theme of the British civil rights legislation, it is the minor themes, contained within the notions of indirect discrimination and positive action, which acknowledge the deep historical and structural roots of discrimination and so contain the greatest potential for effective action.

Strengthening the commitment to substantive measures is only half the battle. Equally important is the removal of the procedural obstacles which hinder effective enforcement. Chapters 4 and 5 take a closer look at the processes of individual litigation, overshadowed by the unequal power relationship between worker and employer. A comparison with the experiences of unfair dismissal applicants reveals the extent to which the factors of class, sex and race combine to produce a low success rate for those who seek to enforce their legal rights. Strategies for reducing the imbalance of power and moderating the effects of the managerial prerogative are considered.

In Chapters 6 and 7 the spotlight turns on the two Commissions, the Equal Opportunities Commission and the Commission for Racial Equality. Given a wide-ranging brief, the Commissions were created for the purpose of launching a systematic attack on those institutions which perpetuate sexual and racial inequality. In comparison with the more limited and haphazard processes of individual litigation, their potential for achievement seemed promising. Yet after some ten years of existence, their impact has been minimal. They have become convenient whipping posts; frequently ignored by government, undermined by the courts and criticized by disillusioned civil rights campaigners. An attempt is made to identify the sources of these difficulties and to consider the measures that would be necessary to rectify them.

This book is addressed to all those who refuse to dismiss the equality laws as nothing more than a confidence trick; to those who do not accept that the victims of discrimination need necessarily wait until 'after the revolution' for an improvement in their situation; and to those who believe that it is important to draw attention to any gap that exists between the declared intentions of the legislators and the law in action. Drawing attention to the gap is one thing; taking steps to close it is another matter altogether. The path to social justice is strewn with obstacles of varying size and complexity. Some could be removed with very little effort, as they would entail little more than minor administrative or legislative adjustments. Others are more intractable; their removal would require a major act of recognition and commitment on the part of the politicians and the judiciary. The rest are insurmountable, as their future is inextricably linked with that of capitalism itself. Having identified the obstacles, it should become possible to reassess the potential role of legislation in establishing a non-sexist, non-racist society.

The Ford dispute: going beyond the law
In 1968, the women who worked as sewing machinists at Ford's River Plant in Dagenham went on strike to protest against the implementation of a new wage structure. Although the blatantly discriminatory category 'women' was to be abolished, the sewing machinists claimed that the new scheme perpetuated sex discrimination by placing them in Grade B, the lowest production grade. They argued that the machining of car seat covers required considerable skill, dexterity and experience; so that the only explanation for the Grade B rating was that the work was invariably performed by women.

The discrimination was compounded by the failure of the new job evaluation scheme to give women equal pay within Grade B; the women's rate was set at 85 percent of the appropriate male rate. The management at Ford, anxious to avoid any challenge to the pay agreement so recently concluded with the trade union negotiating committee, redefined the strike as an 'equal pay' dispute. The unions and the media were attracted to this idea and the transformation from local issue to national campaign was accomplished.

After four and a half weeks Barbara Castle intervened. She invited the strike committee to the Ministry and, over cups of tea, announced her intention to introduce equal pay legislation. The women agreed to return to work for 92 percent of the male rate; the grading issue was to be dealt with by a Court of Inquiry. The eventual outcome of these deliberations was that the women remained in Grade B.

Barbara Castle did not forget her promise to the women at Ford and yet ironically, despite the fanfare and trumpets, the Act that was passed proved to be irrelevant for the group of women who ostensibly provided its inspiration. A woman wishing to claim equal pay had to compare herself with a man employed on the same or 'broadly similar' work. As a consequence of job segregation, there were no men employed on similar work whom the sewing machinists could use as comparators. Seven more years were to elapse before the

European Court of Justice stepped in to declare that the British government had not fulfilled its obligations under the law of the European Economic Community.[8]

As a consequence of the European Court judgment, the government amended the legislation by introducing the Equal Pay (Amendment) Regulations, which made it possible for women whose work was undervalued to claim that their jobs had the same value as those performed by men. Soon after the new regulations came into operation in January 1984, some of the Ford sewing machinists filed an application for equal pay under the amended regulations, claiming that their work was of equal value to that of the Eastman cutters, headliners and welders, all of whom were men. An industrial tribunal dismissed the claim, holding that there were no reasonable grounds for determining that the 1968 job evaluation scheme was discriminatory. Sixteen years after their initial protest, the sewing machinists went on strike again. Their union, the Transport and General Workers' Union (TGWU), brought the issue to a head by refusing to sign the annual pay agreement with the Ford management until action was taken on the women's grievance. The management agreed to refer the matter to an independent job evaluation panel. The ensuing report provided a complete vindication of the women's claim. Using the evaluation system established in 1968, the arbitration panel uprated the sewing machinists' work by 27 points. The women were at last moved from Grade B to Grade C; indeed, they were only three points short of Grade D.

The experience of the sewing machinists provides a classic example of the difficulties that workers encounter when attempting to use the law in order to challenge discrimination in the workplace. For the women at Ford, the equal pay legislation must have looked like a massive diversion, promising a great deal and delivering nothing. In the end, it was through collective action and not through litigation that a successful outcome was achieved. Even so, the legislation did provide an important frame of reference for those involved in the battle for equal pay. Legal action and collective action are not mutually exclusive; in order to obtain maximum benefit for a particular group, it is often necessary to use a combination of both. In the Ford case, there can be no doubt that the equal value regulations provided the inspiration both for the TGWU's intervention and for the deliberations of the arbitration panel.

Notes

1. A similar pattern of events occurred in the United States. Equal Pay Bills were introduced in every Congress from 1945 onwards. An Equal Pay Act was eventually

passed in 1963, just one year before the passing of a wide-ranging and comprehensive measure against discrimination: the Civil Rights Act 1964.

2. The International Labour Organization (ILO) was established after the First World War and is now part of the United Nations. The British government has ratified a number of the ILO Conventions, including (in 1971) the one on equal pay. The government has chosen to 'de-ratify' some of the Conventions in recent years, thereby freeing itself to develop policies in breach of those Conventions (see Wedderburn, 1986: 15–16). Article 119, together with the EEC directives on equal pay and equal treatment, are given in Appendix 2. For an excellent discussion of the relationship between British and Common Market law see Rights of Women Europe, 1983.

3. The key provisions of the equal pay legislation are given in Appendix 3.

4. These campaigns are examined in more detail in Chapter 2. See also Meehan (1985) on the campaigns for laws on sex equality; Lester and Bindman (1972) and Lea (1980) on the background to the 1960s race relations legislation.

5. Some of the major provisions of the Sex Discrimination Act 1975 and the Race Relations Act 1976 are given in Appendix 4. Neither the SDA nor the RRA applies in Northern Ireland (see SDA 1975 s 87 and RRA 1976 s 80). However, an equivalent law on sex discrimination and equal pay does have effect in Northern Ireland: the Sex Discrimination (Northern Ireland) Order, S I no 1042 (NI 15). Northern Ireland also has the Fair Employment Act 1976, which is concerned with employment discrimination on grounds of religion and political opinion. This last piece of legislation is outside the scope of the present book.

6. The Equal Opportunities Commission (EOC) first produced a set of proposals for amending the equal pay and sex discrimination laws in 1981. Subsequently, the EOC abandoned those proposals and started afresh with a consultative document entitled *Legislating for Change? Review of the Sex Discrimination Legislation*. The Commission for Racial Equality began with a consultative paper in 1983 and followed this with a firmer set of proposals: *Review of the Race Relations Act 1976: Proposals for Change*, published two years later. See Appendix 5 for summaries of the most recent contributions from these two Commissions. In 1982, the Northern Ireland EOC published its recommendations for amending the Equal Pay Act and the following year made some proposals regarding the Sex Discrimination Order. (See EOC (NI) June 1982, March 1983.)

7. The information on women's employment is taken from the *New Earnings Survey*, 1970–1985, Part E Table 138, and from the *Employment Gazette*, April 1985 and January 1986. It is re-presented in a convenient form, together with other useful statistical information, in EOC, *Women and Men in Britain, a Statistical Profile*, HMSO, 1986. See also the report of the 1980 Women and Employment survey by Martin and Roberts (1984).

8. The EEC Equal Pay Directive, adopted in 1975, referred to 'equal pay for work of equal value' and so was broader in scope than the Equal Pay Act (see Appendix 2). For a report of the case against the British government, see Commission of the European Communities v United Kingdom of Great Britain and Northern Ireland [1982] IRLR 333.

1 Separate and unequal:
the limits of formal equality

The passivity of the common law

Equality before the law is a formal concept, not a principle which entitles the courts to restrain the strong from oppressing the weak. Its symbolic representation is the figure of justice wearing a blindfold, promising a rational and predictable framework of adjudication within which competitive individualism can flourish. Such a system of law does not undermine existing inequalities of wealth and power, but rather confirms them; so that oppressed groups seeking equal treatment on the basis of common law doctrines have frequently been disappointed. The existence of a written constitution, as in the United States, seems to make little practical difference, except that it becomes more difficult for the judges to blur the issues.

Between 1865 and 1870, three crucial amendments were added to the American Constitution. The thirteenth amendment abolished slavery, the fourteenth guaranteed the equal protection of state laws to all United States citizens and the fifteenth confirmed the right of all citizens to vote, regardless of race, colour or previous status as slaves. Despite this clear declaration of public policy, the American Supreme Court reacted with suspicion and hostility towards legislation inspired by these amendments. In 1875 Congress passed a Civil Rights Act making it illegal to discriminate against members of racial groups in the provision of public accommodations. Eight years later, the Supreme Court declared the Act to be unconstitutional. The Court held that such a law could not be authorized by the thirteenth amendment because:

> It would be running the slavery argument into the ground to make it apply to every act of discrimination which a person may see fit to make. (Civil Rights Cases 109 US 3 [1883])

Nor was it authorized by the fourteenth amendment which referred to state action, not to individual acts of discrimination. Similarly, in the notorious Plessey v Ferguson case (163 US 537 [1897]), the Court held that the provision of 'separate but equal' facilities for different racial groups satisfied the constitutional requirement for equal protection. Presidential initiative in the appointment of Supreme Court judges, combined with wider political and social pressures, eventually produced a judiciary more sympathetic to government policies. The judges began to make such statements as: 'Distinctions between citizens solely because of their ancestry are by their very nature odious to a free people whose institutions are founded upon the doctrine of equality' (Hirabayashi v United States of America, 320 US 81 [1943]) and: 'all legal restrictions which curtail the civil rights of a single racial group are immediately suspect' (Korematsu v United States of America, 323 US 214 [1944]). Despite this strong language, the plaintiffs lost in both cases, which concerned the rights of Japanese–Americans. The Court recognized the 'compelling state interest' of the government during wartime. After the war, judicial scrutiny of racial classifications intensified, culminating in the unequivocal rejection of the 'separate but equal' doctrine.[1]

At the same time as the equal protection rights of minority groups were strengthening, so the need for them declined with the proliferation of state laws against discrimination. Then in 1964 Congress attempted to secure the rights of all citizens by passing a comprehensive Civil Rights Act, a product of intensive protest and racial violence. It became law against the background of marches, sit-ins and the assassination of President Kennedy, its original sponsor. It was passed by a deeply divided Congress after hundreds of hours of debate and numerous amendments.

In Britain, the judges were if anything even more reluctant than their American counterparts to interpret the common law in order to protect individual freedom. For example, although judges were aware that colonial slavery conflicted with British notions of liberty, they held back from decisions that might have threatened the slave trade. Lester and Bindman (1972) examine several cases decided by the Judicial Committee of the Privy Council, in its role as Supreme Court of Appeal for the British Colonies, and discover that:

> legal issues affecting the rights and the liberties of individuals and minorities are treated as linguistic problems to be solved within a moral vacuum.
> (Lester and Bindman, 1972: 39–40)

The technical language used by the judges masked their susceptibility to arguments based on expediency and rooted in prejudice.

A brief examination of some leading cases before the English courts in the period preceding the enactment of the race relations legislation serves to illustrate the combined effects of the common law and judicial timidity. In Weinberger v Inglis ([1919] AC 606), the House of Lords endorsed the right of the Committee of the Stock

Exchange to deprive a man of his membership solely because of his German origins. They chose not to interfere with the Committee's discretion, nor to use the British Nationality and Status of Aliens Act 1914 as evidence that public policy required equality of treatment.[2] In Horne v Poland ([1922] 2 KB 364), the Court allowed the underwriters of an insurance policy to escape their liabilities on the grounds that the insured person had not disclosed his national origins. The underwriters had not specifically required the man to disclose this information and yet the court accepted it as a relevant material fact. In Constantine v Imperial Hotels Ltd ([1944] 1 KB 693), Learie Constantine made use of the common law provision that innkeepers must receive all travellers unless they have reasonable grounds for refusal. He won his claim for damages against the hotel that operated a colour bar against him and his family. This was hailed as a great triumph in legal circles, although he was only awarded the derisory sum of five guineas. Then in Scala Ballroom (Wolverhampton) Ltd v Ratcliffe ([1958] 3 All ER 220), the Court supported the right of the proprietors to maintain a colour bar 'in their own business interests' and also the right of the Musicians' Union to protect its members' interests by persuading them not to perform at the ballroom. This decision meant that discriminatory clauses and actions covering a wide range of activities could be legally justified in terms of self-interest.

With the judges unable or unwilling to provide relief, it has fallen to the politicians to take a stand against discrimination. At first, legislators assumed that a clear statement of public policy would be enough to eradicate the evils of discrimination and only later began to appreciate the difficulties in formulating effective legislative measures.

The battle for formal equality
Historically, women and black people have been regarded as the property of their masters and denied an independent legal identity. With the abolition of slavery, racial discrimination did not disappear but, with the passing of time, assumed a more insidious shape, less susceptible to direct legal challenge. Discrimination against women remained both legally and socially acceptable for a longer period; it was (and still is) rooted in commonly held views of the 'natural' and appropriate roles for men and women.

For women, black and white, American and British, the campaign for legal equality was complicated by their explicit exclusion from the common law doctrine that all men were equal in the eyes of the law. The clearest expression of the legal subordination of women was to be found in marital law:

> By marriage, the husband and wife are one person in law: that is, the very being or legal existence of the woman is suspended during marriage, or at least is incorporated and consolidated into that of the husband under whose wing, protection and cover she performs everything. (Blackstone, 1765, Book 1: 430)

This patriarchal principle was kept very much alive by the judges, who repeatedly excluded women from the category of 'persons' and at the same time presented this exclusion as a privilege. In 1868 substantive arguments were employed to deny British women the right to vote:

> in this country ... chiefly out of respect to women, and a sense of decorum, and not from their want of intellect ... they have been excused from taking any share in this department of public affairs.[3]

Only after a prolonged and bitter political campaign were positive legislative steps taken to change the legal status of women. In 1918 women over thirty were given the vote and ten years later this was extended to women over twenty-one. The Sex Disqualification Removal Act of 1919 enabled women to hold public office. Despite the clear shift in public policy embodied in these pieces of legislation, the judges still dragged their feet. In 1923, the House of Lords refused to allow a Lady who had inherited a peerage to take her seat and they continued to exclude women for more than forty years. Also in the 1920s, a regulation requiring women teachers to resign on marriage was held to be reasonable and lawful, but a local authority which awarded equal pay to its women workers was found to have exceeded its powers. As far as the judge was concerned, the concept of equal pay was a form of political extremism:

> The council would, in my view, fail in their duty if, in administering funds which did not belong to their members alone, they ... allowed themselves to be guided ... by some eccentric principles of socialist philanthropy, or by a feminist ambition to secure equality of the sexes in the matter of wages in the world of labour. (Roberts v Hopwood [1925] AC 578)[4]

However, the judiciary were not wholly immune to the shift in political climate. In 1929 the Judicial Committee of the Privy Council finally broke the circular argument which denied women access to positions of power (in this case, in the Canadian Senate) on grounds of historical practice. Lord Sankey declared that the word 'person' did include women and that the burden of proving otherwise lay with those who wished to exclude them (Edwards v Attorney General for Canada [1930] AC 124).

In formal terms, women had achieved a major victory. Parliament had removed the major legal disabilities and the judiciary had admitted women to the category of 'persons'. For many campaigners for women's rights, the battle was won and the foundations laid for women to move into the full range of traditionally male activities and occupations. The experiences of the Second World War temporarily reinforced this view, as women were positively encouraged to assist the war effort by moving into previously all-male forms of employment. As soon as the war was over, the day nurseries were closed and the restrictions on female employment reimposed. During the period of post-war reconstruction, traditional views of appropriate male and female roles were re-established. The welfare state was created on the basis of strengthening existing family patterns; the gap between the ideal of formal equality and the realities of substantive inequality widened (see Riley, 1979; Wilson, 1980).

In the United States, a similar pattern of events occurred. Despite the constitutional commitment to equal protection, it required a new amendment (the nineteenth, added to the Constitution in 1920) to give women the vote. It declared that: 'The right to vote shall not be abridged on account of sex'. As in Britain, the courts chose to restrict the application of the new policy. For example, it was held that voting rights did not imply the right to jury service:

It is unthinkable that those who first framed and selected the words for the statute had any design that it should ever include women in its scope. When they used the word 'person' to describe those liable for jury service, no-one contemplated the possibility of women becoming so qualified. (Commonwealth v Welosky 276 Mass 398, 284 US 684 [1932])

As recently as 1961, the American Supreme Court accepted that:

A woman should be relieved from the civic duty of jury service unless she herself determines that such service is consistent with her own special responsibilities. (Hoyt v Florida 368 US 57 [1961])

The judges considered that the rights of women to be excused from jury service on the grounds of domestic duties over-rode the rights of a woman charged with a serious crime not to be tried by an all-male jury.

By the early 1970s there was evidence of a growing scepticism on the part of some members of the judiciary towards arguments based on unsupported assertions about gender differences (see Krause, 1974). For many supporters of women's rights however, the judicial change of heart offered too little and came too late. Exasperated by the practice of excluding women from male preserves while presenting this exclusion as a privilege, a substantial part of the growing American feminist movement threw its weight behind a campaign for a new constitutional amendment. The proposed Equal Rights Amendment (ERA) stated that: 'Equality of rights under the law shall not be denied or abridged by the United States or by any State

on account of sex'. Although approved by Congress and the Senate in
the early 1970s, the amendment failed to obtain the necessary ratification from individual states and has now fallen.[5]

The significance of the ERA campaign lay in its unequivocal
acceptance of the idea of formal equality. Laws which treated men
more severely than women, including the liability to do National
Service, were condemned as much as those discriminating against
women. The temporary removal of the judicial blindfold in order to
compensate women for past discrimination is firmly rejected:

> The concept of benign discrimination to make up for past damage to a
> class of course would be fraught with danger if applied to women . . . Any
> permitted difference in treatment as between men and women is likely to
> protect away women's liberties. (Eastwood, 1971: 296)

The supporters of the ERA believed that the only way to undermine the sexual division of labour was to ignore it and so insist that
women and men be treated in an identical fashion by the law. They
considered that any deviation from this strategy would simply perpetuate the view that women were different from and, by implica-
tion, inferior to men. It would give legitimacy to the exclusion of
women from a wide range of activities. In relation to employment,
'protective' legislation was rejected because it reinforced the idea
that women's primary social function was as wives and mothers and
that their role in the labour market was very much a secondary one.
Laws restricting women's hours of employment were used to exclude
them from overtime premiums and from supervisory jobs requiring
overtime work (see Mengelkoch v Industrial Welfare Commission
393 US 993 [1968]).

The limits of formal equality

The sex and colour blindness of the concept of formal equality is both
its greatest strength and its ultimate weakness. On the one hand,
people would undoubtedly benefit from being judged on their merits
rather than on the basis of sex or race. On the other hand, formal
equality is blind to the substantive inequalities that separate people
and prevent them from competing on equal terms. Those involved in
the battle against racial discrimination are constantly reminded of
this limitation, because of the close association between class inequality and racial inequality. The attack on poverty and hence the
recognition of substantive differences in the life chances of people of
different racial origins is an indispensable feature of civil rights
campaigns. Feminists have been much less consistent; some have
drawn attention to the material realities of sexual inequality, while
others, like the ERA campaigners, have taken a conscious decision

to ignore them. In the campaign for the repeal of protective legislation and again in the development of equal pay legislation, we discover the contradictions that flow from assuming that men and women in the labour market compete on equal terms.

Protective legislation

Although there is no precise British equivalent to the ERA campaign, feminists in Britain confront the same dilemma: laws which offer special protection for women purely on the basis of their sex serve to perpetuate and reinforce the myth of female inferiority. Yet the repeal of such laws in the name of formal equality usually means that women sacrifice their legal protection and gain nothing in return. Recent changes in family law are a case in point. The Matrimonial and Family Proceedings Act 1984 was based on the assumption that women had become the 'spoilt darlings' of the law. It therefore aimed to dismantle the 'privileges' of divorced women and so ensure a greater degree of equality, in formal terms, between men and women. In so doing, it disregarded both the operation of welfare laws and the persistence of inequalities in the job market which perpetuate the economic dependency of women and so make a nonsense of formal equality.[6]

Similar considerations apply to protective employment legislation, particularly to those laws which restricted the hours of work of women employed in factories.[7] Although the Sex Discrimination Act 1975 was largely inspired by the principle of formal equality, the government chose not to amend the protective laws at that time. Instead, the Equal Opportunities Commission (EOC) was required by section 55 of the 1975 Act to review the laws and make recommendations to the government. In 1979, the EOC produced its report *Health and Safety Legislation: Should we Distinguish between Men and Women?* After considering the evidence, the working party reached the conclusion that:

> the hours of work legislation constitutes a barrier — often an artificial one — to equal opportunities for women. So long as this legislation remains as it is at present, women workers will be disadvantaged. (EOC, 1979: 29)

They recommended that the legislation be repealed or 'where health, safety and welfare demand it, replaced so that it applies equally to men and women' (p. 96). However, they rejected the extension of hours of work legislation 'as a whole' to men because of the 'undesirable economic effects' and the 'considerable administrative problems' that would be created by the inevitable increase in applications for exemption. (Two of the commissioners with TUC allegiance dissented from this finding, arguing that the legal restrictions on nightwork and shiftwork should be extended to men.) The report recognized the need to protect women already employed in factories from the consequences of repealing the legislation, together with those workers — 'mainly women at the moment' — with responsibility for the care of young or elderly dependents. They recommended the introduction of a code of practice which would recognize 'the substantial domestic commitments' of some workers and would ensure that all workers were fully consulted before shiftwork was introduced.

Unfortunately, the EOC failed to make these suggested reforms a condition of repeal, which made it easier for the Conservative government that came to power shortly after the report was published to adopt the main conclusions while rejecting the safeguards. Repealing the protective laws was not a high priority for the government, but in 1986 an opportunity presented itself with the drafting of a new Sex Discrimination Bill. The primary purpose of the Bill was to amend the 1975 Act following a ruling by the European Court of Justice that the British legislation failed to comply with European law.[8] The European judgment made no mention of the laws imposing restrictions on women's hours of work; nevertheless, measures to remove these restrictions were included in the Sex Discrimination Act 1986 and presented as a further step along the road to sex equality.

This decision presupposes that women no longer need protection; that the conditions of inequality which justified the original legislation have been removed. This is patently not the case: women continue to shoulder the major responsibility for domestic tasks and child care. Women who work in factories are already exploited and vulnerable. To 'liberate' them to work the nightshift is a spurious form of equality. Significantly, the government's proposals for repeal were initially presented in a white paper entitled *Lifting the Burden* (HMSO, 1981). This was not a reference to the burdens on women who work both inside and outside the home, but to the burdens on employers who have to cope with a growing body of governmental regulation. Attempts in both Houses of Parliament to modify the Bill and so reintroduce safeguards for employees (and hence burdens on employers) were not well received, nor was the TUC demand for a 'levelling up' rather than a 'levelling down'; in other words, an extension of protective legislation to men.[9]

If the trade union movement recognizes the full implications of this demand, it may prove possible to prevent history from repeating itself. In the nineteenth century, socialist women had no doubt that the early Factory Acts represented a major victory for the working class, both in reducing the exploitation of women and children and in laying the foundations for improving the working conditions of men.

Eleanor Marx, for example, stressed the importance of organizing 'not as "women" but as *proletarians*, not as female rivals of working men but as their comrades in struggle' (quoted in Draper and Lipow, 1976: 220).

Unfortunately, the majority of male workers did not share this vision of solidarity and so allowed employers to exploit divisions within the workforce. Capitalism, although ostensibly based on a 'free' market in labour, developed within the context of a sexual division of labour and a patriarchal family structure which affected the relative availability of men, women and children for waged labour. In particular, employers were frequently able to use women as a cheap, docile and unskilled labour force to circumvent the demands of male workers for improved pay and conditions. Rather than prevent the women from undercutting wage rates by encouraging them to unionize and by insisting on equal pay, the usual response of the male workers was to try to reduce the competition for well-paid skilled occupations by encouraging the expansion of job segregation based on sex. Protective legislation was occasionally extended to men, but on the whole it remained on the statute books specifically to protect women, who remained a separate and vulnerable part of the workforce. Women were 'protected' from long, arduous work in the factories in order that they could spend more time on equally arduous domestic tasks. Significantly, protection was confined to those categories of employment where the women were in direct competition with the men and did not affect the more 'domestic' types of work considered appropriate to their sex (see Alexander, 1976; Thompson, 1976).

In the short run, certain sections of the male working class benefited by restricting the supply of labour in this way, but it left the employers with a potential source of cheap, unorganized labour whenever job restructuring occurred. Barbara Taylor (1979) gives a vivid account of this process, particularly as it affected the London tailoring trade in the 1830s:

> Whether the weapons employed by capital ... were the glossy new machines of factory industry (as in textiles) or the far less glossy, but equally effective, ones of piecework and sweated outwork (as in tailoring), the outcome was the same: the displacement of skilled (usually male) labour by cheaper, unorganised (usually female) labour, and through this the establishment of a new level of capitalist command over the workforce as a whole. (Taylor, 1979: 29)

The working class women who found themselves being used to challenge male craft domination in several industries did not experience these tendencies as progressive and many gave their support to the idea of a 'family wage' (see Introduction, p.1) for the male bread-

winner and protection for women and children. Barbara Taylor
believes that:

> There is no sense in which this dislocation of the old patriarchal arrange-
> ments could be called 'liberating' for the women involved. It happened at
> a terrible cost in terms of intensification of exploitation and poverty.
> (Taylor, 1979: 28–9)

Protective legislation did not create the sexual division of labour at
work and at home; it was a reaction to it. Repealing the legislation
will not of itself break down the barriers to sex equality, but neither
will its retention. Its extension to men, however, could provide the
basis for a new identity of interests between male and female workers
and so make it more difficult for employers to divide and rule the
workforce.

The reality of racial job segregation
It is the present position of black workers in Britain which provides
the most vivid illustration of the limits of formal equality. The progress of black male workers has not been impeded by any 'protective'
laws; in formal terms they have been free to move into the full range
of occupations open to white males. In practice, this movement has
not occurred and black men are just as locked into low-paid, unskilled jobs as are black and white women (see Table 1.1). Significantly,
male immigrants provided the chief source of night workers in the
textile industry following the prohibition on employing women workers on the night shift.

Historically regarded as a reserve labour force to be used and
discarded as required, black workers continue to be treated as second
class employees. All too frequently, white male workers have colluded in this exploitation in order to restrict access to the highly
skilled, better-paid areas of work. The educational system has done
little to challenge the racist stereotypes which legitimate such inequalities, in the same way that it has been slow to recognize the
significance of sex-role stereotyping.

Section 1(2) of the Race Relations Act 1976 contains a formal
statement against apartheid:

> It is hereby declared that, for the purposes of this Act, segregating a
> person from other persons on racial grounds is treating him less favour-
> ably than they are treated.

In the absence of effective mechanisms for enforcement, such a
declaration is meaningless, as sixteen Asian workers discovered to
their cost. They brought a complaint against their employer under
the 1976 Act, claiming that they were effectively segregated in the

TABLE 1.1
Earnings of different racial groups compared

Male full-time employees by job level	Average gross weekly earnings	
	White (£)	Asian and West Indian (£)
Professional/managerial	184.70	151.80
Other non-manual	135.80	130.40
Skilled manual/foreman	121.70	112.20
Semi-skilled manual	111.20	101.00
Unskilled manual[a]	99.90	97.80
All male employees[b]	129.00	110.20

[a] If employees under the age of 25 are removed from the analysis, the earnings gap between black and white males in the unskilled group increases from £2.10 to £6.60 per week.

Just under one-third of black manual workers are employed as shiftworkers on a regular basis, compared with one-fifth of white manual workers. As shiftworkers are paid considerably more than other manual workers, this 'would lead us to expect the wages of manual workers to be higher for blacks than whites, other things being equal' (Brown, 1984: 168).

[b] For women, it is the sex differential and not the race differential that is paramount. The average gross weekly earnings are £77.50 for white and £78.50 for Asian and West Indian full-time employees. Brown explains the slightly higher wages of black women in terms of West Indian women being more likely to work for public sector employers or large firms, to work unsocial hours and to join trade unions.

Source: The 1982 Policy Studies Institute Survey (Brown, 1984).

paint shop and prevented from transferring to other parts of the factory. They also made a complaint against their trade union (the Furniture, Timber and Allied Trades Union) on the grounds that it had failed to support their efforts to improve pay and conditions or obtain transfers. The industrial tribunal upheld the complaints but the Employment Appeal Tribunal reversed the decision, holding that there was no evidence that the union treated the Asian workers less favourably than any other group of workers and that the de facto separation arose because vacancies in the paint shop were filled by the friends of the existing Asian workforce (FTATU v Modgill and others, Pel Ltd v Modgill and others, [1980] IRLR 142). In other words, because Asian workers sought jobs for their friends, they and not the employers bore the responsibility for the discriminatory practices throughout the factory.

The Appeal Tribunal had no difficulty in reconciling a commitment to formal equality on the one hand with the persistence of entrenched inequality on the other; they were not concerned with the facts of segregation but with the identification of a guilty party. Discriminatory employment practices can rarely be reduced to the motives of individuals in this way; they can only be challenged effectively by moving beyond the frame of reference supplied by the concept of formal equality.

There is no equivalent to section 1(2) of the Race Relations Act to be found anywhere in the sex discrimination legislation. The segregation of men and women is a common feature of social life; it springs directly from widely held beliefs about the 'natural' roles of men and women. Legislation which reflects gender stereotypes (such as family law and welfare law) is socially acceptable; it is those legislators who wish to challenge the operation of such stereotypes that have to tread cautiously. For most women, the sexual division of labour within the home is the central reality of their lives and yet this is specifically excluded from the terms of reference of the Sex Discrimination Act because: 'The government does not and should not seek to intervene in the private relationships of citizens' (*Equality for Women*, HMSO, 1974: 1). Only the 'public' manifestations of sexual inequality are to be subjected to legal scrutiny; so that any threat to the sexual division of labour itself is contained.

Equal pay legislation: separate but equal?
Before 1970, not only were women workers to be found concentrated in low-paid, low-status areas of employment, they were frequently paid the 'female' rate for the job. The more blatant the discrimination, the cruder the legislative response, or so it was with the Equal Pay Act 1970. A woman wishing to file an equal pay application had to compare herself with a man working for the same employer and engaged in the same or broadly similar work, or on work rated as equivalent under a job evaluation scheme. Consequently, the Act could only be used against the grossest forms of pay discrimination; where job segregation flourished, it was an irrelevance. Hence its impotence in the re-grading dispute at Ford.

Between 1970 and 1980, women's average hourly earnings, expressed as a percentage of men's earnings, rose by approximately 10 percentage points, from 63 to 73 percent (see Table 1.2) and this can largely be attributed to the existence of the Equal Pay Act. Its impact would have been even greater, had not many employers used the five and a half year period between the passing of the Act and its implementation in 1975 to circumvent the provisions. Workers were reshuffled so that men and women were not employed on comparable work; grading schemes were introduced which abolished the female rate but placed women in the lowest, unskilled grade (see Snell, 1979; Snell et al., 1981). Far from undermining job segregation, the Equal Pay Act ensured its perpetuation. As employers made the necessary adjustments to bring themselves into line with the new law, its usefulness declined and the number of equal pay applications fell from 1,742 in 1976 to 26 in 1983 (see Ch. 4, Table 4.1).

TABLE 1.2
Women's average gross hourly earnings
as a percentage of men's, 1970–1985

1970	1974	1975	1976	1977	1978	1979	1980	1981	1982	1983	1984	1985
63.1	67.4	72.1	75.1	75.5	73.9	73.0	73.5	74.8	73.9	74.2	73.5	74.0

Source: New Earnings Survey, 1970–1985 Part A, Tables 10 and 11. Reprinted in EOC (1986), *Women and Men in Britain: a Statistical Profile.*

Although the Equal Pay Act had outlived its usefulness in its original form, the impetus for giving it a new lease of life came not from the British government, but from the European Court of Justice (see Introduction). The government was most reluctant to widen the scope of the Equal Pay Act, as such a development was directly opposed to its laissez-faire philosophy of allowing wages to find their own market level. This opposition is reflected in the way in which the government responded to the judgment of the European Court. First, it chose to amend the Equal Pay Act by means of an Order under the European Communities Act 1972. This restricted parliamentary discussion and ruled out the possibility of major revisions to the legislation. The new regulations were presented as a minor addition and an avenue of last resort, only to be used if a claim fell outside the existing provisions. Second, the regulations themselves are a veritable minefield of procedural obstacles likely to deter all but the most persistent applicants.[10]

Third, the government attempted to limit the potential impact of the amendments by widening the terms on which employers could defend themselves against an equal value claim. Employers are given the opportunity at the outset of the tribunal hearing and again at the end, to argue that the variation in pay between the man and the woman is 'genuinely due to a material factor which is not the difference of sex' (see Appendix 3). The case may be lost at this point; if it is not, the employer is permitted to raise the same defence later, after the tribunal has received a report from an independent expert.

This obsession with the 'material factor' defence reflects the government's preoccupation with market forces. Introducing the new regulations to the House of Commons, the Under-secretary of State for Employment had explained the 'material factor' provisions in the following terms:

> What we have in mind are circumstances where the difference in pay is not due to personal factors between the man and the woman, but rather to skill shortages or other market forces. If a man is paid more than a woman for work of equal value because his skills are in short supply, this is not sexually discriminatory, provided the reason is genuine and the employer can show this. (Parliamentary Debates, House of Commons, Vol. 46, col. 486)

As the equal value formula was generated precisely because the market undervalues women's work, this interpretation of the new rules actually undermines their central purpose. Section 1(3) of the original Equal Pay Act had used a different form of words and referred to a 'material factor other than the difference of sex' (see Appendix 3). The 'material factor' formulation in the new equal value regulations was devised in an attempt to escape the consequences of the case law on s 1(3), as established by the Court of Appeal in the case of Fletcher v Clay Cross Quarries [1978] IRLR 361.

The employer in this case had argued that he had been compelled to offer Ms Fletcher's male colleague a higher rate of pay than her in order to attract him from his previous employment. The Court held that such extrinsic factors should be disregarded. Lord Denning acknowledged that if the 'market forces' argument is accepted as a valid reason for not awarding equal pay, the fundamental aim of the law is thwarted. In giving judgment, he referred to Common Market law as well as to the British Equal Pay Act.[11]

The new regulations were widely criticized, both inside and outside Parliament. The House of Lords was so concerned that it passed an amendment, expressing the belief that the regulations failed to meet Britain's obligations under European Community law (Parliamentary Debates, House of Lords, Vol. 445, col. 886). Even so, several hundred women decided to brave the complexities of the law during the first few years of its operation. Although industrial tribunals were intended to provide a cheap, speedy and informal system of justice, adjudicating equal value claims has proved to be inordinately slow.

Some women have been able to expedite matters by achieving a satisfactory outcome without venturing too far into the legal labyrinth. In 1984, three female box-makers who claimed equal value with the male case-makers scored a major success when the company, Pilkington Glass, agreed halfway through the hearing to settle the case. During the first day of the hearing, the tribunal members had reacted with some scepticism to the company's claim that the men's work was more demanding. It was argued that the men used a four-inch nail and the women only a three-inch nail; ironically, this restriction had been imposed on the women in the past in order to protect male jobs! The company, which had planned a reorganization which would have meant redundancy or lower-paid canteen work for the women, granted them equal pay (backdated) and retraining for new packaging jobs.

Julie Hayward, a cook working for Cammell Laird, was less fortunate. The first equal value application to be referred to an independent expert, Ms Hayward's case received considerable publicity and was hailed as a great victory for women. The expert came to the conclusion that the work of a cook was of equal value to that of a painter, a joiner and a thermal insulation engineer. Consequently, the tribunal held that Ms Hayward should be paid at the skilled male craft rate, which meant a backdated pay rise of approximately £30 a week. Cammell Laird's attempt to challenge the expert's report and to raise a new 'material factor' defence was unsuccessful. However, their response to the decision was simply not to pay Ms Hayward, thereby forcing her to return to the tribunal.

This time, the employer argued that Ms Hayward's terms and conditions of employment, considered as a total package (including holiday and sick pay entitlement and meal breaks), was no less favourable than those of her male comparators, so that there was no money due to her. Although the law refers to 'any term of the woman's contract' being less favourable, the tribunal accepted the employer's argument that all the terms should be considered as a package and when Ms Hayward appealed, the Employment Appeal Tribunal (EAT) confirmed the decision. The EAT regarded this approach as 'pragmatic', necessary to avert the danger of 'leap-frogging', whereby the male comparators would demand equality of fringe benefits. Although designed to avoid 'widespread chaos in industry', according to the editor of *Equal Opportunities Review*, the decision could mean that the same disputes:

> will be in and out of the industrial tribunal for years. Any time the relationship between the respective compensation packages of the complainant and any of her comparators is altered, the tribunal will have to undertake a fresh valuation so as to ensure the equality clause continues to be implemented. (*Equal Opportunities Review*, No. 9, Sept/Oct 1986: 34)

An appeal has been lodged against this decision. Whatever the final outcome, the Hayward case demonstrates the impotence of individual litigation to deal with equal value claims which have implications for collective agreements. The government was aware of this problem when introducing the regulations but chose to take no action:

> It is obvious that the decision to award equal pay in individual cases may have collective repercussions. We have not, however, provided any specific mechanisms to deal with those. (Earl of Gowrie, Parliamentary Debates, House of Lords, Vol. 445, col. 885)

The government need not have looked far for a solution if it had wanted to ensure the successful operation of the equal value concept. The Central Arbitration Committee (CAC) had been given a statutory role in relation to equal pay under the original legislation. Section 3 of the Equal Pay Act provided for discriminatory collective agreements to be referred to the CAC by the Secretary of State or by a party to the agreement. In the early days of the legislation, the CAC had adopted a broad and informal role in relation to equal pay. As very few employers continued to operate overtly discriminatory job categories once the legislation was passed, the CAC had included within its frame of reference neutral-sounding grades which were discriminatory in practice.

The Divisional Court brought this process to an abrupt halt in R v Central Arbitration Committee ex parte Hymac Ltd [1979] IRLR 461, when it ruled that there had to be a 'provision specifically applying to men only or women only' before the CAC could become involved. The CAC itself has expressed its concern that if equal pay claims are treated on an individual basis, while the wider collective issues are ignored, the potential stability of existing pay structures is threatened (*CAC Annual Report*, 1982). It would be a simple matter to extend its jurisdiction to cover the collective implications of equal value awards and so minimize the confusion, anxiety and conflict that such awards will frequently engender. Instead, the last vestiges of the CAC's involvement with equal pay were removed when the Sex Discrimination Act 1986 repealed s 3 of the Equal Pay Act.

In the absence of any legal mechanisms for scrutinizing collective agreements, the trade union response to equal value is of paramount importance. Where a union is sympathetic, it can achieve much more on behalf of its membership through collective negotiation than lawyers are ever likely to achieve through individual litigation. In the Ford dispute, the story might have ended with the tribunal's refusal to interfere with the company's grading scheme. Not only did the Transport and General Workers' Union pursue the matter further, it also ensured that the arbitration panel included two women who would be sensitive to the possibility of 'hidden' discrimination. After sixteen years of argument and two strikes, the sewing machinists were at last rewarded with a major act of commitment from their union.

A number of other unions have scored some notable successes. In 1985, the print union, the Society of Graphical and Allied Trades

(SOGAT), concluded a national agreement which gave 25,000 women bookbinders and collators equal pay with male machine assistants. The Banking, Insurance and Finance Union (BIFU) is studying areas where claims could be made involving thousands of employees; secretarial skills, for example, are undervalued in comparison with computing skills and the women who clear the cheques are paid less than the messengers who carry the cheques between floors. The Royal College of Nursing is attempting to show that the skills of company-employed occupational health nurses are undervalued.

These examples provide some measure of the potential impact of the concept of equal value. They also demonstrate some of the limitations of the regulations as presently conceived. The problem of low pay for women workers is most acute in precisely those areas of employment where there is the highest concentration of female labour. The link between job segregation and wage differentials is undeniable; the skills of nurses are undervalued precisely because most nurses are women. The decision to spearhead the equal value campaign by using company-employed nurses is an astute move, as it offers the widest choice of male comparators in a high-salaried, male-dominated area of employment. If this test case strategy is successful, it will create an anomalous situation within the nursing profession and provide powerful economic and moral arguments for use in collective negotiations.

The equal pay and equal value provisions are a response to the discriminatory way in which the labour market operates. As presently formulated, they are an inadequate response. Firmly rooted in the principle of formal equality, they require an individual worker to measure her skills and abilities against those of a fellow worker, as though the factors which have caused her skills and abilities to be undervalued for so long did not exist. The problem is compounded by allowing 'market factors' to be brought into the equation in recognition of specific skill shortages. If job and training opportunities had been equally available to women and men, such shortages would have occurred less frequently. Considerable mental agility is required in order to unravel the multiplicity of factors, some with discriminatory origins and some without, which go to make up a particular pay structure. Even with the help of independent experts, most tribunals have been unable to resolve these issues satisfactorily and are considerably hampered by the timidity and complexity of the present legislation.

Unless they are used as part of a concerted campaign to undermine job segregation, the equal value regulations will have little impact on the labour force as a whole. If they could be used successfully to challenge the tendency to undervalue 'female' skills, employers would lose a major source of cheap labour. This might help to reassure male workers that allowing women into traditionally all-male areas of employment will not depress wage rates. Unfortunately, it is not as simple as this, as the Ford experience demonstrates. There is no evidence (as yet) that jobs other than sewing car seats are becoming available to the women at Ford. This leaves the women as vulnerable as ever; with each development in technology and each pay negotiation, everything is thrown back into the melting pot.

A more fundamental objection to the entire process of claiming equal value is that it draws women into the game of making invidious comparisons between different groups of workers. As grading systems are revised in the light of equal value claims, some women will benefit considerably. The vast majority of workers, men and women, will remain in the lowest gradings. The concept of equal value draws attention to the inequalities which derive from a system of horizontal job segregation, which occurs when a high percentage of the labour force within a particular occupation is either male or female; for example, nurses and secretaries are predominantly female, whereas engineers and construction workers are predominantly male. It leaves intact the system of vertical segregation which ensures that women are concentrated in the less responsible and less skilled positions within each occupation. Their low status and abysmal wages are merely confirmed and justified by the rules of the new equal value game. Perhaps the clearest way to express the limitations of this approach is to point out that it fails to address the problem of low pay for the vast majority of black workers, men and women.

The concept of formal equality is perfectly compatible with a process of 'levelling down', which merely ensures an equal measure of misery for all vulnerable groups. The equal value regulations were introduced against the background of an increasing emphasis on a return to the 'free' market. The devastating consequences of this policy for low-paid workers in general far outweighs any minor gains accruing to certain groups of women workers as a consequence of the equal value regulations. Repealing the protective legislation was only one small part of the process of lifting the burden on employers and allowing 'market forces' to determine wage levels. In 1982, the Fair Wages Resolution, which had been in operation since 1946, was rescinded, with the result that employers tendering for public sector contracts were no longer required to observe minimum standards of pay and conditions. The work of the Wages Councils, which have set minimum standards of pay and conditions for low-paid workers across a range of industries for a number of years, have been severely curtailed; the size of the wages inspectorate responsible for enforcement has been reduced and the protection for workers below the age of twenty-one removed. Other proposals in the pipeline will hit hardest at the most vulnerable groups of low paid workers, as a range of employment rights are stripped away in the name of *Building Businesses . . . not Barriers* (HMSO, 1986).

In response to this frontal attack on workers' rights, the trade union movement is beginning to shed some of its more protectionist and divisive strategies, replacing them with a set of policies designed to improve the general living standards of all workers. The obsession with maintaining pay differentials is being pushed into the background as the problem of low pay is given top billing. In pay negotiations, unions more frequently seek flat rate increases, the abolition of the lowest grades and the establishment of minimum earnings levels (Labour Research Department, 1986: 31–4). The 1986 Conference of the Trades Union Congress witnessed a major departure from the traditional insistence on 'free collective bargaining' when resolutions were passed in favour of a statutory minimum wage and a comprehensive body of legal rights for all workers.[12]

The attack on low pay is no longer couched in terms of the 'family wage' ideal (see Introduction, p. 1), which has been widely discredited on three counts. First, it is premised on the concept of the male breadwinner and his dependents and so is incompatible with a genuine commitment to equal pay for women. Second, it is illusory: no more than 11 percent of all households are composed of a working husband, a wife who does not work and dependent child(ren). (*General Household Survey*, 1983). The vast majority of women workers are not working for 'pin money' and an increasing number are the sole providers for their families (Maclennan, 1984). Third, it is reactionary because it implies that wage earners, rather than the state, should assume responsibility for non-wage earners; in practice it condemns large sections of the working class not supported by a male breadwinner to permanent poverty (see Barrett and McIntosh, 1980). Only when the 'family wage' smokescreen has been lifted does it become possible to consider broader social issues such as the relationship between work and non-work and the distribution of wealth on the basis of need. Such an analysis cannot be contained within the straitjacket of formal equality, as it necessarily involves identifying substantive inequalities and formulating policies designed to reduce them.

Notes

1. The two landmark decisions which overturned the 'separate but equal' doctrine were McLaurin v Oklahoma State Regents 339 US 637 [1950] and Brown v Board of Education 347 US 483 [1954].

2. This point is made by Lester and Bindman, 1972: 50, note 42. The four cases referred to in this section are taken from their account, Ch. 1: 50–63.

3. Chorlton v Lings [1868] Law Reports 4 Common Pleas 374. This is one of the many cases quoted in Sachs and Wilson (1978), who give a full and vivid account of the 'persons' cases and of women's struggle for formal equality in both Britain and America.

4. All these cases are discussed in Sachs and Wilson (1978). The married teachers' cases are Price v Rhondda Urban District Council [1923] 2 Ch. 372 and Short v Poole Corporation [1926] 1 Ch. 66. It is interesting that Griffith chooses to quote from the equal pay case at the beginning of *The Politics of the Judiciary* (Griffith, 1977).

5. The Equal Rights Amendment was approved subject to ratification by the legislatures of three-quarters of the states within seven years. When the seven year period expired in March 1979, thirty-five states had ratified the amendment, three short of the required number. The time period was extended, but then some states attempted to rescind their ratification. The amendment fell in September 1982. The case for the amendment is forcefully argued in a number of articles. See, for example, Temin (1973), Eastwood (1971), Singer (1973), Frankel (1973); also a note on sexual segregation of American prisons in the *Yale Law Journal*, May 1973, and a symposium in the *Harvard Civil Rights — Civil Liberties Law Review*, March 1971.

6. See Brophy (1984). The expression 'spoilt darling of the law' was used by Lord Denning and is quoted by Carol Smart in *The Ties that Bind* (1984: 29). In the second chapter, Smart gives a clear account of the operation of formal and substantive equality in the area of family law. For an analysis of the ways in which the proposed changes in social security law will worsen the position of women, see Land and Ward (1986).

7. The laws are: The Hours of Employment (Conventions) Act 1936, The Mines and Quarries Act 1954 and the Factories Act 1961.

8. Commission of the European Communities v United Kingdom of Great Britain and Northern Ireland [1984] IRLR 29. In the same way that the Equal Pay Act 1970 had been found wanting when measured against the EEC Equal Pay Directive (see Introduction, note 8), so the Sex Discrimination Act 1975 fell short of the requirements imposed by the Equal Treatment Directive, adopted by the Council of Ministers in 1976 (see Appendix 2).

9. Amendments introduced by Lords Wedderburn and McCarthy in the House of Lords, designed to provide safeguards for employees affected by the repeal of the protective laws, were accepted by their Lordships but subsequently removed by the House of Commons.

10. See The Equal Pay (Amendment) Regulations 1983 and Industrial Tribunals (Rules of Procedure) (Equal Value Amendment) Regulations 1983.

11. In a more recent case however, this judgment was overturned. It concerned a woman prosthetist (artificial limb fitter) recruited directly into the National Health Service (NHS) and paid less than a man employed on like work but recruited from the private sector. The House of Lords dismissed the case on the grounds that the woman was not underpaid and that there were 'objectively justified reasons' for paying the man more, in order to attract him and his colleagues from the private sector and so establish a prosthetic service within the NHS (Rainey v Greater Glasgow Health Board, *Equal Opportunities Review*, No. 11, January/February 1987).

12. See 'Big Majority for a Minimum Wage Law', *Financial Times*, 4 September 1986; TUC–Labour Party Liaison Committee (1986). The General, Municipal, Boilermakers and Allied Trades Union has been particularly vigorous in its support of this shift in policy (see GMBATU, 1986).

2 Defining discrimination: a tentative step towards substantive equality

In the United States, the employment rights of women and racial minorities are embodied in the same law, although the legislators had not originally intended it to be so. Ironically, the amendment to include 'sex' along with 'race' in Title VII of the Civil Rights Act 1964 was introduced by a Southern Congressman who regularly voted against civil rights measures and who wished to discredit the Bill. Although discussion on the amendment was punctuated with hysterical laughter, Congress accepted it and the Bill became law.[1]

In a curious historical parallel, it was a Conservative Member of Parliament with strong reservations about civil rights legislation who tabled an amendment during the committee stage of the 1968 Race Relations Bill, in an attempt to bring several new categories (including women) within its scope, and so avoid creating 'a privileged class of victims'.[2] The amendment was ruled out of order because it was beyond the scope of the Bill's long title, and British anti-discrimination measures have continued to apply either to racial minorities or to women.[3]

As in America, it was the issue of racial discrimination which first occupied the minds of the legislators. In some respects the problems of the two countries do not appear to be comparable. People from the West Indies and the Asian sub-continent only began to enter Britain in large numbers on a regular basis after the Second World War and at no time did they constitute a large percentage of the population. Yet after only a few years of immigration from the 'new commonwealth', some striking parallels with the American situation were evident. The traditional British xenophobia, reinforced by colonial prejudice, produced a climate within which racism flourished. Specifically recruited to meet the labour shortages in predominantly low-paid, unskilled areas of employment, the immigrants rapidly became 'ghettoized' in terms of jobs and housing. Whereas previous immigrant groups had to some extent become dispersed and 'assimilated' into the native population with the passing of time, there was little evidence of geographical or social mobility among the groups arriving from the West Indies and Asia.

Members of Parliament were deeply divided on the question of both the need and the desirability of legislation to tackle racism. During the 1950s a series of private members' bills, chiefly concerned with prohibiting racial discrimination in public places, were unsuccessful. It required the violent incidents in Notting Hill in 1958 before politicians gave serious consideration to the issues.

During the 1960s two Race Relations Acts were passed. The 1965 Act made incitement to racial hatred a public order offence and prohibited discrimination in 'places of public resort'. The Race Relations Board was created and given a largely conciliatory role. The 1968 Act extended the scope of the law to cover discrimination in employment, housing and the provision of goods, facilities and services. A new body, the Community Relations Commission, was created and given the task of promoting 'harmonious community relations' and supervising a network of community relations councils. The Race Relations Board was retained and given increased powers, enabling it to investigate complaints and seek legal redress. Even so, this second attempt was seriously flawed, both in the way that discrimination was defined and in the provisions for enforcement.

The first private member's bill to tackle sex discrimination was sponsored in 1967 by Joyce Butler; similar attempts were made every year thereafter until in 1972 two bills were introduced, one in the House of Commons, the other in the House of Lords. Both bills passed the second reading stage, but instead of becoming law, they were referred to separate Select Committees. In contrast to the apparent lack of discussion preceding the inclusion of women in the proposals before the American Congress, the British Parliament seemed reluctant to proceed beyond the discussion stage. Then in 1974, the return of a Labour government was followed by the reappointment of Roy Jenkins to the Home Office and events began to move rapidly.

The government's proposals for a law on sex discrimination were outlined in a white paper, *Equality for Women*, published in September 1974. The paper argued that the long-term goal should be the 'harmonization' of measures on race and sex. In the short term then, it was important to look at the operation of race relations law when drafting a measure on sex equality. The 1960s race relations legislation had adopted the 'administrative agency model', which meant that all complaints of discrimination were handled by the Race Relations Board. There was, however, an alternative model available, embodied in the Equal Pay Act 1970, due to take effect in 1975. This was the 'individual complaint model', which gave the victims of discrimination direct access to the courts. The white paper argued that an exclusive reliance on either model produced its own disadvantages: the latter depended entirely on individual initiative; the former required a vast and costly administrative machinery. If the agency had to investigate all complaints, delays would be inevitable and individuals denied the right to seek legal redress would feel aggrieved. Also, such pressures would distract the agency from playing a wider role in changing discriminatory practices.

To overcome the weaknesses inherent in the two approaches, the new law was to be based on a combination of the models. It would therefore provide for individuals who believed themselves to be the victims of discrimination to make an application to an industrial tribunal, if the complaint related to employment, or to initiate civil proceedings in a county court (or sheriff court in Scotland) in non-employment cases. These individual remedies would be complemented by the strategic role planned for the new administrative body, to be called the Equal Opportunities Commission (EOC). The Commission would be able to assist and represent individual complainants in appropriate cases but its main task was to be the identification and elimination of discriminatory practices. It would therefore be empowered to conduct investigations on its own initiative and to serve a non-discrimination notice, comparable to the American cease-and-desist order, on the person concerned. It would review the general operation of the legislation and play a general research and educational role in the battle against discrimination.

The powers to be given to the EOC were precisely the ones envisaged for the Race Relations Board by those of its supporters who believed that it had no teeth. It therefore came as no great surprise when the 1975 white paper on *Racial Discrimination* offered a similar critique of the individual complaints model and was followed by a new Race Relations Bill, drafted along very similar lines to the Sex Discrimination Act. The Race Relations Act 1976 established a new administrative body, the Commission for Racial Equality (CRE), with an almost identical set of powers to those of the EOC.

In so far as it recognized the shortcomings of the 'individual complaints model' and hence the need for a body which could launch a systematic attack on discriminatory practices, the white paper *Equality for Women* had demonstrated some awareness of the pervasive and persistent nature of discrimination. The same awareness was not, however, reflected in the way in which the white paper defined discrimination:

> to understand the meaning of unlawful discrimination, it is essential not to confuse motive with effect. In the absence of any intention (or inferred

intention) to treat one person less favourably than another on the grounds
of sex or marriage, there will be no contravention of the proposed Bill.
(*Equality for Women*, para. 33)

Such a definition assumed that sexual and racial disadvantage exist as
the result of the cumulative effect of deliberate and conscious individual actions; the existence of institutionalized sexism and racism is
thereby denied.

Fortunately, Roy Jenkins made a visit to the United States shortly
after the publication of the white paper. On his return, the Bill was
re-drafted in order to incorporate two promising American developments. The first of these was the concept of indirect discrimination;
the second involved a modest step towards 'affirmative action' and
provides the subject matter for Chapter 3.

Indirect discrimination
American civil rights lawyers had discovered that they could make
little headway in challenging long-standing discriminatory employment practices on the basis of such a restrictive definition of discrimination as the one employed in the white paper. Long-standing
practices could not be reduced to the motives of individuals; yet
unless such practices could be challenged, the structural basis of
discrimination would remain intact and job segregation on the basis
of sex and race would persist. Although Title VII of the Civil Rights
Act 1964 used the phrase 'intention to discriminate', American
courts increasingly ignored the issue of motive and began to examine
employment practices in terms of their consequences.

The leading judgment at the time of Roy Jenkins' visit was Griggs v
Duke Power Company (401 US 424 [1971]), in which black workers
had brought a 'class action' against their employer.[4] Before the
passing of the Civil Rights Act, the company had only employed
blacks in one department, where wages were considerably lower than
in the other four departments. In 1965, when this policy became
illegal, the company introduced a requirement that all workers seeking employment in any of the four departments would in future be
required to have a high school education and pass two intelligence
tests. Ostensibly, all workers were to be treated in the same way;
in practice, as a consequence of educational discrimination, the
new criteria effectively ruled out black applicants. A unanimous
Supreme Court found no evidence that the new requirements were
related to job performance, as white employees taken on before
1965 continued to perform satisfactorily and achieve promotion.
The Court held that the new arrangements effectively perpetuated
past discrimination and were illegal. The employer's motive was
irrelevant:

absence of discriminatory intent does not redeem employment procedures or testing mechanisms that operate as 'built-in headwinds' for
minority groups and are unrelated to measuring job capability. (Griggs v
Duke Power Co.: 432)

This broader concept of discrimination was incorporated into the
British legislation, so that it now contains a two-pronged definition.
The idea of direct discrimination is retained and covers the situation
in which a person of one sex or racial group is treated less favourably
than a person of the opposite sex or another racial group has been (or
would be) treated. Although the victim has only to show that there
was less favourable treatment on the grounds of sex or race, and not
that the action was intended, in most cases the motives of the alleged
discriminator become the central issue.[5]

In the case of indirect discrimination however, no such limitation
exists. It is not a question of allocating blame, but of identifying the
discriminatory consequences of particular actions and policies. In the
words of the Home Office guides to the two Acts: 'Indirect ...
discrimination consists of treatment which may be described as equal
in a formal sense ... but discriminatory in its effect' (Home Office,
1975; 1977). It thus becomes possible to challenge a requirement or
condition which is ostensibly the same for all employees or prospective employees but is such that only a small proportion of the members of one sex or racial group can comply with it in practice (Sex
Discrimination Act 1975 s. 1(1)(b) and Race Relations Act 1976 s.
1(1)(b): see Appendix 4). The requirement or condition is illegal
unless the employer can justify it. In the words of the Griggs decision:
'The touchstone is business necessity' (ibid: 431).

The concept of indirect discrimination represented a major departure in legal ideology. It broke with the traditional method of reducing social conflict to questions of individual guilt and innocence and
sought instead to identify and remove the historical and structural
impediments to equality. Unfortunately, its impact was seriously
weakened by the way in which it was 'tacked on' as an afterthought to
a legislative framework that had been designed without it. Removed
from the context of American legal institutions and ideology, the
concept of indirect discrimination is a 'legal transplant' which has lost
much of its impact (see Lustgarten, 1980: 187). The Griggs case was
brought as a class action, as are the vast majority of discrimination
cases in the United States. A class action is brought on behalf of a
number of plaintiffs, against a common defendant. The financial and
emotional burden of bringing the case is thereby shared and if the
action is successful, they all derive benefit.

The class action is by no means free of all problems: since it became
widely available in the United States in 1966, with the amendment of

Rule 23 of the Federal Rules of Civil Procedure, a considerable backlog of cases awaiting adjudication has accumulated (Dam, 1975). Furthermore, class actions are binding on all members of the class, who are therefore barred from pursuing individual claims. For this reason, the Supreme Court has ruled that the plaintiffs must take steps to notify other members of the class of the proposed action, however prohibitive the cost (Eisen v Carlisle and Jacquelin 417 US 156 [1974]). Despite these difficulties, the advantages of group litigation are increasingly acknowledged by other common law jurisdictions, notably Australia and Canada (*New Law Journal*, 1979; Van Bueren, 1983; Widdison, 1983; Pannick, 1985: Ch. 10).

In Britain at the present time, the nearest equivalent to the American class action is the representative action. It enables people with a common grievance to be represented by one or more of their number, who bring proceedings on behalf of the whole group. However, the Industrial Tribunal Rules make no provision for this type of action, which is in any event subject to a number of restrictions which make it inappropriate for discrimination cases. Claims arising from a number of separate individual contracts, even if these are identical, cannot be heard as a representative action. Furthermore, the representatives cannot claim damages on behalf of the class but only for themselves, leaving those who were not plaintiffs in the case to sue for damages separately, within the original limitation period (*New Law Journal*, 1979; Pannick, 1985: Ch. 10).

In Britain therefore, the radical edge of the concept of indirect discrimination is somewhat blunted by the absence of group procedures, a situation made worse by the absence of adequate remedies. Although the complainant is required to show that he or she is a member of a group adversely affected by a particular rule, s/he must argue that position as an individual. If the action is successful, then the rule must be changed and others will benefit. Where the discrimination is unintentional however, the applicant will not be entitled to claim damages. If there is no 'guilty' party, there is no-one against whom such a claim could be made (Sex Discrimination Act s. 66(3) and Race Relations Act s. 57(3)).

The American judiciary has played a constructive and creative role in the development of civil rights legislation and British policy-makers have attempted to learn from these interventions. The principle of indirect discrimination established in the Griggs case is enshrined in the British legislation; it does not have to be inferred or invented by the judges. There remains, however, considerable scope for judicial intervention. Complex and detailed provisions require interpretation just as much as open-ended or contradictory ones. An examination of the case law in this area provides a vivid demonstration of the power the judges have, either to make a statute effective or to strangle it at birth.

Indirect discrimination: the development of case law
The initial reaction of the industrial tribunals to the concept of indirect discrimination was one of total incomprehension. The first two cases were both dismissed by the tribunals but reversed on appeal by the Employment Appeal Tribunal (EAT). In the first of these cases, a postwoman had challenged the seniority agreement made between the Post Office and the Union of Post Office Workers. Ms Steel, who had worked for the Post Office for sixteen years, lost her bid for a 'walk' (a postal delivery round), in favour of a young man who became a postman in 1973. The choice of 'walks' was decided on the basis of seniority. The man was considered senior to Ms Steel because she became permanent only in 1975, when the Post Office accepted women into the permanent grades in response to the Sex Discrimination Act. The industrial tribunal had dismissed the case on the narrow grounds that Ms Steel (who had represented herself at this stage) had made no complaint against the Post Office and that her complaint against the Union was misconceived. The tribunal also considered that questions of seniority were matters for the Union and the Post Office to decide, rather than the tribunal.

The members of the Employment Appeal Tribunal disagreed; they held that the proportion of women who could comply with the seniority requirement was considerably smaller than the proportion of men because of the discrimination against women which existed until 1975. Ms Steel was entitled to succeed in her claim unless the Post Office could show that the seniority rule was justifiable on grounds other than sex. The case was remitted to an industrial tribunal for a decision on this point (Steel v The Post Office [1977] IRLR 288). The EAT offered some guidelines to help the tribunal decide the question of justifiability; applying these guidelines, the second tribunal upheld Ms Steel's complaint and recommended that her seniority be backdated to 1969 ([1978] IRLR 198).

Like the American power workers in the Griggs case, Ms Steel was challenging a practice which perpetuated past discrimination. The Appeal Tribunal freely acknowedged its debt to the American case law when it established the principle that a practice 'cannot be justifiable unless its discriminatory effect is justified by the need — not the convenience — of the business or enterprise' ([1977] IRLR 288). Such an approach would require employers to examine their practices with some care.

The second indirect discrimination appeal concerned the Civil Service requirement that applicants for direct entry to Executive

Officer grade should be between the ages of seventeen and a half and twenty-eight. Ms Price complained that the proportion of women who could comply with this requirement was smaller than the proportion of men, because many women in this age group were involved in bearing and rearing children. The tribunal had dismissed the case on the grounds that there are as many women as men in these age groups and that it is irrelevant that fewer women are available in the labour market (Price v Civil Service Commission [1976] IRLR 406). The Employment Appeal Tribunal held that the tribunal had construed the words 'can comply' too narrowly and therefore:

> out of sympathy with the spirit and intention of the Act . . . knowledge and experience suggest that a considerable number of women between the mid-twenties and the mid-thirties are engaged in bearing and rearing children. ([1977] IRLR 291)

The case was remitted for a differently constituted tribunal to consider whether the proportion of women who could comply with the Executive Officer age limit was *considerably* smaller. The second tribunal decided in favour of Ms Price and recommended that the Civil Service alter its upper age limit in time for the 1980 selection procedure ([1978] IRLR 3).

The first successful case of indirect discrimination under the Race Relations Act 1976 followed the lead set by the EAT. The employer had imposed a condition that job applicants should not live in the city centre area because their unemployed friends living nearby would hang around the premises and create a nuisance. As the majority of the city's black population lived in the central area (Liverpool 8), the condition was found to be indirectly discriminatory (Hussein v Saints Complete Home Furnishers [1979] IRLR 337).

However, as the case law unfolded, the courts began to move away from the 'Griggs' criteria and to redefine the word 'justifiable'. When Mr Singh complained that the refusal of Rowntree Mackintosh to employ production workers with beards was indirectly discriminatory against Sikhs, the tribunal accepted the company's argument that the requirement was justifiable in the interests of hygiene. The Employment Appeal Tribunal sitting in Glasgow agreed with this decision, holding that: '. . . an employer must be allowed some independence of judgment as to what he deems to be commercially expedient' (Singh v Rowntree Mackintosh [1979] IRLR 199).

The use of the term 'expedient' represents a significant shift away from the guidelines established in the Steel case. As Rowntree Mackintosh applied the 'no beard' rule in only two of their eight factories, they could hardly argue that the rule was necessary. In a similar case against Nestle, where a no-beard rule also operated in some but not all of the Nestle factories, the applicant suggested other ways of ensuring hygienic conditions, such as requiring that beard protectors be worn, but neither the tribunal nor the Appeal Tribunal was convinced. Mr Justice Slynn considered that the discriminatory effect of the requirement had to be balanced against the employer's reasons for making the requirement and he interpreted the word 'justifiable' as establishing a much weaker test than implied by the word 'necessary' (Panesar v Nestle [1980] IRLR 60).

Worse was yet to come. The case of Wong v GLC (EAT 524/79, unreported) hinged on the interpretation of the phrase 'considerably smaller'. The Appeal Tribunal decided that if no members of a particular racial group were able to comply with the requirement or condition in question, then the considerably smaller test could not be applied and the requirement was legal. In other words, a requirement or condition which it is difficult for members of a racial group to meet can be scrutinized, whereas an impossible requirement cannot![6]

From this line of cases, it begins to look as though the judiciary is particularly resistant to the concept of indirect discrimination when it is used on behalf of black applicants. The courts are sometimes able to recognize the structural impediments that flow from the sexual division of labour; they are less prepared to acknowledge the existence of institutionalized racism or to take any effective remedies against it. It is no more of an imposition to require one employer to revise his rules on factory hygiene than it is to require another to revise the age limits for job applicants. Even so, the Steel and Price decisions did not open the floodgates to the victims of either sex or race discrimination. These two favourable judgments were destined to remain in splendid isolation for some time to come, as the victims of indirect discrimination fought unsuccessfully to extend their application to other areas.

Recognizing the sexual division of labour

(i) Part-time workers

A number of early sex discrimination cases involving part-time workers foundered, because the Equal Pay and Sex Discrimination Acts were treated as two quite separate pieces of legislation. Although the two Acts were intended to be complementary, some applications slipped between the two and were covered by neither. A part-time secretary who believed she was entitled to the same hourly rate of pay as the full-time secretaries could not argue her case under the Equal Pay Act because all the secretaries were female. She managed to convince the tribunal that she was a victim of indirect discrimination as fewer women could comply with the requirement to work full-time. However, matters relating to pay were excluded from this provision because they were covered by the Equal Pay Act; and so the case was dismissed (Meeks v National Union of Agricultural and Allied Workers [1976] IRLR 198).

A part-time machinist who claimed the same hourly rate of pay as a full-time male machinist lost her claim because full-time workers of both sexes were paid at a higher rate. The Appeal Tribunal accepted the company's argument that part-time employees made a lower contribution to the profitability of the company (Handley v Mono [1978] IRLR 534).

When Ms Durrant accepted a full-time position with the North Yorkshire Area Health Authority, her claim for removal expenses was refused on the grounds that she was transferring from a part-time job. As her application involved the payment of money, it was considered under the Equal Pay Act, but she also invoked the in-direct discrimination provisions of the Sex Discrimination Act, in order to show that the requirement to work full-time was one with which fewer women could comply. Although it had been known for the Appeal Tribunal to treat the two Acts as a 'harmonious code', Mr Justice Slynn remained unimpressed and Ms Durrant's appeal was dismissed (Durrant v North Yorkshire Area Health Authority [1979] IRLR 401).

Against this background, when another part-time worker, Ms Jenkins, filed a claim for the same wage rates as full-time workers, her prospects of success looked bleak. Halfway through the appeal however, a change of strategy was adopted. The application under the Equal Pay Act was withdrawn and the Tribunal asked to consider only the relevance of Community law. The EAT decided to refer a number of questions to the European Court of Justice, the third British case to be referred in this way.[7]

This time the European response was unhelpful and contradictory, but the EAT had a new president, Mr Justice Browne-Wilkinson. He in effect ignored the European ruling and instead re-examined the rights conferred under the British legislation. Whereas Mr Justice Slynn had refused to consider the two Acts together, the new president did precisely that; and so concluded that the Equal Pay Act should be construed to accord with the indirect discrimination provisions of the Sex Discrimination Act. Even if the employers had no intention of discriminating against women, they must show that:

> the difference in pay between full-time and part-time workers is reasonably necessary in order to obtain some result (other than cheap female labour) which the employer desires for economic and other reasons. (Jenkins v Kingsgate [1981] IRLR 388: 390)

(ii) Women with children

Soon after taking up his post as president of the EAT, Mr Justice Browne-Wilkinson heard the appeal of a woman refused employment as a waitress because she had young children. The industrial tribunal had dismissed her complaint on the grounds that the employer's rule applied also to men with young children and that the rule was justifiable in the interests of the business. Reversing the decision, the EAT held that the woman had suffered unjustifiable indirect discrimination: first, there was no evidence that the proprietor discriminated against *men* with young children; second, the tribunal itself, in considering whether the condition was justifiable, examined evidence relating solely to *women* with young children and had thereby applied double standards. According to the EAT:

> Parliament has legislated that women with children are not to be treated as a class but as individuals. No employer is bound to employ unreliable employees, whether men or women. But he must investigate each case and not simply apply a rule of convenience, or a prejudice, to exclude a whole class of women or married persons because some members of that class are not suitable employees. (Hurley v Mustoe [1981] IRLR 208)

In 1984 the twin issues of part-time employment and employees with young children converged in an important case against the Home Office itself. Following the birth of her first child, Ms Holmes experienced considerable difficulty in continuing to work full-time. After the birth of her second child, Ms Holmes asked if she could return to work on a part-time basis. The Home Office rejected the request, on the grounds that there were no part-time posts available within her grade. An industrial tribunal held that the Home Office had indirectly discriminated against Ms Holmes and had failed to justify the requirements. The EAT under Mr Justice Waite upheld the tribunal's decision but was clearly concerned to limit the consequences of the ruling:

> The present case stands very much upon its own. It is easy to imagine other instances, not strikingly different from the present case, where the result will not be the same . . . All such cases will turn upon their own particular facts. (Holmes v The Home Office [1984] IRLR 299)

There is a bitter irony in this picture of the government department which gave birth to the brilliant new concept 'indirect discrimination' making a supreme effort to strangle its growing infant. The willingness of certain members of the judiciary to collude in this enterprise reflects an antipathy towards litigation which has wider economic and social implications beyond the immediate facts of a particular case.

(iii) Selection for redundancy

As evidence of the deteriorating economic climate, during the early 1980s the tribunals were asked to consider a number of cases involving the selection of workers for redundancy. In the case of Clarke and Powell v Eley Kynoch, the company had a long-standing agreement with the trade union that workers would be selected on a last-in, first-out basis, except that part-time workers would be selected first, regardless of length of service. In October 1981 all 60 part-time workers (all of whom were women) and a smaller number of full-time workers (of both sexes) were made redundant. Two of the part-timers, Ms Clarke and Ms Powell, complained of indirect discrimination. The tribunal upheld Ms Powell's application but dismissed that of Ms Clarke on the grounds that as her children were grown up, she could have complied with the requirement to work full-time. On appeal, Mr Justice Browne-Wilkinson and his colleagues at the EAT extended the tribunal's finding to Ms Clarke, holding that the question of why the women worked part-time was irrelevant. As both women had been unfairly dismissed, the case was remitted to the industrial tribunal to consider compensation and reinstatement of the two women ([1982] IRLR 483).

In February 1985 the Employment Appeal Tribunal performed a complete somersault in order to dismiss the appeal of a female employee who, like Ms Clarke and Ms Powell, had been selected for redundancy because she worked part-time. Unlike his predecessor at the EAT, Mr Justice Waite belonged to the school of thought which believed that the industrial tribunals should be allowed to make 'common sense' decisions without being bombarded with 'guideline authority' from the superior courts.[8] In this particular case however, it was extremely difficult to follow the 'common sense' reasoning of the industrial tribunal at all. Ms Kidd argued that the requirement to work full-time in order to avoid redundancy was one which women in general and married women in particular were frequently unable to meet because of child-care commitments. Ignoring the statistical evidence which overwhelmingly supported Ms Kidd's contention, the tribunal decided that the appropriate population to provide the basis for comparison were households in which there were young children requiring care. The tribunal considered that 'given the changing conditions of modern life', it was no longer safe to assume that a greater proportion of women than men or of married women rather than single women regularly undertook the child-caring role and so were unable to accept full-time employment.

The tribunal then added insult to injury by holding that even if the requirement were discriminatory, it was justifiable because of the 'marginal advantages' to the employer of operating one shift of full-time workers rather than two shifts of part-time workers. The Appeal Tribunal refused to interfere with any of these arguments, insisting that: 'Every case will depend upon its own facts, as judged by the industrial tribunals' and admitting that: 'A degree of uncertainty as to how a particular tribunal will react to particular circumstances is therefore inevitable' (Kidd v DRG (UK) Ltd [1985] IRLR 190 at 192).

Justifying indirect discrimination

Despite Mr Justice Waite's aversion to 'guideline authority' there can be no doubt that the judgments emanating from the EAT and the Court of Appeal had important consequences for the way in which the tribunals interpreted the provisions on indirect discrimination. The EAT's approach varied considerably, depending on whether or not the judge presiding in the case was sympathetic to the aims of the legislation. The judgments of the Court of Appeal were, however, consistently negative. As a result of the Court's intervention, the provision which gave an employer the chance to justify the discriminatory practice became a gaping hole through which almost any complaint of indirect discrimination could be lost.

The first indirect discrimination case to be considered by the Court of Appeal involved two African students offered places on a polytechnic management course but refused MSC grants because they lacked appropriate industrial experience. Both the tribunal and the Appeal Tribunal had accepted that it was more difficult for black applicants to comply with the requirement that they must have previous management experience, but considered the requirement to be justifiable. Dismissing the appeal, the Court of Appeal denied the relevance of American case law and took objection to the blurring of the distinction between 'justifiable' and 'necessary' that had occurred in the Steel decision. The Court enunciated an even weaker definition of 'justifiable' than the one used to dismiss the complaints against Rowntree Mackintosh and Nestle:

> If a person produces reasons for doing something which would be acceptable to right-thinking people as sound and tolerable reasons for so doing, then he has justified his conduct. (Ojutiku v Manpower Services Commission [1982] IRLR 418)

Using this criterion, it is hard to see how an employer could fail to justify almost any practice.

In Perera v Civil Service Commission, the EAT had followed its own ruling in the Price case to find that an upper age limit for administrative trainees did constitute indirect discrimination against black applicants and that elaborate statistical evidence was not required for the case to be proved. Mr Perera had also complained of discrimination in relation to another appointment within the Civil Service, but this complaint was dismissed. He (rather unwisely, as it turned out) appealed against this part of the EAT decision. Not only did the Court of Appeal dismiss his appeal, they went further and restricted the meaning of the term 'requirement or condition', by insisting that a requirement has to be an 'absolute bar' to appointment, not merely one factor among others taken into consideration by the employers ([1983] IRLR 166).

The House of Lords' excursions into indirect discrimination law have so far been restricted to the educational arena. The effect of this intervention has been to moderate the wilder excesses of the Court of Appeal but has done little to advance the development of case law. In Mandla v Lee, a Sikh boy was refused admission to a school because he wore a turban. The Court of Appeal held that Sikhs were not a racial group and so had no remedy under the Race Relations Act. In any event, the judges doubted whether the words 'can comply' were intended to refer to a condition which arose by choice; it was not physically impossible for a Sikh to remove his turban and cut his hair. The Court also considered that the headmaster was entirely blameless and had himself been treated oppressively by the Commission for Racial Equality (Mandla v Lee [1983] IRLR 17). The House of Lords overturned this decision, holding that Sikhs were a racial group, that the words 'can comply' were intended to cover 'can in practice . . . consistently with the customs and cultural conditions of the racial group' and that the no-turban rule was a form of indirect discrimination that could not be justified. They added that the CRE's action in supporting the complainant was perfectly correct (Mandla v Lee [1983] IRLR 209).

In Mandla v Lee, the House of Lords had refrained from offering any general guidelines on the concept of 'justifiability'. In the case of Orphanos v Queen Mary College ([1985] IRLR 349), they were more forthcoming. Mr Orphanos was a Greek Cypriot who complained of indirect discrimination when he was obliged to pay fees around eight times those charged to students resident in the UK or another EEC country. The House of Lords accepted that the residence requirement was a form of indirect discrimination against people without EEC nationality but held that Mr Orphanos had no remedy, because the discrimination was unintentional. In the course of the decision, the House of Lords also insisted that a particular racial group has to compare itself with all those who are not members of that particular group. A Cypriot therefore has to compare himself or herself with all non-Cypriots, 'consisting of all persons . . . of every nationality from Chinese to Peruvian inclusive'. It would follow therefore, that the point of comparison for a person of West Indian origin would not be white people but people of all races, excluding West Indians. As if this were not enough damage to inflict in one decision, their Lordships also decided to define 'justifiable' as 'capable of being justified'. As the editor of the *Industrial Relations Law Reports* points out, the combined effect of these pronouncements is likely to ensure that 'the law prohibiting indirect discrimination will not be worth the paper that it is written on'.[9]

The limits of indirect discrimination
The concept of indirect discrimination became part of British law approximately ten years ago. During that time, an occasional judgment has allowed us a tantalizing glimpse of its potential impact, but for the most part, the courts and tribunals have reacted unsympathetically to the new jurisdiction. Industrial tribunals have received no clear guidance from the superior courts on how to interpret the complex provisions, as the judges themselves have been so deeply divided. Indirect discrimination is difficult to identify and even more difficult to prove, requiring the presentation of complex legal and statistical evidence. If the employer is then provided with a wide escape route, the whole exercise will have been to no avail. In view of these difficulties, it comes as no surprise to discover that the vast majority of discrimination cases heard by industrial tribunals are concerned solely with questions of direct discrimination. On average, only 15 percent of such cases are brought under the indirect discrimination provisions.

The concept of indirect discrimination was created in the United States, not by the legislature, but by the Supreme Court. In Britain, it seemed as if nothing had been left to chance when the concept was explicitly built into the statutes. Unfortunately, the measure was too tentative; in particular, the choice of the word 'justifiable' rather than 'necessary' made it easier for the judges to dilute the provision so as to render it meaningless.

The equality legislation was intended to provide a powerful source of ammunition in the battle against discrimination. In the course of drafting, however, it devolved into a balancing exercise between the rights of the victims of discrimination on the one hand and the rights of the employer on the other. The more radical the provisions, the greater the tension between these two conflicting principles. Wherever the tribunals and courts have resolved this tension in favour of the employers, they have thwarted the primary purpose of the legislation.

If the measures on indirect discrimination are to fulfil their original purpose, it will be necessary to devise a more rigorous test for employers who seek to retain discriminatory practices. The CRE and EOC would both like to see the concept of indirect discrimination redefined to include any practice which has a 'significant adverse impact' on the members of one sex or racial group and which could not be demonstrated to be 'necessary' (CRE, July 1985: 5–6; EOC, October 1986: 14). Employers will invariably insist that the viability of their business is threatened by changes imposed from outside. It is often possible to demonstrate that their fears are unfounded; indeed, new employment practices are likely to result in a more efficient use of human resources. Such an approach does, however, evade the central question of whether employers should be allowed to dictate the terms of reference in this way. It presupposes that the profit motive necessarily takes priority over other considerations. It denies the possibility of an alternative set of values in which wriggling out of the commitment to build a non-sexist, non-racist society would become unthinkable.

Notes

1. Title VII of the Civil Rights Act 1964 is the section which deals with employment discrimination. See DeCrow (1974) and Friedan (1977). Once the law was passed, feminists then had to campaign to ensure that the provisions in respect of women were taken seriously (see Eastwood, 1971; DeCrow, 1974).

2. Quintin Hogg, 9 May 1968, Official Report, House of Commons Standing Committee B, col. 58. In response to this interpretation of his intervention, Quintin Hogg (now Lord Hailsham, the Lord Chancellor) writes that he considers it foolish to speculate about motives and that the analogy between the House of Commons Standing Committee and proceedings in the American Congress is entirely misleading (private communication, 19 July 1984).

3. Acts of Parliament have a short title by which they are cited, for example, Race Relations Act 1968, and a long title, which describes their scope and purpose. The long title of the RRA 1968 was: 'An Act to make fresh provision with respect to discrimination on racial grounds, and to make provision with respect to relations between persons of different racial origins'. It is possible for the long title of a Bill to be altered if the government so wishes. The long title of the Sex Discrimination Bill 1986 was altered to include discriminatory requirements in public entertainment licences, following the acceptance of a government amendment while the Bill was in committee (see Ch. 8, p. 161).

4. The American class action is discussed more fully below.

5. The Commission for Racial Equality has expressed its concern on this point and has asked for an amendment to the Race Relations Act to make clear that direct discrimination does not necessarily involve a racial motive. The Commission gives the example of employers who appoint no black staff and explain this in terms of supposed customer dislike rather than their own personal feelings on the matter (CRE, July 1985: 3–5).

6. Not until 1985 was this interpretation challenged in a case of indirect sex discrimination. A barmaid suspended from her job at an all-male social club was denied the right of appeal against suspension because as a woman she was ineligible for mem-

bership of the club. The EAT held that a claim of indirect discrimination could still succeed:

> It would in our view run counter to the whole spirit and purpose of the ... legislation if a requirement or condition which otherwise fell within the definition [of indirect discrimination] because a negligible proportion of women as against men could comply with it was held to lie outside the legislation if the proportion was so negligible as to amount to no women at all. (Greencroft Social Club v Mullen, [1985] ICR 796)

7. The other two cases were Macarthys v Smith [1980] IRLR 210 and Lloyds Bank v Worringham [1981] IRLR 178. In both these cases, the employers had possible escape routes under the domestic legislation not available under Article 119 of the Treaty of Rome nor under the Equal Pay Directive. The Jenkins case was more problematic however, as there is no reference to 'indirect discrimination' in either the Article or the Directive (see Appendix 2).

8. The evolution of the Employment Appeal Tribunal from a highly interventionist to a less interventionist body is examined in more detail in Chapter 5.

9. Rubenstein, *IRLR Highlights*, August 1985: 332. See also *Equal Opportunities Review*, No. 2, July/August 1985: 40 and 48. The situation has improved slightly since the Orphanos decision, thanks to developments in Common Market law. As a result of the Rainey decision (see Ch. 1, note 11) the more stringent standard of 'objectively justified reasons' has been imposed. Although this was an equal pay case, the House of Lords accepted that the same standard of justification would apply to s 1 (3) of the Equal Pay Act and to the indirect discrimination provisions of the SDA. The standard was established by the European Court in interpreting Article 119 in a case referred by Germany (Bilka-Kaufhaus v Weber von Hartz, *Equal Opportunities Review*, No. 9, September/October 1986: 29). It is possible, then, for the law on race discrimination to benefit from EEC law, albeit by a convoluted route.

3 Positive action: another tentative step

Prior to his American trip in the winter of 1974–5, Roy Jenkins had rejected the idea of positive discrimination, on the grounds that it contradicted the principle of formal equality which would underpin the new legislation (see Meehan, 1985: 52). The primary purpose of the new law was to ensure that members of both sexes were treated equally. Positive discrimination compromised this purpose by appearing to favour one sex at the expense of the other. As a result of his experiences in America however, the Home Secretary shifted his position just enough to allow a modest measure of 'positive action' to be included in the Sex Discrimination Bill. Explaining the new provisions to the House of Commons, he said:

> I believe that we should not be so blindly loyal to the principle of formal equality as to ignore the actual and practical inequalities between the sexes, still less to prohibit positive action to help men and women to compete on genuinely equal terms and to overcome an undesirable historical link. (Parliamentary Debates, House of Commons, Vol. 889, col. 514)

He used a similar form of words when introducing parallel provisions for racial minorities the following year (Parliamentary Debates, House of Commons, Vol. 906, col. 1558).

Positive action in the United States

Roy Jenkins's visit came at a high point in the American experiment with affirmative action. This had begun somewhat hesitantly in 1964 with the passing of the Civil Rights Act. The divisions of opinion within Congress on this issue were reflected in the contradictory measures which co-existed within the law and which the courts were left to interpret as they saw fit. Title VII contained a provision which insisted that no employer should be required to 'grant preferential treatment' on the basis of race or sex (section 703j). Yet the legislation also provided for a court to 'order such affirmative action as may be appropriate' if it found evidence of unlawful employment practices (section 706g).

The American government strengthened its commitment to affirmative action in the years that followed. Executive Order 11246 issued in 1965 made it illegal for government departments and firms holding government contracts to discriminate against racial minorities and established the Office of Federal Contract Compliance (OFCC) to enforce the non-discrimination clause in contracts. Companies holding contracts worth more than 50,000 dollars were required to draw up and implement affirmative action plans. In 1968 the Executive Order was amended to include sex discrimination. More specific instructions for employers were contained in further executive orders in the early 1970s. Where women and racial minorities were under-represented in the workforce, the employer was required to set goals and timetables for the company, indicating the numbers of such workers to be employed in specified grades by a specified date.

The powers of the Equal Employment Opportunities Commission (EEOC), restricted in 1964 to those of investigation, persuasion and conciliation, were extended in 1972. The Commission was permitted to initiate civil action where conciliation failed and also where it had 'reasonable cause' to believe there existed a 'pattern and practice of discrimination'. The mere existence of these powers had a most persuasive effect on the majority of employers, who preferred to draw up affirmative action programmes as part of a negotiated settlement, rather than risk a court judgment against them. It was not simply a question of public image; a finding of discrimination would almost certainly involve the payment of considerable sums of money to the victims, including substantial pay arrears.

Administrative action by the OFCC and the EEOC had an immediate impact on the employment practices of a much wider range of companies than the courts could reach through litigation, even class action litigation. Judicial decisions were, however, vital in order to establish the parameters and ground rules for affirmative action programmes. In 1970, the Supreme Court struggled with the problem of how to overcome the effects of a discriminatory seniority system in an equitable fashion:

> The [legislative] history leads the court to conclude that Congress did not intend to require reverse discrimination; that is, the Act does not require that Negroes [sic] be preferred over white employees who possess employment seniority. It is also apparent that Congress did not intend to freeze an entire generation of Negro employees into discriminatory patterns that existed before the Act. (Local 189, United Papermakers and Paperworkers v United States 397 US 919 [1970])

The Court rejected the 'freedom now' approach (the immediate implementation of minority representation at all levels) because it would involve displacing white workers from senior positions, but it also denounced the 'status quo' option, which would ignore the present consequences of past practice altogether. It compromised with the 'rightful place' approach: non-discriminatory criteria would operate for all future appointments and the existing seniority system would cease to operate.

It looked as though the Americans had hit on the perfect formula which made possible an immediate, wide-ranging and radical improvement in the employment prospects of women and racial minorities without giving the white male majority grounds for complaint. Affirmative action programmes were presented as a temporary expedient; once the effects of past discrimination had been remedied, they would no longer be required.

Unfortunately, the white male majority did not always see it in these terms. The 'rightful place' approach meant that people already ensconced in senior positions were secure. The brunt of the new policies was borne by people who were themselves relatively disadvantaged. Van den Berghe voiced the sense of injustice felt by those who saw themselves as the casualties of affirmative action policies: 'There is no way of being benign to one group without being malign to another, if they have to compete for the same scarce resources'.[1] Van de Berghe's primary target on this occasion was not employment policy but educational policy, specifically the University of Washington's special education and ethnic studies programme.

In 1978 the contradictions implicit in the 'rightful place' strategy were brought to a head and again it was educational affirmative action in the firing line. Mr Bakke, a white American, applied for admission to the University of California medical school at Davis and was rejected. The School reserved sixteen of its 100 places each year for minority group applicants and the students admitted under this policy were less well qualified than Bakke. He sued the University under the Civil Rights Act, claiming that he was the victim of reverse discrimination, and under the equal protection clause of the fourteenth amendment.

The diversity of opinions expressed by the nine Supreme Court judges in this case reflects the complexity of the issues involved. Four of the judges found in Bakke's favour under the Civil Rights Act. The other five held that the constitutional question had priority over the Civil Rights Act and proceeded to consider whether the Davis quota system violated Bakke's equal protection rights. Four of them felt that 'benign' racial classifications should be examined in the light of public policy objectives and so concluded that the medical school's purpose of 'remedying the effects of past societal discrimination' was constitutional.

The decision of the ninth judge was crucial as the deciding opinion in a Court otherwise split equally for and against Bakke. He held that explicit quotas like the Davis scheme were unconstitutional because they were not required to achieve goals of 'compelling importance'. However, he added that it would be lawful to operate more flexible schemes that took account of race and other characteristics in order to ensure diversity in the student population. The outcome was a political compromise in the sense that Bakke obtained a place in medical school but affirmative action programmes were held to be lawful, so long as they were based on the diversity argument and did not impose rigid quotas (Regents of the University of California v Bakke 438 US 265 [1978]).

The following year, the Supreme Court was required to pronounce on the legality of an affirmative action programme in employment. Under the programme in question, 50 percent of new vacancies and 50 percent of in-plant craft training places were to be reserved for minority group workers. A white employee whose application for training was rejected claimed that such a practice was illegal, because it used race as the basis for selection. This time the Court concentrated on the employment provisions of the Civil Rights Act and the majority (with two judges dissenting) concluded that the programme did reflect the policy objectives of the legislation. The judges reached the conclusion that white employees were treated fairly as there were to be no job losses and half the training places were still available to them. Furthermore, the policy would cease to operate as soon as the racial profile of the workforce within the factory reflected the racial composition of the local population (United Steelworkers of America v Weber 443 US 193 [1979]).

With some reservations then, the court had declared in favour of affirmative action programmes and an increasing number of companies and organizations, rather than wait for an expensive class action lawsuit to be launched against them, began to alter their employment practices. The companies making the greatest effort, however, were undoubtedly those which stood to lose valuable government contracts if they did not. An OFCC survey of 77,000 companies employing 20 million workers found that during the period 1974 to 1980, women and racial minorities made greater gains, both numerically and in terms of status, in companies holding government contracts (see Stamp and Robarts, 1986: 118).

Under the Reagan administration, commitment to affirmative action has undoubtedly waned and Executive Order 11246 is under threat. It may well be that this backlash comes too late, however. Employers have grown accustomed to living with anti-discrimination policies and have even begun to acknowledge their positive effects in the shape of a more efficient use of labour power. Stability and predictability are high priorities in the world of business; any attempt to reverse gear on positive action after twenty years becomes a potential source of disruption without recognizable benefits.[2]

Positive action in Britain

Although Roy Jenkins was evidently impressed by the American policies, it can hardly be said that he allowed himself to be swept away by them. The 'positive action' provisions added to the Sex Discrimination Bill on his return and subsequently included in the Race Relations Act, were a pale shadow of the American measures. First, the provisions contain no element of compulsion. Training bodies and employers are permitted to provide training for members of one sex or for particular racial groups if they have evidence that members of those groups are under-represented in those areas of employment for which the training is intended. Such training schemes are exempted from the requirement that members of both sexes and all racial groups be treated equally.[3]

Second, where such 'positive action' schemes are operated by an employer, they can only be made available to the existing workforce. It is illegal to recruit members of one sex or particular racial group in order to send them for special training. As though in anticipation of the Bakke case, such a practice was condemned as 'reverse discrimination' and was specifically rejected. The Home Office guide is unequivocal:

> The Act does not permit 'reverse discrimination': for example, it is unlawful to discriminate in favour of women in recruitment or promotion on the grounds that women have in the past suffered from adverse discrimination and should be given a chance to 'catch up'. (Home Office, 1975 para. 7.10. See also Home Office, 1977: para. 7.7)

Quotas, of the kind approved by the Supreme Court in the United Steelworkers case, are illegal in Britain. The only exception is that elected bodies of trade unions are permitted to reserve a specified number of seats for one sex, or make extra seats available through election or co-option (Sex Discrimination Act 1975, s 49). There is no similar provision in the Race Relations Act, although if racial minorities are under-represented, trade unions can take steps to recruit minority group members and provide training facilities which would enable them to apply for official posts within the union (Race Relations Act 1976 s 38 (3)).

The positive action provisions are little more than a goodwill gesture. They have provided a limited framework within which people and organizations already committed to the fight against discrimination can develop programmes for action. They offer no incentive to those without such a commitment to take up the challenge. On the contrary, the cautious wording of the measures is likely to act as a deterrent. Until 1986, organizations wishing to make use of the training provisions, other than specified government bodies such as industrial training boards and the Manpower Services Commission, had to seek designation from the Secretary of State. The Sex Discrimination Act 1986 removed the designation requirement for single-sex training but not for racial minority training (see note 3). In both cases, the training can only be offered if the members of one sex or particular racial group(s) have effectively been excluded from the areas of work for which the training is intended, during the previous twelve months.

The Open University ran foul of these restrictions soon after the passing of the Sex Discrimination Act and had its knuckles rapped by the Equal Opportunities Commission (EOC) when a man excluded from a course reserved for female students complained of reverse discrimination. The first tribunal applicant backed by the EOC was also a man challenging an illegal quota system. The Burnham agreement that the second master or mistress of a school should be of the opposite sex to the deputy head was declared illegal. In the opinion of the Commission: 'Quota systems can excuse people from facing the full consequences of equality' (EOC Press Notice, 11 October 1976).

Ten years later, an industrial tribunal held that the London Borough of Hackney unlawfully discriminated against white job applicants by considering only black and ethnic minority applicants for two gardening apprenticeships (Hughes and others v London Borough of Hackney, *Equal Opportunities Review*, No. 7, May/June 1986).

Hackney is not the only local authority whose attempts to remedy the effects of past discrimination are constrained, rather than advanced, by the cautious wording of the positive action provisions. A number of local authorities have taken their duties under section 71 of the Race Relations Act seriously, although the wording of this section is sufficiently vague for most authorities to take no action (or very little action) with impunity. Section 71 confers on local authorities the duty to 'make appropriate arrangements' to ensure that they carry out their functions 'with due regard to the need (a) to eliminate unlawful racial discrimination; and (b) to promote equality of opportunity, and good relations, between persons of different racial groups' (see Appendix 4). Although there is no equivalent section in the Sex Discrimination Act, local authorities who develop equal opportunities policies usually do so in relation to women as well as to racial minorities. If they wish to take full advantage of the positive action provisions but stay within the law, the main thrust of their energies will be directed towards the processes by which existing employees are selected for retraining and promotion. In the case of new applicants, they can advertise the posts in a way which will encourage applications from women and black people, but they are not allowed to discriminate at the point of selection.

Some local authorities have also attempted to persuade other employers to adopt non-discriminatory practices by adopting the American strategy of 'contract compliance'. This entails the use of purchasing power in order to ensure that companies holding contracts with them have exemplary employment policies. Traditionally, such clauses in local authority contracts have focused on fair wage levels, trade union rights and health and safety records; only recently have policies regarding the employment of women and black workers been subjected to similar scrutiny.

Such a strategy can only be successful where the authority has considerable purchasing power, as was the case with the Greater London Council; even then, it is most effective against small employers. Larger companies may prefer to withdraw their tender rather than submit to the requirements, or they may be able to resist them if they are indispensable to the purchaser as sole supplier of essential goods or services. The experience of the GLC prior to its abolition is instructive: although the Council did exclude a number of companies from its approved list of contractors, the majority provided the information requested and welcomed the advice offered. When the Council was abolished in March 1986, the Contract Compliance and Equal Opportunities Unit was taken over by the Inner London Education Authority. As this authority does not have the same purchasing power as the GLC, the potential impact of the policy is inevitably weakened (see Stamp and Robarts, 1986: 78).

Closing the gap between policy and practice

In the absence of direct legal sanctions, or financial sanctions in the form of contract compliance, persuading recalcitrant employers to adopt a positive action programme is largely a game of bluff. Even if a finding of illegal discrimination is made against an employer, following a tribunal hearing or an investigation by one of the Commissions, the employer is only required to cease discriminating and cannot be ordered to adopt a particular course of action. Even so, the Commission's powers of persuasion are considerably enhanced in such circumstances and they do have a useful role to play in encouraging the development of positive action programmes. In this connection, a useful addition to the Commissions' persuasive repertoire was provided by the legislators, apparently as an afterthought.[4] The EOC and the CRE are empowered to issue codes of practice on employment, following consultations with employers' and workers' organizations. Although not legally binding, the codes are to be admissible in evidence and any relevant provisions taken into account by industrial tribunals. Both Commissions have devised codes of practice and received parliamentary approval for them. The CRE codes have been in operation since April 1984 and those of the EOC since April 1985. Positive action features in both codes as an example of a voluntary but highly recommended policy available to employers.

Developments at Austin Rover provide a perfect illustration of the combined effects of legal and persuasive powers, together with a rare example of co-operation between the two Commissions. Although Austin Rover (formerly known as British Leyland) regarded itself as an equal opportunity employer, the CRE received a number of complaints of racial discrimination and in the late 1970s conducted a formal investigation into the company's employment practices. The adverse publicity which accompanied the serving of two non-discrimination notices on the company and on two shop stewards was too much for Austin Rover, which decided to negotiate an equal opportunities agreement with the trade unions. The central feature of the agreement, signed in October 1985, is that it establishes procedures for monitoring the workforce. A voluntary questionnaire issued to all employees asks them to categorize themselves according to sex, marital status, ethnic origin, age, job grade and length of service. If they choose not to complete the questionnaire, supervisors and trade union representatives will supply the required data. Employees will be able to check the information about themselves, which will be held on computer. The results of the monitoring are to be used to identify where women and black people are under-represented within the company and to draw up positive action plans to rectify these inequalities.[5]

Despite the lack of legal compulsion, a number of employers have begun to describe themselves as 'equal opportunity employers'. Their initial involvement may well begin as a public relations exercise, and if no further action is taken, the statement will have no practical consequences. Only when a genuine attempt is made to translate the statement into active policies within the organization can the company claim to be involved in a positive action exercise. Many employers, somewhat naively, believe that with a little goodwill, patience and education, inequalities will begin to disappear. When it becomes apparent that nothing less than a fundamental shake-up of the entire workforce is involved, they may get cold feet and settle for a small number of 'token' women and black workers in jobs and grades which were formerly a white male preserve. A research project, commissioned by the Department of Employment in the early 1980s to investigate 'successfully' operating equal opportunities policies for racial minorities within the private sector, was unable to find a single employer that had translated a formal statement of policy into effective practice (see Hitner et al., 1982; Knights and Hitner, 1982). Since then it has become possible for the two Commissions, armed with their codes of practice, to provide encouragement and practical advice, so that it becomes more difficult for the organization to beat a retreat.

One of the first British employers to become involved in a positive action project on a voluntary basis was Thames Television, which agreed in 1980 to take part in a project initiated by the National Council for Civil Liberties and funded by the Equal Opportunities Commission. The project officer, Sadie Robarts, discovered that the vast majority of the female workers at Thames were to be found in the traditionally female areas of employment: they were either secretaries or production assistants or confined to the make-up or catering departments. Upper managerial and technical positions were a largely male preserve. These differences were reflected in the salary structure, with 67 percent of the female employees but only 17 percent of the male employees earning less that £10,000 a year. Although the work of production assistant (an all-female position) could be regarded as an ideal training ground for the posts of producer and director, very few women held such posts (Robarts, 1981).

Following Ms Robarts' recommendations, Thames Television appointed a women's employment officer and formed a positive action committee. Training courses were introduced for members of staff responsible for promotion and recruitment decisions and a code of practice was produced, drawing attention to the factors that might discourage women from applying for certain types of job and requiring a fresh scrutiny of job specifications, methods of advertising and interview procedures. Steps were taken to encourage existing women employees to apply for technical and management training schemes and the availability of financial assistance for child care was more widely advertised. The career development of women who have participated in training schemes is to be monitored and company statistics will show job movement within the organization over time. In 1984 the programme was widened to include positive action for ethnic minority workers and the company has since added ethnic monitoring to its activities. However, no targets for the recruitment of women and black workers into particular grades have been set; the company argues that as labour turnover is low and no expansion is planned, it would be a mistake to set 'unrealistic' targets which might jeopardize the entire project.

When British Rail, another self-designated equal opportunity employer, invited the EOC to study women's employment within BR, the resulting report sent shock-waves reverberating throughout the organization. It would be difficult to imagine a wider gulf between the professed commitment to equality and the blatantly discriminatory practices uncovered during the project. Women comprise only 6 percent of the workforce at British Rail and are to be found working almost entirely as clerks, secretaries, cleaners and canteen staff. A mere handful of women have penetrated the skilled manual and technical grades and the only female train driver at the outset of the research was a man who had had a sex-change operation (male to female). Those women with the courage and tenacity to break into this male domain are subjected to daily abuse and harassment and deprived of toilet and washing facilities.

Although the report concentrated on sex discrimination, the researcher also found evidence of racism. At one depot, where showers were provided for the men but not for the women, the drivers apparently refused to use these facilities 'because the coloured people do' (Robbins, 1986: 56). Similar attitudes were to be found at managerial level, where local autonomy over staff appointments leaves managers free to indulge their own prejudices in defiance of head office policy: 'At the end of the day managers must manage. We *do* get edicts from on high for example about race — but I ignore them' (Robbins, 1986: 6, emphasis in the original).

These managers are not trained in recruitment techniques. Their favoured method of filling a vacancy is to 'ask around' among existing staff. The concept of the 'railway family' means that sons and brothers of existing employees are highly regarded. This source of applicants is supplemented by letters from young male enthusiasts, writing in on the offchance of a job. Women are only considered for jobs where sexual attractiveness is regarded as an asset, where routine, monotonous tasks need to be done or where domestic skills are required. As one manager put it: 'You can't beat a woman on carriage-cleaning. I suppose it's their domestic nature' (Robbins, 1986: 22). Yet this work is heavy, dirty and dangerous and often used as a form of degradation for male workers, for example to discipline a drunken driver. Nor were sexist attitudes confined to the manual grades; BR was proud of its graduate trainee programme and considered it the main route by which women could reach senior positions. In 1984 however, there were only 325 trainees throughout the whole of British Rail, of whom a mere 37 were female. The discrimination against women was reinforced by a system of patronage for promotion and an age limit of 25 for all forms of training.

If the gap betwen policy statements and day-to-day decision making at British Rail is to be closed, a fundamental overhaul of employment practices is undoubtedly required. BR's initial response however was confined to making one senior appointment, an equal opportunity project manager, and instituting a series of awareness training workshops and seminars. Awareness training that is not part of a comprehensive programme of positive action is unlikely to have any impact on the composition of the workforce. Indeed, there is a serious risk that such training will merely 'change the professional veneer', so that arguments for retaining discriminatory practices become more sophisticated.[6]

Given the co-operative nature of the British Rail research project, the EOC can do little to speed the process of change. A similar difficulty faced the CRE when it uncovered widespread discrimination at the National Bus Company. Although this enquiry had started life as a formal investigation, the proceedings were brought to a halt when the House of Lords gave judgment against the Commission in another similar case (see Ch. 6, p. 121). However, National Bus agreed that the Commission should go ahead with the publication of its findings, because of their significance for the whole of the transport industry. The report revealed that three-quarters of the ethnic minority workers at NBC were either drivers or conductors (mostly conductors) and that very few were employed as mechanics, office workers or in supervisory or managerial positions. The Commission found extensive word of mouth recruitment and the use of inappropriate tests with indirectly discriminatory consequences. It recommended a change in recruitment procedure and the use of positive action to provide training and encourage applications for promotion (CRE, November 1985). Now the Commission can only wait and hope.

It is tempting to dismiss these 'voluntary' exercises as a waste of time and resources, but they do have a potential value. First, they help to open up the debate about discrimination. Once the existence of widespread discriminatory practices within a particular sector of employment is made public, employers can no longer wriggle out of their obligations with bland assurances that their hands are clean. In the face of incontrovertible evidence and a recommended programme of action to remedy the situation, they are forced either to respond positively or to admit that their priorities lie elsewhere. Second, some employers may genuinely wish to discard discriminatory practices, in which case they will need help in identifying and removing them. Any relevant research will then be welcomed, rather than regarded as a threat. For example, the Express Foods Group made use of the CRE's formal investigation report on Unigate to review its own employment practices. Similarly, London Regional

Transport responded positively to the CRE's promotional work following the formal investigation into the Bradford Metro. More generally, employers wishing to inform themselves about the racial composition of their workforce soon discover that the processes of ethnic monitoring are fraught with difficulty and are pleased to draw on the experiences of others.[7]

If one employer is prepared to take the plunge, others may be prevailed on to follow. The banking industry is a case in point; attempts to develop and generalize best practices in this area are inspired by a unique blend of enlightened policies and legal persuasion. NatWest were the pioneers: in the early 1970s, one senior manager took up the question of career opportunities for women in response to a number of research projects revealing widespread sex discrimination within the banks. The Midland followed closely behind and in 1978 appointed a manager with special responsibilities for equal opportunities for women, a role subsequently extended to include the employment of ethnic minorities and people with disabilities. Barclays were only precipitated into action when the EOC considered undertaking a formal investigation into the bank's recruitment practices. The Commission had received complaints that the bank was more favourably disposed towards boys with the General Certificate of Education at Advanced level than towards girls with this standard of education. The proposal to investigate was dropped when Barclays agreed not to discriminate in the future and to supply the Commission with the necessary statistics to enable it to monitor the situation over a four year period. NatWest, the Midland and Barclays have all begun to monitor the ethnic origin of job applicants.

Bringing up the rear is Lloyds Bank. Lloyds have lost two major sex discrimination cases; one on equal pay, which it contested all the way to the European Court of Justice, the other on maternity rights. Faced with further litigation under the equal value regulations, in 1986 Lloyds at last appointed a manager to develop an equal opportunities policy.[8] The Banking, Insurance and Finance Union (BIFU) has played an active part in these developments. With a membership that spans the finance industry, it is well placed to press any advantage, so that gains become generalized throughout the industry. BIFU is particularly concerned that unless there is a radical and immediate overhaul of recruitment practices, career opportunities and pay structures, any improvements will simply be wiped out by the introduction of new technology.[9]

Trade union involvement
The trade union movement has a crucial role to play in making positive action effective. A plan of action negotiated through collec-

tive bargaining procedures and vigilantly monitored by the unions would be more difficult to shelve and (hopefully) more responsive to the needs of the workforce than one initiated solely by management. Unfortunately, many employers decide to go it alone, either because they regard policy decisions as a managerial prerogative, or because they believe that consultations with the unions will be time-consuming and unproductive. Although the EOC and CRE codes of practice place the primary responsibility for developing equal opportunity policies firmly at the door of the employer, they do acknowledge that the involvement and commitment of the unions is important. At Austin Rover, all twelve trade unions are signatories to the Equality Agreement and at Thames Television the unions were actively involved in the project from the outset. Local authority initiatives on positive action appear always to be taken in conjunction with the relevant unions, but a number of other organizations have set up steering committees to implement policies on equality and have not included trade union representation.[10]

Unless trade unions become actively involved in these developments, they will be identified with the forces of reaction. They will be seen as impeding rather than facilitating the development of positive action policies and as affording an easy scapegoat for employers reluctant to introduce changes. Thus managers at British Rail are most insistent that the railway unions constitute the greatest obstacle to change (Robbins, 1986: 42). Clearly then, some of the unions have a great deal of work to do, to put their own houses in order. The Society of Graphical and Allied Trades (SOGAT), for example, despite the use of a standard equal opportunities agreement in its negotiations with employers and its worthy efforts on the equal value front, has been exposed by the EOC as a persistent discriminator.[11] The same lack of consistency operates with regard to racial issues. In its code of practice, the CRE considered it necessary to warn employers against limiting recruitment to trade union sources, where this might exclude members of certain racial groups (CRE, 1983, Code of Practice: 10).

In general, it is not membership as such that is the problem, but rather the absence of women and black members from the decision-making bodies of the unions. Although the proportion of women workers who join trade unions is lower than that of male workers, the gap has closed considerably in recent years and women now constitute more than a third of the total union membership. West Indian and Asian workers have tended to join unions more frequently than white workers, a tendency which is particularly noticeable for black women workers.[12]

Table 3.1 shows the extent to which women are still under-

TABLE 3.1
Representation of women in trade unions, January 1986

Union	Membership		Women Executive members (% of total)	Women full-time officials (% of total)	Women TUC delegates (% of total)
	Number of women	% of total			
Amalgamated Engineering Union (AEU)	100,000[a]	10–12[a]	0	1	2
Assoc. of Professional, Clerical & Computer Staffs (APEX)	50,000	54	20	4	45
Assoc. of Scientific, Technical & Managerial Staffs (ASTMS)	84,000	24	9	9	13
Banking, Insurance & Finance Union (BIFU)	82,000	52	10	25	40
Confed. of Health Service Employees (COHSE)	184,000	80	14	12	21
Civil and Public Services Assoc. (CPSA)	105,000	70	41	21	50
General, Municipal, Boilermakers & Allied Trades Union (GMBATU)	256,000	31	3	4	4
National and Local Government Officers Assoc. (NALGO)	391,000	52	32	13	29
National Union of Public Employees (NUPE)	449,000	67	42	7	34
National Union of Teachers (NUT)	153,000	72	16	10	19
National Union of Tailors & Garment Workers (NUTGW)	71,000	90	79	14	71
Transport & General Workers Union (TGWU)	229,000	16	3	2	4
Union of Shop, Distributive & Allied Workers (USDAW)	239,000	61	19	13	27

[a] Union estimate.

Sources: Labour Research, April 1986; EOC (1986), *Women and Men in Britain: a Statistical Profile.*

represented within the union hierarchy six years after the TUC adopted a ten point charter designed to alter this situation (see Appendix 1). There are signs of improvement however, and in some unions the changes have been quite spectacular. For example, in 1981, only 3 percent of full-time officials and only 28 percent of TUC delegates in the Civil and Public Services Association were women, although women comprised some 70 percent of the total member-ship; by 1986, these percentages had risen to 21 and 50 respectively. Although women are still under-represented in the higher echelons of the unions, their involvement at local level has increased, so that unions are becoming more responsive to the needs of women mem-bers. Positive action to increase women's participation is taking a variety of forms, for example: providing special training courses for women, reserving seats for women on decision-making bodies and assisting with child care to facilitate attendance at union meetings (see *Labour Research*, April 1986: 13–15).

As trade unions do not record the ethnic origin of their members, it is not possible to obtain a precise picture of ethnic minority participa-tion. According to the Policy Studies Institute survey however, black union members attend branch meetings just as frequently as white members, but are much less likely to have held an elected post (Brown, 1984: 170). A report produced by the Lancashire Associa-tion of Trades Councils in 1985 found no black full-time union officers in Lancashire and an almost universal lack of knowledge about the TUC Charter for Black Workers and the CRE's Code of Practice at shop steward site and branch levels (LATC/CRE, 1985).

The Black Workers' Charter was adopted by the TUC in 1981. It recognized the need to combat racism in the workplace, including trade union racism, and outlined the steps that should be taken to encourage black membership and participation (see Appendix 1). It also reproduced a model equal opportunities clause (see Appendix 1). Some unions have responded positively in the form of working parties, race relations committees and equal rights officers, but a wide gap still exists between official statements of policy and their rigorous and effective implementation. In 1983 the Labour Research Department found that only a few unions had issued statements against racism and set up bodies to monitor these policies and only one (the GMBATU) had held national meetings and conferences on the issue of racism (*Labour Research*, July 1983). In a survey of thirty-three major national unions two years later, *Labour Research* reported that thirteen had black full-time officials, an improvement on the findings of an earlier TUC survey; it also pointed to a rela-tionship between black representation and a union's willingness to take up issues of concern to black members (Labour Research

Department, 1985). Once a union has taken steps to ensure the adequate representation of women and black workers within its own organization, it is well placed to pursue positive action at the workplace.

Increasing the pressure on employers

After ten years of legislation which opened the door to positive action programmes but did nothing to entice or push anyone through the door, there is very little progress to report. The plans recently set in motion by a number of public and private sector employers are still in their infancy and have as yet borne little fruit. This time, the finger of blame cannot be pointed at the judiciary. On the contrary, the major potential strength of a positive action programme lies in its ability to tackle direct and indirect discrimination at the workplace in a systematic fashion, without waiting for the judges to decide precisely what these terms mean.

The weakness of the measures lies in the absence of any incentive to implement them, combined with the practical difficulties of doing so at a time of rising unemployment and a shrinking labour force. For a brief period, the Greater London Council provided us with a glimpse of what might be possible, given an expanding workforce and a single-minded commitment to positive action. Not only did the GLC implement a contract compliance policy to persuade other employers to develop equal opportunities policies, it also pursued a vigorous programme of positive action for its own employees. Equality targets were set in each department, new recruitment and selection procedures were established and training courses provided in an effort to open up new areas and levels of employment for women and black workers. After four years, the Council was able to report an increase in the percentage of ethnic minority employees from 7 to 11 percent and an increase of around a quarter in the proportion of women, so that they constituted 21 percent of the workforce. Despite the 'impressive' increase in the number of women holding senior positions and a 33 percent rise in the number of ethnic minority employees entering the non-manual grades, the report recognized that a great deal more needed to be done (GLC, July 1985). Unfortunately, the abolition of the GLC brought many of these experiments to a halt and it has been left to others to take up the challenge of positive action.

Local authorities in general are coming under pressure from central government to put services out to tender, rather than employ labour directly; the attachment of any conditions which might deter employers from submitting competitive tenders is discouraged. In other words, although contract compliance is legal, the current emphasis on privatization and de-restriction does nothing to facilitate it.[13]

Although one might expect public sector employers to be leading the field in developing positive action programmes, the record is patchy. The Civil Service has conducted a review of women's employment opportunities within the Service and is also collecting data on the ethnic origins of existing staff and job applicants.[14] Following the publication of the CRE report which revealed a serious under-representation of black employees working for the Kirklees Borough Council (CRE, June 1984), several other local authorities in multi-racial areas have begun to scrutinize their own employment practices. In 1986 however, *Labour Research* reported that of the forty local authorities with a higher than average population originating from the 'new commonwealth' or Pakistan, only ten were monitoring an equal opportunities policy to see how it operated in practice and only nine had introduced contract compliance (*Labour Research*, May 1986). Similarly, a survey of London's thirty District Health Authorities found that although twenty-one of them had an equal opportunities policy, only five were attempting to implement action programmes in line with the CRE's code of practice; the rest had not even begun the process of data collection, an essential prerequisite for an effective programme of action (London Association of Community Relations Councils, 1985). Within the private sector, although a small number of employers are leading the way, the CRE admits that there are still many companies which are content with paper exercises and are making no effort to review their employment practices (CRE, *From Words to Action*, July 1985).

For positive action to make a serious and long-lasting impact on patterns of employment, the measures would need to be strengthened and backed by sanctions. Sanctions with immediate financial consequences, such as contract compliance and the withholding of licences, would be an important component of such an enforcement strategy. Employers in both the public and private sector would be required to collect the necessary workforce statistics, establish programmes of action and set targets for rectifying any sexual and racial inequalities revealed by the statistics. The EOC and the CRE would prove invaluable at this stage as they would have the necessary expertise to identify the sources of the discrimination and prescribe the appropriate remedial action. Full co-operation between the two Commissions would be essential in order to avoid an unnecessary duplication of effort.

Although a system of quotas produces rapid and dramatic results, its application in the job market would tend to accentuate rather than dissipate racial hostility. If it entailed the selection of people with inferior qualifications merely because they were black or female (or both), those selected might feel patronized and those not selected might see themselves as a new class of victim. Hence the importance of training schemes which would render such preferential treatment unnecessary.

American and British experiences with positive action show that a sustained political commitment is even more important than a strong legal framework, although both are required for maximum effectiveness. If there is a genuine determination to fight sexism and racism, progress can be made even if the enforcement procedures are inadequate. If the political will is lacking, even strong legislative measures are ineffective. This second scenario is vividly portrayed by the fate that has befallen a British statute of more than forty years standing: the Disabled Persons (Employment) Act 1944. Initially designed to secure jobs for the war disabled at a time of acute labour shortage, the Act established a quota system which positively discriminated in favour of workers with disabilities. All firms with more than twenty employees are required to ensure that at least 3 percent of their workforce are registered as disabled and that adequate records on this are kept. An employer who is below quota is supposed to offer any vacancy to a registered disabled person. If such a person cannot be found, the employer can apply for a permit to employ a worker who is not disabled. It is an offence to dismiss a registered employee if that would place the firm below quota.

As the moral fervour and economic conditions that inspired the 1944 Act evaporated, so did the political will to ensure its enforcement. The percentage of private employers fulfilling their quota declined from just over 60 percent in 1960 to just over 30 percent in 1982. An increasing number of firms are issued with block permits so that they do not have to offer vacancies to workers with disabilities. Government departments, although not legally bound by the Act, had agreed to accept the same moral responsibility but only one — the Royal Mint — was meeting its 3 percent quota in 1983. In the first forty years of the Act, there were only ten prosecutions. Fines, amounting to £334 in total, were imposed in only seven cases. The 1944 Act has not been repealed; it has simply been allowed to remain dormant. The emphasis has shifted from compulsion to persuasion, with the introduction of a 'fit for work' campaign, a voluntary code of practice and a system of awards to encourage employers to make a positive response (Lonsdale and Walker, 1984).

The limits of positive action
In order to mollify the harsher consequences of competitive individualism, capitalist democracies have been forced to compromise

the principle of formal equality by making a series of pragmatic excursions into the area of substantive equality. However tentative, such excursions are fraught with difficulty. First, there is no simple formula which will resolve the competing claims of people with special needs. For example, if war veterans are awarded extra points on occupational tests, this discriminates against women, who are less likely to have served in the armed forces. To take another example: if a re-drawing of electoral boundaries is required in order to protect the voting rights of the non-white population, what are the rights of Hasidic Jews, who, formerly located in one electoral district, now find themselves split between a number of different districts?[15]

Second, the protective arm of the state brings with it some loss of 'citizenship' and welfare recipients find themselves in a gift relationship, in which benefits are exchanged for freedom of action. A similar stigma attaches itself to positive discrimination, if it is presented as the triumph of ascriptive criteria over the search for merit. Hence the British preference for the term 'positive action', regarded not as a departure from meritocratic principles but as a refinement of them. Positive action ensures the more efficient distribution within the meritocracy by drawing on previously neglected areas of talent. Although quotas are rejected as demeaning and unfair, setting goals and devising strategies for achieving these goals are essential components of an effective positive action programme (see Stamp and Robarts, 1986: 1).

Positive action measures are an important step on the road to justice, but they will not by themselves guarantee the production of a just society. The commitment must be sustained and total, otherwise there is the danger that a few 'token' individuals, the least disadvantaged members of the disadvantaged group, will be co-opted into the ranks of the privileged, merely increasing the despair of those left behind. Positive action may help us to integrate a larger number of women and black people into existing structures, but unless that is seen as the first step in a fundamental re-shaping of the structures themselves, then those people will simply be replaced by yet another disadvantaged group.

Notes

1. From a letter to *The Daily* (University of Washington) in July 1971, quoted in Scheingold (1974).

2. The National Association of Managers has expressed its support for the retention of Order 11246 in its present form; 95 percent of the largest American corporations have indicated that they will make no changes in their affirmative action programmes, whatever happens to the Order (see Stamp and Robarts, 1986: 119). However, the Reagan 'backlash' is not always so easily neutralized. Through the control of funding and appointments, not least those of the Supreme Court judges,

many of the fragile gains of the previous decades have been eroded during the 1980s (see Meehan, 1985: 99, 101, 128, 144. On Reagan's Supreme Court appointments see Hoggart, *The Observer*, 22 June 1986).

3. The Sex Discrimination Act 1986 widened this provision to allow 'any person' to offer single sex training. At the same time, it removed the need for those providing such training to seek designation from the Secretary of State. The words 'training body' in Section 47 of the SDA 1975 (see Appendix 4) are therefore replaced by the words 'any person'. The equivalent provision of the RRA, Section 37 remains unchanged.

4. Section 47 of the Race Relations Act was inserted into the Bill when the deliberations of the standing committee were well advanced. An equivalent section, s. 56A, was then added to the Sex Discrimination Act (see Race Relations Act 1976, Schedule 4: Amendments to the Sex Discrimination Act 1975). Section 47 of the RRA is reproduced in Appendix 4.

5. See Stamp and Robarts, 1986: 71. The Austin Rover equality agreement is reproduced in *Equal Opportunities Review*, No. 6, March/April 1986: 24. The implications of the Data Protection Act 1984 for keeping records on the ethnic origins of employees are discussed in *Equal Opportunities Review*, No. 3, September/October 1985: 15–18.

6. This point has been made forcibly by Derek Hooper of the Southwark Institute's Industrial Language Unit. See 'Training to Overcome Prejudice', in *Equal Opportunities Review*, No. 3, September/October 1985: 8–14. Mr Hooper's views are given on pp. 13–14 of the article.

7. The Express Foods Group is one of the employers discussed by David Wainwright (1986). Details of positive action at London Regional Transport are given in *Equal Opportunities Review*, No. 2, July/August 1985. The problems of collecting statistics on the racial origins of employees and job applicants are discussed in 'Ethnic Monitoring: Issues and Practice', *Equal Opportunities Review*, No. 7, May/June 1986: 6–12.

8. Most of the information on the banking industry is taken from an article entitled 'Industry Focus: Banks and Equal Opportunity', in *Equal Opportunities Review*, No. 9, September/October 1986: 4–11. See also *Equal Opportunities Review*, No. 4, November/December 1985, for articles on the Midland Bank equal opportunities manager and on the agreement between the EOC and Barclays. The two tribunal cases involving Lloyds Bank are Worringham v Lloyds Bank 1981 IRLR 178 and Lloyds Bank v Secretary of State for Employment 1979 IRLR 41.

9. BIFU has been especially vigilant on behalf of its women membership, both in the pursuit of equal value claims and in seeking to break down the barriers of job segregation. On the latter, see BIFU (1984).

10. See for example 'Achieving a Balanced Workforce 1: Recruitment of Ethnic Minorities', *Equal Opportunities Review*, No. 1, May/June 1985, where Littlewoods, Massey Ferguson and the West Yorkshire Passenger Transport Executive are all quoted as developing equal opportunities programmes without involving the trade unions.

11. SOGAT's intervention on behalf of the women bookbinders is referred to in Chapter 1: an account of the EOC's enforcement action against SOGAT can be found in Chapters 6 and 7.

12. According to the Policy Studies Institute survey conducted in 1982, 61 percent of West Indian and Asian male workers were members of a union, compared with 57 percent of the white male workforce. For women workers the percentages were 48 and 35 respectively (see Brown, 1984).

13. In February 1985 the government published a green paper entitled *Competition in the Provision of Local Authority Services*. The paper includes a proposal to declare void any term or condition in a contract if it is not directly related to the 'required performance' of the contractor 'in respect of the quality, timing or cost of the specified goods and services' (para 16(a)). If such a proposal were to become law, it would, to say the least, create a dilemma for those local authorities which have taken seriously their duties under s 71 of the Race Relations Act. For further discussion of the Local Government Bill which will enact the green paper proposals see postscript, pp. 165–6.

14. See *Equal Opportunities for Women in the Civil Service*, a report by the Joint Review Group on Employment Opportunities for Women in the Civil Service, HMSO 1982. The Civil Service model code of practice on ethnic monitoring is reproduced in *Equal Opportunities Review*, No. 3, September/October 1985: 16–17.

15. The war veteran example is taken from Miller (1974). The second example is provided by the case of United Jewish Organizations v Carey 430 US 144 [1977]. The majority opinion of the Court was to regard the Hasidim as part of the white population and so to dismiss the complaint.

4 The individual route to equality: industrial tribunals

The history of legislative reform teaches us that it is not enough to devise radical new concepts and then sit back and wait for the social transformation to unfold. The procedures used for implementing the new policies are every bit as important as the policies themselves. If the new measures cannot be fitted comfortably into the practices and ideologies of the people responsible for enforcement, they may be diluted beyond all recognition.

The choice of enforcement mechanisms for a new piece of legislation is usually a matter of expediency: there may seem to be little point in devising new mechanisms if it is possible to make use of existing ones. When, therefore, the decision was made to allow the victims of discrimination to bring legal proceedings on their own behalf, the suggestion that special anti-discrimination tribunals be created for this purpose was rejected in favour of using existing legal structures. Industrial tribunals were given jurisdiction in cases of employment discrimination; complaints of discrimination in other areas were to be dealt with by the county courts.

The employment provisions of the sex discrimination and race relations legislation were thus firmly located within the framework of industrial relations law, a decision to some extent pre-empted by the way in which the Equal Pay Act had been devised in 1970.[1] The Equal Pay and Sex Discrimination Acts were to take effect on the same day (29 December 1975) and were seen as complementary. As complaints about equal pay were to be handled by industrial tribunals, the simplest solution was to extend their jurisdiction yet again to cover sex discrimination in employment. This would simplify the problem of untangling equal pay and sex discrimination disputes where they overlapped. Conciliation officers from the Advisory, Conciliation and Arbitration Service (ACAS) would have the same duties in respect of both types of dispute, as would the Equal Opportunities Commission. Appeals from the industrial tribunals on points of law would be heard by the new Employment Appeal Tribunal (set up under the Trade Union and Labour Relations Act 1974 in place of the much despised National Industrial Relations Court). The arrangements had an appealing symmetry and opposition was muted, even when the same formula was extended to the Race Relations Act. Some commentators did however regret the absence of legal aid for industrial tribunal applicants (see for example Bindman, 1976).

Absence of legal aid was not an oversight on the part of the policy-makers. Industrial tribunals, first established under the Industrial Training Act 1964 to hear appeals from employers against levies imposed by training boards, were intended to dispense justice informally, cheaply and rapidly; legal representatives would tend to impede this process. The practical experience of the two lay members, drawn from 'the two sides of industry' was considered just as important to the conduct and outcome of the hearing as the skills of the lawyer who would chair the proceedings.

The workload of industrial tribunals was transformed by the Redundancy Payments Act 1965 and again by the Industrial Relations Act 1971, so that the bulk of the caseload no longer consisted of claims made by employers against administrative decisions by government bodies. Instead, it was the employers who were called to account as increasing numbers of workers filed claims against them in relation to redundancy payments and unfair dismissal. In the view of the first president of industrial tribunals, it would be a mistake if this shift in emphasis were to signal the advent of greater formality. On the contrary, tribunals should dispense 'simple, informal justice in an atmosphere in which the ordinary man [sic] feels he is at home'. They were to be, in effect, the 'people's courts'.[2]

So how successful are these 'people's courts' in dispensing 'simple, informal justice'? A useful starting point for answering this question is to see how many people file complaints under the sex and race discrimination legislation and what proportion of these emerge at the other end with a tribunal decision in their favour. Table 4.1 reveals that the majority of applicants fall by the wayside; more than half never reach a tribunal hearing and, of those that do, only a handful are successful in winning their cases. The individual route to equality is evidently strewn with pitfalls. Before the tribunals can play an effective role in eradicating employment discrimination, we need to identify and remove as many of these pitfalls as possible. First, therefore, we need to consider why such a large proportion of cases is withdrawn before the tribunal hearing and second, why so many applicants are unable to convince the tribunal of the merits of their complaint. Third, it would be useful to discover what distinguishes the successful applicants from the others and how effective are the remedies awarded to them.

TABLE 4.1
Outcome of tribunal applications

	Equal Pay		Sex discrimination		Race discrimination	
	Number	Percent	Number	Percent	Number	Percent
1976						
Applications	1,742	100.0	243	100.0		
Total heard	709	40.7	119	49.0		
Dismissed	496	28.5	95	39.1		
Upheld	213	12.2	24	9.9		
1977					**1977/78**[a]	
Applications	751	100.0	229	100.0	146	100.0
Total heard	363	48.3	77	33.6	66	45.2
Dismissed	272	36.2	60	26.2	61	41.8
Upheld	91	12.1	17	7.4	5	3.4
1978					**1978/79**	
Applications	343	100.0	171	100.0	364	100.0
Total heard	80	23.3	67	39.2	188	51.6
Dismissed	56	16.3	53	31.0	130	36.0
Upheld	24	7.0	14	8.2	58	16.0
1979					**1979/80**	
Applications	263	100.0	178	100.0	426	100.0
Total heard	78	29.7	59	33.1	203	47.6
Dismissed	65	24.7	45	25.3	181	42.5
Upheld	13	4.9	14	7.9	22	5.0
1980					**1980/81**	
Applications	91	100.0	180	100.0	330	100.0
Total heard	26	28.6	69	38.3	137	41.5
Dismissed	22	24.4	15	30.6	120	36.4
Upheld	4	4.4	14	7.8	17	5.1
1981					**1981 (July/Dec)**[b]	
Applications	54	100.0	256	100.0	172	100.0
Total heard	27	50.0	89	34.8	71	41.3
Dismissed	21	38.9	73	28.5	65	37.8
Upheld	6	11.1	16	6.3	6	3.5
1982					**1982**	
Applications	39	100.0	150	100.0	273	100.0
Total heard	13	33.3	56	37.3	124	45.4
Dismissed	11	28.2	32	21.3	105	38.5
Upheld	2	5.1	24	16.0	19	7.0

	Equal Pay		Sex discrimination		Race discrimination	
	Number	Percent	Number	Percent	Number	Percent
1983						
Applications	35	100.0	265	100.0	310	100.0
Total heard	15	42.8	116	43.7	166	53.5
Dismissed	6	17.1	54	20.3	131	42.3
Upheld	9	25.7	62	23.4	35	11.3
1984						
Applications	70	100.0	310	100.0	364	100.0
Total heard	24	34.3	118	38.0	158	43.4
Dismissed	13	18.5	66	21.3	129	35.4
Upheld	11	15.7	52	16.8	29	8.0
1985 (Jan/Mar)[c]						
Applications	65	100.0	26	100.0	69	100.0
Total heard	2	3.0	9	34.6	37	53.6
Dismissed	2	3.0	4	15.4	29	42.0
Upheld	–	0	5	19.2	8	11.6

[a] For the first four years, the race statistics were calculated from 1 July to 30 June.
[b] In 1981, an adjustment was made so that subsequent figures could be presented for the calendar year.
[c] In 1985, a further adjustment prepared the way for all three sets of statistics to be presented for the financial year, April–March.
Source: Department of Employment Gazettes and EOC (1985), *Annual Report*: 49.

Applicants who withdraw

Some applicants will withdraw their cases because the employer concedes that their complaint is justified and agrees to make amends; others will withdraw on discovering that their case falls outside the scope of the law. These explanations, however, account for only a small minority of applicants who withdrew. All the research evidence relating to this group demonstrates that the vast majority still believe in the merits of their complaints but withdraw as a result of various pressures.[3]

Such pressures might come from the employer, who often feels insulted by the suggestion that he[4] has discriminated; if he is not inclined to compromise, he is in a position to make life very uncomfortable for an employee who insists on pursuing the case. Although the law offers protection for workers who are victimized as a consequence of pursuing their rights under the anti-discrimination laws (see section 4 of the SDA and section 2 of the RRA, reproduced in Appendix 4), almost no cases are brought under these provisions; yet there is evidence that victimization is a frequent occurrence (see

Graham and Lewis, 1985: 48; Kumar, 1986: 22). Pressures may also come from friends and relatives concerned for the physical and mental well-being of the applicant. Workmates who had offered their services as witnesses will often have second thoughts and may themselves be subjected to pressure by the employer.

Given the vulnerability of the individual employee and the employer's monopoly over information which may be vital for presenting the complaint, it seems very clear that unless the employee is guaranteed a considerable amount of support and assistance, the whole idea of filing a complaint is simply a non-starter. As Margaret Legum put it when the third Race Relations Act became law:

> The mind boggles at the almost lunatic kind of courage an ordinary black citizen would need to go into court on his [sic] own against lawyers employed by a large institution on which his future may depend. (Legum, 1977)

ACAS is the only agency that has information on all tribunal applications and is therefore strategically placed to take action in all cases. Yet ACAS conciliation officers are not in a position to provide a supportive role for applicants; their brief is to act impartially, to convey information and explore the common ground between the two sides in the hope of arranging a settlement. Many applicants are understandably eager to settle the dispute and so avoid the agonies of litigation. Unfortunately, the intervention of the conciliation officer does not ensure that the best settlement terms are obtained; the rights and wrongs of a particular case are subordinated to the over-riding concern with conciliation. The 'impartial' role of the officer does nothing to redress the imbalance of power between the complainant and the employer. On the contrary, many applicants (and some employers) regard the officer as the employer's representative and claim that his or her (usually his) advice was the decisive factor in their decision to withdraw. Two examples, the first taken from a study of equal pay and sex discrimination applicants and the second from a similar study of race discrimination applicants, provide a graphic illustration of the kind of pressure that is exercised by some conciliation officers.

A woman advised by the conciliation officer to drop her case wrote:

> He said that if you take a case to the tribunal, the onus is on you to produce the evidence to prove your case. If you lose the case you have to pay the costs and you can't ask for a reference from your employers if you leave. He said that the number of cases which go through successfully are virtually nil. All this information succeeded in putting me off. He also asked me who had told me I could make a complaint about sex discrimination and I told him the Jobcentre had. He said they shouldn't do that.

In fact, Jobcentres are an important source of information on tribunal rights and procedure (see Gregory, 1982 for a full discussion of this and similar cases).

The researcher in the race discrimination study recounts a similar experience:

> The information given to the applicant was entirely negative. [The conciliation officer] advised the applicant of the low overall success rates in such cases, said that the employers had a good case and that if he lost it might cost him £200 in legal costs. His impression was that the officer was only interested in getting the applicant to withdraw the case: 'he talked to me for a few minutes and then handed me the form to withdraw'. The applicant did not want to withdraw the case there and then but preferred to seek some advice and so the officer left the form with him, stressing that withdrawal was best. The applicant did not in fact seek independent advice before withdrawing but completed the form a few days later after receiving daily telephone calls from the officer asking him if he had filled out the form yet. Asked why he withdrew he said he was 'fed up' and felt pressurised by the officer both at the meeting and because of the frequent 'phone calls which gave him, he said, no chance to think on his own. (Byrne, 1982: 38)

Even if the vast majority of conciliation officers perform their duties more sensitively than the officers in these two examples, the simple act of imparting information, whether it takes the form of messages from the employer, or facts on tribunal procedure and success rates, may well have an intimidating effect on the applicant.

Other sources of support are available to some tribunal applicants but not all. Many will seek help from their trade union although this is not a realistic option for those who are unemployed (as is often the case where the complaint relates to an application for work). By no means all those who do seek union backing are satisfied with the quality of help they receive. Responses range from those which give glowing reports of union involvement to those claiming that the union was in league with the employer. The absence of union involvement is particularly striking in cases involving black workers. In equal pay and sex discrimination cases, union members are equally divided between those who found the union helpful and those who did not (see Gregory, 1982: 78; Graham and Lewis, 1985: 36). In race discrimination cases however, only 8 percent of complainants were assisted by their union, although nearly a quarter had regarded the union as their first source of help (Kumar, 1986).

Union officials who seem to be unsupportive may well be colluding with the management in opposing an equal pay claim or defending a discriminatory agreement; in cases of racial or sexual harassment, they may be acutely embarrassed by the involvement of union members on both sides. Others may simply be incompetent or apathetic, reflecting a lack of understanding of, or commitment to, anti-discrimination issues.

The EOC and the CRE have discretionary powers to assist tribunal applicants in a number of ways, including giving advice in preparing a case for the tribunal and providing representation at the hearing itself. The support provided by the Commissions is generally of a high quality, but unfortunately is not offered to all those who seek it. Many applicants do not even approach the Commissions for assistance, often because they are unaware that this service is available. Although ACAS claims that 'the conciliation officer draws the complainant's attention to the help which is available from the EOC and the CRE' (ACAS, 1979: 8), in practice there seems to be an extraordinary reluctance to do this.

In the present circumstances, it is not possible for the Commissions to provide a system of support for all the victims of discrimination. Given scarce resources and a range of other statutory powers and duties, the Commissions have to be selective. The process of selection does, however, leave much to be desired. There is no obligation on the Commissioners to explain why requests for assistance are turned down. Such a rejection might have nothing to do with the merits of a particular case. A negative decision might derive from a belief in the competence of the applicant to conduct his or her own case, or result from a particular case strategy in operation at the time. Such processes are mysterious to the applicant, so that it comes as no surprise to learn that a high proportion of cases rejected by the Commissions is subsequently withdrawn.

Every research study that has considered the question of why so many applicants withdraw their cases before they can be heard by the tribunal reaches the same conclusion: without an adequate system of support and representation, it is virtually impossible for an employee to enter this procedural minefield and emerge triumphant at the other end with a decision in his or her favour. Applicants who represent themselves are handicapped at every stage of the proceedings and are more likely to abandon their cases even if the employer has made no offer (or only a derisory offer) to settle the complaint.

Recent changes in tribunal procedure have made the need for a system of representation all the more urgent. Whereas in the past the applicants' fears that costs might be awarded against them were largely unfounded as such an award was only made in cases found to be 'vexatious and frivolous', this rule was broadened in 1980 to cover any party 'acting unreasonably'. At the same time, provision was made for a 'pre-hearing assessment', a private meeting of the tribunal at which a decision could be taken to issue a costs warning (The Industrial Tribunals (Rules of Procedure) Regulations 1980, S I No.

884). More recently, the government has proposed that all tribunal applicants be charged a fee of £25 when making the application, refundable if the case were to be successful or the claim withdrawn (see *Building Businesses . . . Not Barriers*, HMSO, 1986). This proposal is designed to reduce the number of complaints brought against employers; it has nothing to do with ensuring that the victims of discrimination are provided with an effective means of redress.

Applicants who lose

If the rate of withdrawals seems high, the failure rate of cases which do reach a tribunal hearing is simply staggering. Even though we have just cast doubt on the view that it is necessarily the weaker cases that drop by the wayside, we might have expected a fair proportion of those cases surviving the preliminary 'cooling out' stages to be successful. Also, we might have expected some improvement over time, with the development of case law and increasing familiarity with the concept of discrimination. Table 4.1 shows that over the years, the vast majority of cases have been dismissed by industrial tribunals. For sex discrimination cases, there has been some improvement in recent years, but for cases under the Race Relations Act the failure rate remains high.

A major difficulty faced by applicants in presenting their case to the tribunal is that they have to shoulder the burden of proof and convince the tribunal that the treatment they received was discriminatory. This is a departure from the practice established by the Trade Union and Labour Relations Act 1974 in relation to unfair dismissal cases. In such cases, once the employee has established that he or she has been dismissed, the burden of proving that the dismissal was fair rests firmly with the employer.[5] The 1974 white paper *Equality for Women* proposed a similar arrangement: the complainant had only to show that unfavourable treatment had occurred, then it would fall to the employer to prove that the detrimental action had not been taken on 'grounds of sex or marriage' (HMSO, 1974: para. 86). This proposal was dropped at the last minute on advice from the Scottish Law Office (see Meehan, 1985: 67) and the burden of proof in direct discrimination cases was left with the complainant.[6]

This may seem to be a somewhat technical argument. Surely, if the members of the tribunal wish to unravel the facts of a particular dispute, they will seek the necessary evidence from both parties, so that the burden of proof in practice would shift back and forth during the hearing. Unfortunately, tribunal hearings rarely conform to this pattern, partly because of the adversarial nature of the proceedings. As in any civil action, a contest takes place between two adversaries; when it is over, the judges (or tribunal) decide on the balance of probabilities who is the winner. Tribunals are extraordinarily reluctant to interfere in this process, in case they appear to be biased. They tend therefore to play a relatively passive role, even if the employer is legally represented and the employee is not.

Another major disadvantage of the present arrangements for adjudicating discrimination cases has been identified in a recent piece of research by Alice Leonard (1987a). Although her study was confined to equal pay and sex discrimination applications, it seems likely that many of her comments would apply equally to race discrimination cases and there is some evidence for this in the CRE study to which we have already referred (Kumar, 1986).

Analysing all tribunal decisions on equal pay and sex discrimination made during 1980, 1981 and 1982, Leonard discovered that the cases were distributed so widely across the tribunal membership that no-one was able to develop any expertise of this jurisdiction. Two hundred and fifteen cases were distributed among 116 different chairpersons (usually men), so that the majority only chaired one or two such cases during the three year period and only seven people chaired more than one case a year. The selection of the 'lay' membership was just as broad, with the result that very few of those chosen heard more than one equal pay or sex discrimination case during the three year period. Given the lack of formal training and the complexity of the legislation, it comes as no surprise to discover that the quality of decision making was extremely low. Leonard found a complete lack of uniformity in the way the law was interpreted and even found a number of cases in which the tribunal had misapplied or misunderstood the legislation. Perhaps understandably, the tribunals tended to draw on their much greater experience with unfair dismissal cases and consequently applied the wrong legal standard. They would consider whether the employer had behaved reasonably rather than whether he had treated his employees equally. Many cases fell as a result of this concept of the 'reasonable employer', although the treatment accorded to the women was patently unequal and therefore illegal. For example, one tribunal accepted that a woman given a car mileage allowance when her male colleague had a company car was treated reasonably.

Leonard also comments on the general paucity of evidence presented to the tribunals, so that most cases are lost by default. The better and more specialized the evidence, the greater the chance of applicant success. In the great majority of cases, the tribunal considered only verbal testimony occasionally supported by a few documents. The success rate in these cases was only 25 percent. In the few cases where the tribunal was presented with detailed, specially prepared documentation and expert witnesses, the success rate rose to

46 percent. Other positive factors associated with success rate were presence of a full-time rather than a part-time chairperson and the presence of a woman on the tribunal. Leonard points out that in Scotland, where the tribunal included a woman and a full-time chairperson in every case, the success rate was 42 percent. The finding that applicants appeared to receive a more sympathetic hearing from a woman confirms the feelings of many applicants that women have a greater understanding of discrimination issues.

In race discrimination cases, which are normally heard by full-time chairpersons and members with some expertise in race relations, applicants are more sceptical about the value of black tribunal members. In the CRE study, a third of the applicants reported the presence of an Asian or Afro-Caribbean member on the tribunal, but opinion was equally divided as to whether this made any difference to the outcome of the case (see Kumar, 1986: 14). Unfortunately, the research report does not provide an answer on this point.

It is clear from this research that a number of minor administrative changes would improve markedly the chance that applicants would receive a fair hearing. A shortlist of appropriate people to hear discrimination cases could be compiled. Steps could then be taken to ensure that they were adequately trained and given the chance to develop expertise in this jurisdiction. More radical proposals for change should also be considered. Corcoran and Donnelly (1984), for example, have conducted a comparative study of the methods for bringing discrimination cases in the various EEC countries. They reached the conclusion that an inquisitorial system is more appropriate than an adversarial system for discrimination cases. Under an inquisitorial system of justice, it is the court or tribunal which directs proceedings from the outset, requesting the evidence and asking the questions. In France, the court is assisted in this process by officials known as 'rapporteurs', who examine the evidence and order the production of documents and the attendance of witnesses accordingly.

There can be no doubt that there is an urgent need to improve the quality of the evidence available to the tribunal before it reaches a decision. Adopting an inquisitorial system might, however, prove to be a leap out of the frying pan into the fire. An inquisitorial system places the parties to the dispute very much at the mercy of the court or tribunal, whose discretionary powers are greatly enhanced. A better strategy would be to retain the present system but provide an adequate method of representation so that the adversaries are more evenly matched. Nor is there any reason why tribunals in an adversarial system should not be assisted in assembling the necessary evidence. A useful precedent exists in the form of 'independent experts' created under the equal value regulations. Inevitably, this would cause some delay in the proceedings, but if the end result is a greater measure of justice for the victims of discrimination, it is a price worth paying.

Applicants who win: the price of success
At last we turn to the small group of people for whom the nightmare of litigation has proved to be worthwhile — or has it? Another excellent study by Alice Leonard (1987b) turns the spotlight on 70 of the 151 equal pay and sex discrimination claimants who won their tribunal cases during the five years from 1980 to 1984 inclusive. She discovers that many of them paid a very high price for their victory, both in terms of emotional stress and a souring of relationships, and financially. The greatest financial costs were not so much those directly associated with the case in the form of legal fees and related expenses, but arose because so many of the applicants left their jobs and had difficulty in securing alternative employment. Only seventeen of the seventy applicants stayed with the employer after their victory at the tribunal hearing; five of these left within six months and a further two during the next two years.

Those applicants who had never worked for the employer — because their complaint related to discrimination in recruitment practices — reported a lower level of stress in bringing the case than did other applicants. Some only filed their complaint after they had ceased working for the employer, either because their application related to dismissal or redundancy or because they obtained employment elsewhere. Several others had left by the time the case was heard, believing that they had no future with the company or simply because working conditions had become intolerable. The rest were forced by the employer to leave: they were dismissed or made redundant as a direct consequence of their application (victimized). Some who stuck it out until after the hearing left shortly afterwards because the situation became unbearable. The following description is typical:

> Life was made difficult. Two or three months after my tribunal the company informed the staff and shop floor that there were to be some redundancies. Several shop floor workers and myself were made redundant. I was offered work in another department as a typist. I have no typing ability and the salary was lower. My job which I fought for equal pay for, was divided between two men who I had worked with. The atmosphere was tense and after a few months I requested my redundancy and it was granted. (Leonard, 1987b: 24)

The severing of all relationships with the employer against whom the case was brought did not necessarily end the hostilities. Many applicants experienced tremendous difficulty in obtaining another job, especially if they were unable to delete the incident from their employment record. The two following examples provide a vivid illustration of this problem:

> As this is a small town, it is inclined to be small-minded. Mine is the only sex discrimination case ever, against a local employer. The case was reported in the paper. I think it spoilt my chances as soon as I mentioned my name. I am still unemployed.

> I cannot write for a reference and every job you apply for wants a reference. Most employers probably look upon me as a trouble maker. (Leonard, 1987b: 26)

It may be necessary at this point to remind ourselves that this punishment is being meted out to people whose complaints were upheld by the tribunal! Clearly then, we need to discover what award the tribunal made to the victims that compensated for all this suffering and also prompted such a vindictive response from the employers. In fact, the remedies available to industrial tribunals in discrimination cases are severely limited. The following courses of action are open to them:

(1) They can make an order declaring the rights of the complainant.
(2) They can order the employer to pay compensation, including compensation for injury to feelings.
(3) They can make a recommendation that the employer take action within a specified period to obviate or reduce the adverse effect of the discrimination. If he fails to comply and can offer no reasonable justification for this failure, the tribunal may increase the amount of compensation (see SDA section 65 and RRA section 56).

If we look at the tribunal statistics for the years 1980–1984 inclusive, we can discover what use the tribunals made of these powers on finding that a complaint of discrimination was justified. In sex discrimination cases, financial compensation was awarded to half the successful complainants; recommendations were made in 40 percent of the cases, while the remaining 10 percent had to make do with orders declaring their rights. In race discrimination cases, the proportion receiving financial settlements was higher: almost two-thirds of the applicants were awarded sums of money. Recommendations were made in most of the remaining cases, so that the percentage of orders fell to below four.[7]

The compensation awarded to the victims of discrimination can only be described as paltry. In 40 percent of the sex discrimination cases the award was less than £200 and in only 29 percent of the cases did the compensation exceed £1,000. The amount of compensation offered to the victims of racial discrimination is even more disgraceful. More than half the awards in such cases were below £200 and only 15 percent were offered a sum in excess of £1,000.

It is clear, then, that the price of discriminating is exceedingly low. Whereas tribunals are limited in the amount of compensation they are permitted to award, most of the time their awards came nowhere near these limits.[8] In its review of the Race Relations Act, the CRE refers to a case in which a young man who lost a Youth Training Scheme work placement as a result of discrimination and whom the tribunal described in its decision as 'shattered' was awarded the sum of £30 as compensation for injury to feelings. The CRE report points out that:

> Save for one exceptional award of £5,000 made in 1985 to a medical consultant not appointed because of discrimination, the highest sum previously awarded so far as we are aware was £750 in 1982 to each of three white applicants who had been discriminated against by a Nigerian-owned company. The compensation is generally regarded as too low by complainants, as a survey of our own shows. The Commission shares that view. The level of compensation for injury to feelings in racial discrimination cases has trivialised the whole matter and enabled people to make light of a serious hurt. (CRE, July 1985: 27)

Even more extraordinary is the apparent lack of interest on the part of those involved in the tribunal system in ensuring that its decisions are respected. One might have assumed that the compensation would be paid by the employer to the tribunal office, which would forward it to the applicant. In practice, it is left to the applicants themselves to collect the money. In Leonard's study of successful applicants, more than half the applicants had still not received the money due to them two months after the decision. Many employers delayed payment as long as possible, some lodging an appeal simply as a delaying tactic. Several were pursued through the county court, involving the claimant in further expense; some had ceased trading before the money could be paid. Even those applicants who had impeccable sources of support throughout the proceedings found themselves abandoned at this crucial stage. Consider, for example, the experience of a woman unfairly dismissed as a result of sex discrimination and awarded over £1,400 by the tribunal:

> (She) found the employer would not pay. But she was told by the solicitor that she could no longer represent her as the EOC would not pay her fees. She explained that the EOC cannot pay for efforts necessary *after* the hearing simply to collect the financial award. The applicant therefore went to another solicitor, paid £30 to register the affidavit needed by the

county court, another £30 for enforcement, and lost a day's wages while seeing the solicitor. At the time she answered the questionnaire, she had still not received the award money. (Leonard, 1987b: 18, emphasis in the original)

If the most tangible of the three remedies available to the tribunal can be so flagrantly flouted by the employers, it does not bode well for the practical enforcement of the two remaining remedies, declarations and recommendations. If the recommendations are ignored, the onus is on the applicant to go back to the tribunal and seek financial compensation. Any award made by the tribunal is likely to be small and may prove impossible to collect. As so very few applicants remain with the same employer after the hearing, it appears that employers can ignore tribunal decisions with impunity. In Leonard's study, of the seventeen who stayed with the employer *not one* believed that her employment situation had improved (see Leonard, 1987b: 25).

The CRE has argued for a strengthening of the remedies available to industrial tribunals in race discrimination cases, including raising the ceiling on compensation and empowering the tribunals to order the employer to appoint or promote the applicant in appropriate cases. At the present time the tribunal can order an employer to re-engage or reinstate an employee who has been unfairly dismissed. The CRE would like to see an extension of this power to cover all employees who have left their jobs as a consequence of discrimination (see CRE, July 1985: 26–9).

There can be no doubt that at the present time industrial tribunals are largely ineffective in meeting the challenge of employment discrimination. This is partly because their powers are inadequate, but also because no effective mechanisms exist for ensuring that their decisions are put into practice. The trade unions are ideally situated to take on this role, but it is difficult to see how they can be compelled to undertake it in the absence of any commitment to do so. It is, however, essential that this burden be removed immediately from the complainant. The EOC and the CRE should therefore be given the duty to follow up on all successful applications and to report any recalcitrant employers to the tribunal instantly.

Conclusion
Comparisons are often made between the ways in which the tribunal system deals with unfair dismissal claims and the way in which it deals with discrimination complaints. The inference is drawn that the system is equipped to handle the former but not the latter. It is argued that lay members can make use of their industrial relations experience in assessing whether or not the employer has behaved reason-

ably in dismissing an employee. In discrimination cases, on the other hand, it is precisely the common-sense approach to employment decisions that is being challenged. Far more employees file unfair dismissal applications every year: some 30,000 compared with two or three hundred discrimination cases. Such employees are likely to better informed of their rights through trade unions and jobcentres; also they do not have to face the employer every day at work while awaiting the tribunal hearing. ACAS certainly feels more at home with unfair dismissal cases, believing that there is a better chance of reaching a compromise. A smaller proportion of such cases is withdrawn without a settlement and more people come away from the tribunal with a favourable decision and a higher level of compensation.

However, it is possible to recognize that the problems are accentuated in discrimination cases without claiming that the tribunal system works perfectly in other jurisdictions. Indeed, the findings of those who have carried out research on unfair dismissal have a familiar ring. It is said that conciliation officers do not seek the best possible terms for applicants but, as in discrimination cases, encourage acceptance of the employer's first offer. Of those cases reaching a tribunal hearing, two-thirds lose and in the remaining third, employees rarely get their jobs back. Although the tribunal is empowered to order reinstatement or re-engagement, this power is hardly ever used. The easy option of terminating the employment relationship, with a payment of compensation to the employee, is the preferred course of action.[9]

When we have stripped away the factors that differentiate discrimination cases from unfair dismissal cases, we find that essentially the underlying process is the same. It is rooted in the principle of formal equality, which assumes that the contest takes place between two equal parties and steadfastly ignores the power differences that divide them. The tribunal members collude in this charade when sifting the evidence presented to them. They usually have to decide the facts of the case on the basis of two very conflicting accounts of what has occurred. In resolving this conflict, they seem to be operating within a 'hierarchy of credibility'. This concept was formulated by Becker (1967), to suggest that the definitions of reality projected by people in positions of authority are accepted in preference to those of their subordinates. The doctor's opinion carries more weight than the patient's; the police officer's description of events is more readily believed than that offered by the accused; the employer's knowledge and evaluation of the workforce is superior to that of a single employee bearing a grudge. With the support of workmates and the assistance of a representative with industrial and legal expertise, an applicant may be able to reduce the effects of the hierarchy; without such support, the odds against him or her are overwhelming.

Although the lay members are drawn from the 'two sides' of industry, so that a trade union nominee and a CBI nominee sit on each tribunal, the hierarchy of credibility proves more powerful than industrial allegiance. The tribunals achieve a remarkable degree of consensus, so that 96 percent of their decisions are unanimous. This contrasts sharply with the political strategy of the French trade unions. According to Napier, the Confédération Générale du Travail 'quite openly and unashamedly expects its nominees who are "conseillers" to deliver decisions which will favour the interests of the working class at the expense of the employers'. The main employers' association in France operates with the same 'polarised view of industrial relations' (Napier, 1979).

To adopt such a strategy in the context of British industrial relations would be to turn tribunal applicants into political footballs, without improving their chances of success. There would simply be an increase in the number of majority decisions. The most effective way of dealing with the hierarchy of credibility is to operate within it, by improving the quality of evidence and representation that is presented to the tribunal. This should help to shift the credibility stakes in the applicant's favour. At the same time, it should help to provide a more effective challenge to the prevailing legal ideology which, as we shall see from the next chapter, militates against the victims of discrimination in a number of ways.

Notes

1. There was a considerable degree of inter-departmental rivalry between the Department of Employment, which had initiated the equal pay legislation, and the Home Office, the department responsible for the Sex Discrimination Act. It was the Department of Employment that insisted that the Equal Pay Act be retained, virtually unaltered, as a separate schedule to the Sex Discrimination Act and also put pressure on the Home Office to allow the TUC and CBI each to have three nominees on the EOC.

2. The expression 'the people's courts' is used by Dickens (1985). The president's comments were made in a paper given to a conference in 1971 (Conroy, 1971).

3. The research evidence on which this section is based is derived from a number of sources: on sex discrimination, Kingman (1978), Gregory (1982) and Graham and Lewis (1985); on race discrimination, Byrne (1982) and Kumar (1986).

4. The use of the masculine pronoun here is not an involuntary lapse into sexist language; rather it reflects the fact that the vast majority of employers are male. At no stage in my own research did I encounter an equal pay or sex discrimination case against a female employer.

5. This burden was reduced to some extent by the Employment Act 1980. The question of whether a dismissal was fair or unfair now depends on whether, 'in the circumstances (including the size and administrative resources of the employer's

undertaking) the employer acted reasonably or unreasonably' (Employment Act 1980 section 6). Nevertheless, the burden remains on the shoulders of the employer. As Griffiths LJ pointed out in Maud v Penrith Council [1984] IRLR 24: 'This is obviously sensible; the employer knows why he dismissed the employee, but the employee may not'.

6. In equal pay and indirect discrimination cases, the situation is more complicated. A woman claiming equal pay has to show that her work is the same or broadly similar to that of a man. Then the burden shifts to the employer to justify the difference in pay. (In equal value cases, he is given this opportunity at the outset of the case and again later; see Ch. 1, p. 23.) Similarly, in cases of indirect discrimination, the applicant must show that the condition or requirement is one with which it is difficult for members of a particular sex or racial group to comply. At that point, the tribunal will ask the employer to justify the requirement.

7. These percentages are derived from information appearing annually in the *Employment Gazettes*. Although the tables are accompanied by the statement: 'some applications upheld include more than one remedy', only one remedy is given for each case. It is impossible to know how many decisions do involve more than one remedy without examining the decisions themselves.

8. The amount of compensation awarded in discrimination cases is limited by paragraph 20 of Schedule 1 to the Trade Union and Labour Relations Act 1974 (see Sex Discrimination Act section 65(2) and Race Relations Act section 56(2)).

9. On conciliation, see Lewis (1982). For a discussion of conciliation in relation to unfair dismissal and sex discrimination, see Gregory (1986). On tribunal remedies, see Dickens et al. (1981) and Williams and Lewis (1981). For a comprehensive appraisal of unfair dismissal procedures, see Dickens et al. (1985).

5   The individual route to equality: the right to appeal

For most victims of discrimination, the tribunal decision is the end of the road. In a minority of cases, however, the unsuccessful party makes use of the appeals system to challenge the decision on a point of law. This entails lodging an appeal with the Employment Appeal Tribunal (EAT), which may confirm the original decision, reverse it or remit it to an industrial tribunal for further consideration, 'having given guidance on the particular question of law at issue' (*Employment Gazette*, November 1984: 492).[1] If either party is dissatisfied with the deliberations of the EAT and still wishes to pursue the matter, the case may be taken to the Court of Appeal and even to the House of Lords, although permission to take the case this far may be refused. Beyond this lies the European Court of Justice, whose opinion has been sought in a small number of equal pay and sex discrimination cases.

The significance of the appeals system extends beyond its impact on specific cases, because the decisions of the superior courts are binding on the tribunals and will therefore largely determine their approach to the law. It has a multiplier effect which cannot easily be measured. It is interesting to note, however, that in terms of the percentage of successful cases, the net effect of the appeals system is to reinforce the employer advantage that we observed in operation in the early rounds of the contest.

If the pattern of appeals precisely reflected the work of the industrial tribunals, we would expect to find the EAT caseload consisting mainly of unfair dismissal cases. In practice, we find that unfair dismissal cases do dominate the work of the EAT but that the rate of appeals is higher in discrimination cases, with approximately 10 percent of such cases going forward to appeal, compared with 5 percent of unfair dismissal and equal pay cases.[2]

Given the low success rate, we would also expect to find that at least three-quarters of the appeals would be lodged by employees. This time, the differences are to be found between discrimination cases on the one hand and unfair dismissal and equal pay cases on the other, with a disproportionate number of employers lodging appeals in this second group. In the discrimination jurisdiction however, the ratio of employer to employee appeals is a more accurate reflection of the tribunal success rate. Table 5.1 shows that 42 percent of unfair dismissal appeals and 39 percent of equal pay appeals come from employers, whereas this drops to 29 and 14 percent respectively when we consider sex and race discrimination appeals.

TABLE 5.1
Appeals to the Employment Appeal Tribunal, April 1977–May 1986

Jurisdiction	Appeals by employers		Appeals by employees		Total	
	Number	Percent	Number	Percent	Number	Percent
Unfair dismissal	1,694	42	2,314	58	4,008	100
Equal pay	26	39	40	61	66	100
Sex discrimination	24	29	60	71	84	100
Race discrimination	21	14	125	86	146	100

Source: Based on information obtained from the Registrar's Office, EAT.

It looks as though employers appeal when an adverse decision hurts them financially. The rates of compensation awarded to workers who have been unfairly dismissed are higher than those awarded to the victims of discrimination. Similarly, an equal pay case may well have far-reaching repercussions on company pay structures, so that it becomes worthwhile to challenge an adverse decision. Lack of employer interest in challenging successful discrimination complaints is almost certainly related to the weakness of the remedies awarded by the tribunals.

Table 5.2 reveals that in unfair dismissal cases 22 percent of employers but only 12 percent of employees won on appeal. The same pattern occurs in other jurisdictions, although here the percentages need to be interpreted with some caution, in view of the smaller number of appeals in total. As only twenty-one employers lodged appeals in race discrimination cases over the period covered by the table, a 43 percent success rate refers to only nine employers. Even so, when we remember the extremely low success rate in cases of racial discrimination, it is worth noting that only eight of the twenty-one employers had their appeals dismissed out of hand.

Only a handful of employment cases have reached the Court of Appeal. Table 5.3 shows the outcome of the Appeal Court's intervention in the cases heard so far. For this particular group of cases, the EAT's intervention was positive as far as the complainants were concerned. The triumph was, however, short-lived, as the effect of

TABLE 5.2
Outcome of appeals to the Employment Appeal Tribunal, April 1977 to May 1986

Jurisdiction	Dismissed		Allowed		Remitted		Total	
	Number	Percent	Number	Percent	Number	Percent	Number	Percent
Unfair dismissal								
Appeals by employers	1,065	63	369	22	260	15	1,694	100
Appeals by employees	1,703	74	274	12	337	14	2,314	100
Equal pay								
Appeals by employers	12	46	5	19	9	35	26	100
Appeals by employees	21	52.5	4	10	15	37.5	40	100
Sex discrimination								
Appeals by employers	11	46	9	37	4	17	24	100
Appeals by employees	32	53	12	20	16	27	60	100
Race discrimination								
Appeals by employers	8	38	9	43	4	19	21	100
Appeals by employees	95	76	24	19	6	5	125	100

Source: Based on information obtained from the Registrar's office, EAT.

TABLE 5.3
Outcome of Court of Appeal cases

Decision at each stage	Industrial tribunal	EAT	Court of Appeal
Six equal pay cases			
Employer wins	2	1	3
Employee wins	4	5	3
Nine sex discrimination cases			
Employer wins	5	3	7
Employee wins	4	6	2
Five race discrimination cases			
Employer wins	4	2	4
Employee wins	1	3	1

As far as I am aware, this table includes all the employment cases to reach the Court of Appeal at the time of writing. It excludes appeals from county court decisions under the non-employment provisions. It also excludes appeals relating to the CRE's enforcement powers; these are considered in the next chapter.

the subsequent appeal reversed this process, leaving the employees in a less favourable position overall than they had been at the start of the appeals procedure.

The system of allowing appeals to ordinary courts of appeal has been described as the 'curse of European labour law' (Wedderburn and Davies, 1969). On the basis of these figures, it is difficult to disagree. The negative impact of the Employment Appeal Tribunal is particularly worrying. Although it can hear appeals only on points of law, it was intended to be rather more than an ordinary court of appeal. Its composition is similar to that of industrial tribunals. The legally qualified person is now a high court judge, but he [sic] sits with two 'wing' members selected for their industrial experience, one within the trade union movement and the other within management. From time to time the suggestion is made by lawyers and others, impatient with the low quality of decisions emanating from industrial tribunals, that the EAT be given an original jurisdiction to hear discrimination cases, thereby cutting out the tribunals altogether.[3]

How could such a step be justified, in view of the gloomy picture of EAT involvement presented in Table 5.2? — particularly as the Court of Appeal would then become the first step in the appeals structure. In order to construct a convincing case for referring all discrimination complaints directly to the EAT, it would be necessary to argue that the Appeal Tribunal is presently hampered by the requirement that an appeal can only be made on a point of law. If the damage is done when the industrial tribunal examines the evidence, the EAT is often powerless to intervene, although some cases are remitted to be considered again. This limitation would not exist if the EAT was the first tribunal to hear the case. It would also ensure that a smaller number of people developed a wider experience of discrimination cases.

Enthusiasm for this idea has waxed and waned depending on the EAT's most recent decision; the idea will be shelved in the wake of a disappointing judgment and resurrected following a favourable and well-reasoned judgment. It is impossible to understand the love–hate relationship that has developed between the EAT and those practitioners and commentators interested in discrimination law, without taking a closer look at the work of the Appeal Tribunal over a period of time.

Some early decisions: the Employment Appeal Tribunal points the way

When the first cases to be filed under the discrimination laws reached the hearing stage, the tribunals were frequently out of their depth and some decisions floundered badly. There can be no doubt that in the early days the EAT, under the presidency of Mr Justice Phillips, launched a rescue operation and provided some useful guidelines for the tribunals to follow. In addition to the two tribunal cases involving Ms Steel and Ms Price (discussed in Ch. 2), there were a number of equal pay cases in which the intervention of the EAT encouraged the tribunals to adopt a broad view of the 'like work' provisions. The Appeal Tribunal criticized the tendency of some tribunals to consider questions not prescribed by the Act, such as whether a particular type of work was 'suitable for women' and insisted that:

> trivial differences, or differences not likely in the real world to be reflected in the terms and conditions of employment, ought to be disregarded. (Capper Pass v Lawton [1976] IRLR 366)

The first applications under the Race Relations Act were not made until June 1977, so that the first appeals under this jurisdiction also came later. Once again, the signs were propitious. A barmaid dismissed because she refused to comply with an instruction not to serve black customers had lost her case at the industrial tribunal on the grounds that she herself had not been subjected to racial discrimination. The Appeal Tribunal reversed this decision, expressing the view that it could not have been the intention of Parliament to deny justice to someone victimized for refusing to carry out an unlawful instruction to discriminate (Zarczynska v Levy [1978] IRLR 532).

The Court of Appeal applies the brake

It was when the Court of Appeal began to intervene that the EAT seemed to lose its sense of purpose and direction. The Appeal Court's pronouncements on the new legislation came like a cold shower, dousing the enthusiasm of those below. The strength of this hostility was particularly unexpected, in view of the relatively innocuous nature of the complaint before the Court. Mr Peake had complained of sex discrimination because women workers were allowed to leave the factory premises five minutes earlier each day than he was. The industrial tribunal had dismissed the case, on the grounds that the earlier leaving arrangements, which applied also to handicapped men, were 'a concession granted to persons who for physical reasons are less capable of withstanding the rush at leaving time' (Peake v Automotive Products Ltd COIT 14290/76 (unreported)).

Mr Peake had appealed to the EAT, where Mr Justice Phillips had used the same broad approach as the one he had adopted in equal pay cases. He admitted that the initial reaction of the EAT members had been to reject the complaint as absurd, but on reflection, they had recognized the legitimacy of the grievance:

> In truth, no guidance can be got from instinctive feelings: rather the reverse. Such feelings are likely to be the product of ingrained social attitudes, assumed to be permanent but rendered obsolete by changing values and current legislation. Accordingly, we have put on one side our preconceptions and taken the Sex Discrimination Act 1975 as the only reliable guide. (Peake v Automotive Products Ltd [1977] IRLR 105)

The appeal was upheld and the tribunal decision reversed. When Automotive Products appealed against the EAT ruling, the Appeal Court judges upheld the appeal and restored the decision of the industrial tribunal. Unlike Mr Justice Phillips, their Lordships chose not to set aside their 'ingrained social attitudes' but rather to insist that:

> The natural differences of sex must be regarded even in the interpretation of an Act of Parliament. It is not discrimination for mankind to treat womankind with courtesy and chivalry . . . Arrangements which are made in the interests of safety or in the interests of good administration are not infringements of the law. (Automotive Products v Peake [1977] IRLR 365)

This judgment provoked an angry response from Francis Bennion who had drafted the Sex Discrimination Act. In a letter to *The Times*, he protested that the decision offended 'both the letter and the spirit of the Act'. It established 'the dangerous principle that the Act does not necessarily mean what it says'. The Court of Appeal had not complained that the Act was unclear, but rather had elected to 'disregard its plain meaning'. In his view: 'That has disturbing implications for Parliamentary democracy and the rule of law' (*The Times*, 15 July 1977). Mr Bennion expressed the hope that the House of Lords would reverse the decision. In fact, the Lords refused leave to appeal on the grounds that the discrimination was *de minimus*: in other words, too trivial to merit their attention.

The Peake judgment seemed to have an unsettling effect on the EAT. The two appellants whose cases were heard immediately following the Peake decision were both unsuccessful. In the case of Saunders v Richmond Borough Council [1977] IRLR 362, the tribunal had dismissed Ms Saunders's claim that the Council had discriminated against her in failing to employ her as a golf professional and in the manner in which they had made the appointment. The EAT was understandably reluctant to interfere with the tribunal's findings of fact, but Ms Saunders claimed that several of the questions asked at her interview were in themselves discriminatory. Mr Justice Phillips disagreed, holding that it was necessary to consider the circumstances in which the questions were asked:

> In the present case, though the questions asked reflected what is now an out-of-date and proscribed attitude of mind, the industrial tribunal were entitled to find on the evidence that they were not asked with the intention of discriminating against the appellant on grounds of her sex. (p. 362)

In Schmidt v Austicks Bookshops Ltd [1977] IRLR 360, the appellant complained of sex discrimination because her employers dismissed her for failing to observe their rule that she wear overalls and a skirt and not wear trousers while serving the public. Dismissing the appeal, Phillips J. made two references to the Court of Appeal decision in Peake. On the first occasion he used it to deny that the clothing rule constituted a 'detriment' within the meaning of the SDA: 'something can only be said to constitute a detriment when there is something serious or important about it' (p. 360). On the second occasion, he used it to declare that: 'an employer is entitled to a large measure of discretion in controlling the image of his establishment, including the appearance of staff' (p. 361). Any employer who had begun to fear that the sex discrimination legislation might be developing some teeth could breathe easily once more!

In the first equal pay case to reach the Court of Appeal, the bond of sympathy between the Court and the employer was strengthened. In National Vulcan Engineering v Wade [1977] IRLR 109, the employer admitted that Ms Wade was employed on like work with her male comparator, but explained that the two workers were placed in different grades as a result of an individual assessment scheme.

Neither the industrial tribunal nor the Appeal Tribunal was convinced that the variation in pay was genuinely due to a material difference other than the difference in sex. The EAT was perturbed by the subjective nature of the management's assessment scheme, particularly as the company admitted that it had in the past discriminated against women and so upheld the decision in favour of Ms Wade. The company appealed against the decision and the Court of Appeal found in its favour. Lord Denning insisted that: 'A grading system according to skill, ability and experience is an integral part of good business management' ([1978] IRLR 225).

The discovery cases
The Court of Appeal struck another severe blow against the anti-discrimination laws in its deliberations on the issue of 'discovery'. In order to discharge the burden of proof, complainants in discrimination cases will often require access to information that only the employer can provide. The employer is likely to resist such a request on grounds of confidentiality, particularly where the information relates to other job applicants or employees.

Applicants in discrimination cases (but not in equal pay cases) can make use of a 'questions procedure' in order to elicit information from the employer. The results of this exercise are admissible in evidence, so that if the employer declines to answer or gives an evasive reply, the tribunal may draw any inference it considers 'just and equitable' (SDA section 74 and RRA 1976 section 65). Under the rules of procedure for industrial tribunals, the complainant may also apply to the tribunal for 'discovery' of the relevant documents. The tribunal is empowered to order discovery if such an order is considered necessary for disposing fairly of the proceedings.[4]

In the early months of 1978, the EAT was asked on three separate occasions to consider whether the tribunals were exercising this power correctly. To the embarrassment of the Commission for Racial Equality, the first 'discovery' case to reach the EAT was a case brought against the Commission by a Mr Rasul, who had been shortlisted for a post with the Commission. The job was not offered to Mr Rasul, but to a white candidate. Mr Rasul applied to the industrial tribunal for discovery and inspection of twelve separate documents. The CRE voluntarily submitted some of them and the tribunal made an order for discovery of a further four. Mr Rasul appealed to the EAT for discovery of the remaining documents. The Appeal Tribunal allowed his appeal in so far as it related to the other candidates shortlisted for the post (Rasul v CRE [1978] IRLR 203).

In the second case, Ms Nasse, who worked for the Science Research Council, believed that she had not been recommended for promotion because she was a married woman. She applied to the industrial tribunal for permission to inspect the confidential reports on two fellow workers who had been selected for interview, together with the minutes of the meetings at which it was decided to recommend them for a promotion interview and not to recommend her. The tribunal ordered that the documents be made available to Ms Nasse and rejected a request from the Council that disclosure be postponed until the tribunal hearing.

The appeal was heard by the same three members of the EAT who had dealt with the CRE case. Once again, they decided in favour of the applicant (SRC v Nasse [1978] IRLR 201). Mr Justice Bristow pointed out that: 'It was unlikely ever to be easy for an applicant to discharge the burden of proving discrimination'. As far as the Appeal Tribunal was concerned: 'the paramount consideration was that justice should be able to be done on the issues raised by the applicant'. They did not favour postponing disclosure until the hearing, because the complainant would have to open her case blind and would probably require an adjournment. They were confident that adequate safeguards existed against abuse, in the form of contempt procedures and the provision that costs could be awarded against applicants who brought vexatious cases.

In the third case, Mr Vyas had complained of racial discrimination when his application for a transfer from one division of Leyland's Cowley works to another was unsuccessful. His application for discovery was allowed in part, but the tribunal declined to order the release of confidential information relating to the men interviewed for transfer. When Mr Vyas appealed, the EAT followed its own ruling and ordered discovery of the confidential documents.

The CRE accepted the judgment of the Appeal Tribunal but the employers in the other two cases, the SRC and Leyland Cars, decided to pursue the matter further. The Court of Appeal heard the two cases together and overturned the EAT's ruling, holding that: 'general orders for discovery should never be made'. Reports and references received in confidence should not be disclosed:

> except in the very rare cases where after inspection of a particular document, the Chairman [sic] decides that it is essential in the interests of justice that the confidence should be overridden; and then only subject to such conditions as he shall think fit to impose. ([1978] IRLR 352)

Lord Denning took the opportunity to launch an attack on the 'immense powers' of the two Commissions, the EOC and the CRE, which were represented at the hearing separately from the other parties to the dispute. Lord Denning referred to their 'inquisitorial powers of a kind never before known to the law'. He emphasized the need for fairness not only to the complainants but to the public services and industrial concerns of this country. They have to cope with these problems of discrimination and should be trusted to deal with them fairly. The statutory Commissions should not treat them as if they were miscreants seeking to evade the law . . . If the statutory Commissions seek to pull the rope too tight, they will find that it will lash back against them. (p. 357)

As in Peake, Lord Denning gave expression to a deep-rooted hostility to the new legislation.

The situation in relation to the release of confidential documents was transformed overnight as orders for discovery came to an abrupt halt. Deprived of the ammunition necessary for presenting a convincing case, a number of complaints waiting in the pipeline fell or were withdrawn. Sixteen months later, after considerable damage had been inflicted, the House of Lords softened the blow slightly. They confirmed the Court of Appeal's decision that a general order for discovery should not be made. However, they took objection to the Court's ruling that discovery should not be permitted except 'in very rare cases' and held that the Tribunal should inspect the documents to decide whether disclosure was necessary. The more extreme formulation was modified and the discretion of the tribunals reinstated (Nasse v SRC and Vyas v Leyland Cars Ltd [1979] IRLR 465).

The EAT goes into reverse
By the autumn of 1978, it was no longer possible to perceive the EAT as blazing a trail in discrimination law. The Court of Appeal had put an effective stop to this intervention and now the EAT had a new president, Mr Justice Slynn, who was much less sympathetic to the aims of the legislation than his predecessor. In Chapter 2, we saw how his interpretation of the indirect discrimination provisions made it increasingly difficult for applicants to win. His approach to cases of direct discrimination was equally restrictive; it was Mr Justice Slynn who presided over the racial segregation case discussed in Chapter 1, and he was also responsible for a decision involving victimization. Mr Kirby was a Jobcentre clerk, who in the course of his work encountered a number of employers discriminating against black applicants. He reported them to the local Community Relations Council. When the senior manager of the Jobcentre realized what the clerk was doing, he transferred him to a less desirable position which involved no interviewing. Mr Kirby filed an application of victimization against the Manpower Services Commission (MSC) but the industrial tribunal dismissed the claim. The EAT concurred, on the grounds that Mr Kirby was transferred for giving away confidential information. The manager had treated him no less favourably than he would have treated any other employee who revealed confidential information (Kirby v Manpower Services Commission [1980] IRLR 229).

The consequence of these mental contortions is that a man who has quite clearly been victimized is left with no right of redress, in contrast to the barmaid, whose case was discussed on p. 90. Furthermore, the real culprits escape without punishment. The Manpower Services Commission was as culpable as the employers identified by Mr Kirby. In its obsession with confidentiality, the MSC colluded with employers who chose to discriminate, rather than using its position to expose them.

Mr Justice Slynn proved equally unsympathetic towards the victims of direct sex discrimination.[5] A woman employed by a travel agency had been dismissed after marrying a man who worked for a rival agency. The two companies, fearing that confidential information was at risk, agreed that 'as the man was the breadwinner' the wife should lose her job. An industrial tribunal found that the employers had discriminated against the woman on the basis of her sex and marital status and awarded her compensation for unfair dismissal. Perversely, the EAT overturned this decision, holding that: 'there there was no evidence to suggest that, had the complainant been a man, the employers would not have dismissed him' and that:

> the industrial tribunal had erred in assuming that because the close association arose from the marriage this was discrimination on the grounds of her marital status. (Skyrail Oceanic v Coleman [1980] ICR 597)

It is an indication of just how far Mr Justice Slynn had moved away from the principles underlying the anti-discrimination laws that when Ms Coleman appealed against this judgment, she met with a positive response from the Court of Appeal. In a majority decision (Lord Justice Shaw dissenting), the Court agreed with the industrial tribunal that:

> an assumption that men are more likely than women to be the primary supporters of their spouses and children is an assumption based on sex. ([1981] IRLR 399)

However, the £1,000 compensation for injury to feelings awarded by the tribunal was 'out of all proportion to the injury proved' and was therefore reduced to £100.

Mr Justice Browne-Wilkinson resuscitates the legislation

The growing body of unfavourable case law emanating from the EAT and the Court of Appeal threw the tribunals into a state of confusion and also effectively discouraged applicants from lodging an appeal, however convinced they were of the merits of their complaints. For equal pay claimants, the best strategy was to argue their cases under European Community Law, where there were fewer loopholes and exemptions to ensnare them. Indeed, as we moved into the 1980s, the judgments coming back from the European Court of Justice provided the only source of good news on the equality front. Mr Justice Browne-Wilkinson took over as president of the EAT in March 1981, just in time to sort out the more equivocal of these messages from Europe and to breathe new life into the discrimination laws. In addition to his favourable judgments in the cases of Ms Jenkins and Ms Hurley (see Chapter 2), the new president also upheld an applicant's appeal in a case of racial discrimination.

Mr Khanna had been passed over for promotion in favour of a white man with much less experience but known personally to two of the three members of the promotion board. The industrial tribunal drew the 'unavoidable inference' of racial discrimination, so that the burden of proof shifted to the employers to provide an explanation. At this point, the tribunal allowed itself to be seduced by the hierarchy of credibility:

> the promotion board consisted of senior men who are in the civil service or ... have retired from it ... They appear to the tribunal to be honest witnesses. They have sworn on oath that they were not racially motivated in any way.

The Appeal Tribunal was not satisfied with this explanation and remitted the case to the tribunal for the evidence to be examined again and offered the following guidance:

> If the primary facts indicate that there has been discrimination of some kind, the employer is called on to give an explanation and, failing clear and specific explanation being given by the employer to the satisfaction of the industrial tribunal, an inference of unlawful discrimination from the primary facts will mean the complaint succeeds. Those concepts are most easily understood if concepts of shifting evidential burdens are avoided.
> (Khanna v Ministry of Defence [1981] IRLR 331)

In Horsey v Dyfed County Council [1982] IRLR 395, Mr Justice Browne-Wilkinson once again overturned an industrial tribunal decision which had been decided in favour of the employer, causing the editor of the *Industrial Relations Law Reports* to comment on:

> the growing sensitivity and sophistication of the Employment Appeal Tribunal in understanding the real issues underlying discrimination.
> (*October Highlights* [1982] IRLR 394)

Ms Horsey, a trainee social worker, was refused secondment to a course in the London area where her husband was employed, because the employer assumed that she would remain in London on completing her studies and so not return to Wales. Ms Horsey complained that the Council had discriminated against her. The tribunal dismissed the application on the grounds that there was no evidence that the employers discriminated against women; indeed, more women than men were seconded to training courses in 1980. They accepted that the secondment was refused on the basis that Ms Horsey was unlikely to return to Wales and not because she was married. Reversing the decision, the EAT points out that:

> Most discrimination flows from generalized assumptions and not from a simple prejudice dependent solely on the sex or colour of the complainant. (p. 395)

In this case, the employer's action was based at least in part on 'the generalized assumption that married women follow their husband's jobs'; it followed that a married man would have been treated differently. The employers had no evidence, other than these generalized assumptions, that Ms Horsey would not return to Wales and had therefore unlawfully discriminated against her.

Consistency or flexibility?

After nearly a decade of case law development and three different presidents at the EAT, it was still impossible to predict case outcomes with any degree of certainty. Such a lack of consistency in interpreting the law created problems even for the experts, both in giving advice to the victims of discrimination and in persuading employers to develop non-discriminatory practices. As the 1980s unfolded, there were no signs that the situation might improve; indeed, all the indications pointed in the opposite direction. Part of the problem resided within the EAT itself, with each president serving only two to three years before moving on to obtain experience of another jurisdiction.[6]

A more serious obstacle has been created by the Court of Appeal. Its own lack of consistency in discrimination cases has not helped, nor has its generally restrictive view of the legislation. In addition, the Court has taken steps to circumscribe the activities of the EAT in a way which can only impede the development of case law.

Mr Justice Phillips had perceived the role of the EAT as providing guidelines for industrial tribunals in order to introduce a degree of uniformity and predictability into their proceedings. He had adopted a very wide view of what constituted a question of law, confident that the presence of lay experts made interference with the decisions of the tribunals much more acceptable. He goes so far as to say that:

> if we, that is the judge, the representative of the employers and the representative of the workers, are individually and collectively satisfied that the decision is 'wrong', judged by the standards of good industrial practice, we feel justified in saying the decision is a contrary one, and is wrong in law. (Phillips, 1978)

Such a bold approach is no longer possible. On several occasions, the Court of Appeal has curbed these interventionist tendencies and complained that the wealth of guidance issuing from the EAT actively hampers the work of the tribunals. The Court believes that the tribunals lose sight of the factual evidence on which a case must be decided and become bogged down in legal technicalities.

Although the comments of the Appeal Court judges arose in the context of unfair dismissal cases, they have affected the work of the EAT in all jurisdictions. In Hollister v The National Farmer's Union [1979] IRLR 238, Lord Denning objects to what he regards as the tendency to 'dress up' points of law in order to encourage appeals and adds:

> It is not right to go through the reasoning of these tribunals with a toothcomb to see if some error can be found here or there — to see if one can find some little cryptic sentence.

Similarly, Lord Justice Browne refers to the 'vast accretion of case law' which has prevented the tribunals from fulfilling their role as 'quick commonsense tribunals which would deal with matters without technicalities' (Thomas and Betts Manufacturing v Harding [1980] IRLR 255). In Bailey v BP Oil Kent Refinery [1980] IRLR 287, which centred on the interpretation of a particular section of the Employment Protection (Consolidation) Act 1978, the Court of Appeal held:

> It is unwise for the Appeal Court or the EAT to set out guidelines, and wrong to make rules and establish presumptions for industrial tribunals to follow or take into account when applying s 57(3).

The consequence of this line of decisions has been to curtail the role of the EAT, thereby sacrificing uniformity on the altar of flexibility, with each industrial tribunal giving effect to its own views. Mr Justice Browne-Wilkinson has referred to this as 'palm tree' justice and argued that: 'the present imbalance between certainty and flexibility must be adjusted if industrial relations law is to develop in a healthy way' (Browne-Wilkinson, 1982: 73). He can see nothing objectionable in guidelines, so long as they are not regarded as immutable.

Towards the end of 1983, Mr Justice Waite became the fourth president of the EAT and seemed more than willing to slot into the role defined for him by the Court of Appeal. At the first opportunity, he launched an attack on legalism and judicial guidelines (Anandarajah v Lord Chancellor's Dept [1984] IRLR 131). His preferred course of action was to allow tribunal decisions to stand but to discourage other tribunals from following their lead. Hence his apparent inconsistency in the two cases of part-time workers complaining of indirect discrimination: Ms Holmes's victory against the Home Office was allowed to stand and so was the adverse decision in Ms Kidd's case. In both cases, he insisted that the facts should not be generalized beyond the particular case (see Ch. 2).

The only positive contribution made by Mr Justice Waite to the development of discrimination law during his term as EAT president was his intervention on the issue of pregnancy. Pregnant women treated unfairly by their employers had effectively been denied a remedy under the SDA since 1979, when the EAT had dismissed such a complaint, on the grounds that since a man cannot become pregnant, it was not possible to claim that the woman had been treated less favourably than a man would be treated! (Turley v Allders Department Stores Ltd [1979] IRLR 4). One of the members of the EAT (Ms Smith) had dissented from this absurd decision, arguing that the correct point of comparison was a hypothetical male worker who required time off for medical reasons. Mr Justice Waite and his colleagues agreed with Ms Smith's interpretation of the law and upheld the appeals of two women dismissed after informing their employers that they were pregnant. In both cases, the tribunals had considered themselves bound by the earlier decision but the EAT, having given new guidance on the law, remitted the cases for the tribunals to look at the evidence again.[7]

Deciding questions of fact and law
Mr Justice Waite would no doubt regard the pregnancy cases as providing further support for his view that 'legalism' should be banished from the tribunals and each case decided on its individual facts. If the tribunals in the two cases reviewed by him had not considered themselves obliged to follow the Turley decision, they would have examined the facts in more detail and might have reached a different conclusion. Undoubtedly, the quality of factual evidence is crucial in determining case outcomes; ample support for such a view was presented in Chapter 4. However, the quality of legal evidence is equally important. If the attack on legalism means that the role of legal interpretation is underestimated, then it is a sham.

In every case that comes before an industrial tribunal, however preoccupied the members may be with establishing the facts, at some point they will have to consider how to apply the law. Although in formal terms the opinion of each member carries equal weight, the lay members acknowledge their subordinate role. Not only does the chairperson conduct the proceedings and take charge of the documentation, but at the end of the day practical considerations take second place to legal ones. The apparent emphasis on informality and common sense is an illusion, which leaves unrepresented applicants feeling that somehow they have failed to present their case adequately (see Dickens, 1983; Dickens et al., 1985: Ch. 3).

This problem is accentuated when the case goes to appeal, as questions of law necessarily occupy the centre stage. Applicants will be deterred from lodging an appeal unless they have union backing or another source of support, such as the EOC or the CRE. If the employer lodges an appeal and engages a lawyer to argue the case, an unrepresented applicant will be completely at the mercy of the Court, unless a successful application for legal aid has been made.[8]

The value of legal representation is acknowledged by the judges. EAT decisions make frequent reference to the 'helpful submissions' of the solicitor or counsel and when remitting a case will sometimes stress the desirability of applicant representation at the second tribunal. Lord Denning even went so far as to blame his mistaken decision in the case of Peake v Automotive Products on the fact that Mr Peake was representing himself at the hearing. Two years later, he modified his ruling in that case in the course of giving judgment in another appeal:

> I think we were under a disadvantage, because Mr Peake appeared in person: and we were not referred to some of the relevant parts of the statutes. (Ministry of Defence v Jeremiah [1979] IRLR 436)

It is no coincidence that in the only discrimination case in which Lord Denning reversed an EAT decision in a favourable direction for the employee, the relevant provisions of both domestic and Common Market law were carefully explained to him by a Queen's Counsel (QC) with considerable experience of discrimination law.[9] Legal representation may well be a necessary condition for winning a complex case; it is not, however, a sufficient condition. It is worth noting that the same QC found himself on the receiving end of Lord Denning's gratuitous attack on the two Commissions in the discovery cases!

The one who pays the piper calls the tune
We seem to be in a Catch 22 situation. On the one hand, industrial tribunal decisions are inadequate, inconsistent and confused. On the other hand, when the tribunals turn to the appellate courts for guidance, the messages are contradictory and unhelpful. In Chapter 2, we saw how a restrictive approach to the law on indirect discrimination actually displaces the central aim of the legislation and gives priority to other considerations. The same processes are at work in the case law on direct discrimination, where the courts are most reluctant to interfere with the employers' freedom to run their enterprises as they think best. The judiciary seems more concerned with

policing the equality laws to ensure that they do not ride rough-shod over the employers, than with policing employers to ensure that the laws are observed.

The same preoccupation with defending the managerial prerogative is a dominant theme in unfair dismissal cases. In discrimination cases, it is compounded by the apparent inability of the judiciary, who are almost exclusively elderly, white, male and upper class, to comprehend the nature of discrimination. A graphic illustration of the uphill struggle faced by lawyers and others attempting to persuade the courts to give practical effect to the laws against discrimination is provided by the harassment cases.

Sexual and racial harassment
The terms sexual and racial harassment do not appear in the legislation, so that the victims of harassment have to rely on the provision that makes it unlawful to subject an employee to 'any other detriment' (SDA section 6(2)(b) and RRA section 4(2)(c): see Appendix 4). The tribunals and courts have been remarkably reluctant to recognize harassment as a detriment and the case of Kingston v British Railways Board provides a particularly vivid example of the Appeal Court's failure to take the question of racial harassment seriously.

There can be no doubt that the consequences of this particular case were extremely serious for the employee. He was sentenced to three months imprisonment for assaulting a police officer. The officer was a member of the Transport Police and therefore an employee of British Rail. Mr Kingston complained that the constable had racially harassed him over a period of time prior to the incident for which he was imprisoned. The Court of Appeal subsequently quashed Mr Kingston's conviction, but by then he had lost his job. He filed a complaint against British Rail for unfair dismissal and racial discrimination. The tribunal dismissed the complaint on the grounds first, that the employers were entitled to dismiss Mr Kingston in view of the length of his prison sentence and the seriousness of the offence, and second, that they had received no oral evidence from the police on which to base a finding of discrimination. On appeal, the EAT agreed that the dismissal had been fair, given the information available to the employers at the time. They were, however, perturbed about the finding of no racial harassment, particularly as a strike had occurred shortly before Mr Kingston's arrest, in which workers protested of racial harassment by Transport Police in relation to another black worker. Mr Justice Browne-Wilkinson and his colleagues believed that on the available evidence Mr Kingston should win his claim, but decided to remit the case in order to give the police an opportunity to state their side of the story (Kingston v British Railways Board [1982] IRLR 274).

When British Rail appealed, the Court of Appeal upheld the decision of the industrial tribunal on both counts, agreeing that the dismissal was fair and disagreeing with the EAT's decision to remit the case. The Court held:

> If the EAT's interpretation were correct, it would demonstrate a serious error by the industrial tribunal, but having regard to the fact that the tribunal had a legally qualified chairman, it was unlikely that this was the meaning they were intending to convey . . . Given the length of time since the incident in question and the industrial tribunal hearing, justice would not be done by remitting the case to the industrial tribunal for further findings or clarification. On the basis of the material before the court, the allegation of unlawful discrimination had not been made out. (Kingston v British Railways Board [1984] IRLR 146)

The first breakthrough in the case law on harassment came in a case of sexual harassment heard in Scotland. Ms Porcelli was sexually harassed by two male colleagues who took a dislike to her, so that she was forced to apply for a transfer. An industrial tribunal dismissed the case on the grounds that if the two men had taken a dislike to a male colleague, they would have treated him just as unfavourably. The EAT sitting in Edinburgh overturned this decision, pointing out that the sexual overtones of the men's conduct made it quite distinctive and that Ms Porcelli had undoubtedly suffered a detriment as a result of this conduct, as she had been forced to seek a transfer. They added that if she had decided to stay where she was, she would have suffered no detriment and have had no remedy, as the SDA did not outlaw sexual harassment as such (Porcelli v Strathclyde Regional Council [1984] IRLR 467).

When Strathclyde Council appealed against this decision to the Scottish Court of Session, the appeal was dismissed. The Court accepted that sexual harassment was 'a particularly degrading and unacceptable form of treatment which it must have been the intention of Parliament to restrain' (Strathclyde Regional Council v Porcelli [1986] IRLR 134).

In the meantime, a case of racial harassment had reached the Court of Appeal in London. Ms de Souza's complaint of racial discrimination had included the fact that she had overheard one of the managers referring to her as a 'wog'. An industrial tribunal dismissed the case and the EAT agreed, holding that:

> It was impossible to say that the use of the phrase 'wog' by one manager to another, even though overheard by the appellant, could properly be described as a 'detriment'. (De Souza v the Automobile Association [1985] IRLR 87)

Although Ms de Souza lost again at the Court of Appeal, the Court did make some useful comments on the definition of a 'detriment'. Referring to the EAT decision in Porcelli v Strathclyde Council, the Court held that if the discriminatory treatment had an adverse effect on the employee's working environment, it could be illegal, 'even if the employee was prepared to work on and put up with the harassment'. In Ms de Souza's case however, one racial insult was by itself insufficient evidence of an adverse environment (De Souza v the Automobile Association [1986] IRLR 103). Although the Court of Appeal made a step in the right direction, the CRE believes that it did not go far enough. Appalled by the notion that someone referred to as a 'wog' had no redress under the law, the Commission proposes that the word 'detriment' be defined in the legislation to prevent such a narrow construction (CRE, July 1985: 42).

The Court of Appeal's pronouncements in the de Souza case should mean that if a worker is subjected to continuous sexual or racial harassment and is courageous enough to stick it out and put up with the harassment, he or she should have a legal remedy.[10] Given the tentative nature of so many judicial pronouncements on discrimination law, together with the tendency of the courts to change their minds, this development in case law is very fragile. It would be safer to incorporate the concept of harassment, clearly defined, into the statutes and not to rely on the judges to interpret the law creatively.

Conclusion

Complex legislation often results from a desire on the part of the legislators to minimize the discretion of the courts and tribunals, on the argument that the more detailed the provisions, the fewer the gaps that remain for the judiciary to fill. In the case of the equality laws however, the complexity arises largely from the need to pacify those who would otherwise oppose it. The result has been to increase the discretion of the tribunal members and judges. Required by the legislators to balance conflicting considerations, their own predispositions have proved crucial in resolving those dilemmas. A careful re-drafting exercise is necessary, making it more difficult for hostile judges to frustrate the aims of the law. To ensure that applicants are given access to the information they require in order to present a case, new rules of evidence on the discovery of documents are also needed.

Reforming the tribunals along the lines suggested in Chapter 4 will be less effective if their decisions continue to be overturned by the superior courts. On present performance, it is tempting to suggest that the right of appeal be removed, but in almost any other context this would be regarded as a retrograde step. More constructively, we need to ensure that whenever a case is the subject of an appeal, high quality legal representation is available to the complainant. At the end of the day, however, unless we can find a way of transforming the legal system so that the judiciary becomes more representative of the people whose fate it decides, the principle of equality will continue to be stifled by the dictates of the managerial prerogative.

Notes

1. When a case is remitted to an industrial tribunal, it does not necessarily follow that the party who lodged the appeal will win. In some cases, the tribunal (who may or may not be the same three people as before), having re-examined the evidence in the light of the EAT's comments, will reach the same conclusion as before. In my own study of thirty-one remitted cases, twelve were withdrawn before the re-hearing; in ten cases the decision of the first tribunal was reversed and in the remaining nine the first decision was confirmed. Overall, there was no clear net advantage to either side (Gregory, 1984).

2. These percentages have been calculated very roughly, for the discrimination jurisdictions by comparing the totals in Table 5.1 with the totals in Table 4.1 and for the unfair dismissal jurisdiction on the basis of Table 5.1, together with tribunal statistics appearing in various issues of the *Employment Gazette*.

3. This idea has been given serious consideration by a number of practitioners and commentators involved in discrimination law. See, for example, Bindman (1985). See also the discussion by Rubenstein on the CRE's proposals for reform of the tribunal system, although he himself rejects this particular option ('Opinion', *Equal Opportunities Review*, No 7, May/June 1986: 48).

4. The Rules of Procedure for industrial tribunals give them the same powers in relation to discovery as those of the county court. See Rule 4(1) of the Rules of Procedure scheduled to the Industrial Tribunals (Labour Relations) Regulations 1974, SI 1974 No 1386 and Order 14, Rules 2 and 3 of the County Court Rules 1936.

5. Mr Justice Slynn is best known to feminists for his comments in the Court of Appeal in a case of sexual assault in 1977. Agreeing with his fellow judges to allow the appeal of a guardsman against a three year sentence for brutally attacking a young woman who refused to have intercourse with him, Mr Justice Slynn implied that the victim should have succumbed to the rape and so avoided injury. He saw the offender as exhibiting an over-enthusiasm for sex rather than criminality and considered that a six month suspended sentence would be appropriate (see Pattullo, 1983: 19–20). From the point of view of sex discrimination applicants hoping for a sympathetic hearing, such a decision did not bode well.

6. Mr Justice Phillips, the first president of the EAT, served from March 1976 to July 1978. He was followed by Mr Justice Slynn who held the position until March 1981 and then by Mr Justice Browne-Wilkinson who served for the same length of time. Mr Justice Waite was appointed in November 1983 and Mr Justice Popplewell took over from him at the beginning of 1986. Although the president will not necessarily hear all the discrimination appeals occurring during his term of office, as there are twelve other High Court judges available to hear EAT cases, in practice most of the significant discrimination cases have been heard by the president.

7. The two appeals, heard together, were Hayes v Malleable Working Men's Club and Maughan v NE London Magistrates Court Committee [1985] IRLR 367. As neither Ms Hayes nor Ms Maughan could meet the two year qualifying period for

bringing a complaint under the unfair dismissal law, they had to use the SDA despite the unfavourable precedent established in the Turley case.

8. Although legal aid is not available for tribunal cases, it is available at the appeal stage. My attempts to discover how many employees, if any, apply for legal aid have met with a complete blank. The Legal Aid annual reports do not give separate figures on legal aid for the EAT; they are included in the 'miscellaneous' category. Telephone calls to the Law Society on these questions have proved unhelpful, except that the person handling appeals from people refused legal aid said that it was her impression that the refusal rate in employment cases was high, but she was unable to supply any figures. A letter to the Law Society evoked no response whatsoever.

9. A Queen's Counsel is a senior barrister appointed on the recommendation of the Lord Chancellor. A QC takes precedence over other barristers in court. The case which Lord Denning reversed in favour of the applicant was that of Fletcher v Clay Cross Quarries (see Ch. 1, p. 24).

10. This would bring us into line with American case law on this issue. In the case of Bundy v Jackson in 1981, the District of Columbia Court of Appeals held that sexual harassment was unlawful discrimination where the employer permits 'a substantially discriminatory work environment regardless of whether the complaining employee lost any tangible job benefits as a result of the discrimination' (CADC (1981) 24 FEP Cases 1155). This judgment is quoted in Sedley and Benn (1984). See also Rubenstein (1983).

6 The administrative route to equality: formal investigations

The processes of individual litigation outlined in the preceding chapters offer an inefficient and uncertain route to equality. The development of case law is dependent on the chance availability of individuals determined to take up the challenge and pursue it, whatever the personal costs. Aware of these difficulties, the proponents of anti-discrimination legislation have always insisted on the need for an administrative body which would have resources and powers superior to those of individual complainants. This was the rationale behind the Race Relations Acts of 1965 and 1968, which relied exclusively on the administrative option and made no provision for individuals to have direct access to the courts. All complaints of racial discrimination were channelled through the Race Relations Board which was required to investigate and attempt conciliation, initiating civil proceedings only as a last resort. The Board could not require witnesses to appear before it; nor could it determine the main thrust of its activities, as its chief function was to respond to individual complaints.

In Britain and America, the history of administrative enforcement of civil rights laws has followed a similar pattern. Initially, the agency is given weak powers of enforcement and only when these weaknesses have been clearly demonstrated over a period of time does it become possible to launch a rescue operation and give the agency some teeth.

In the United States, the Equal Employment Opportunities Commission (EEOC) was created for the purpose of enforcing the employment provisions (Title VII) of the Civil Rights Act 1964. Originally, it was to be given 'cease and desist' powers, but it had to bear the main brunt of the compromises necessary before Congress would pass the legislation. In the version which finally became law, the Commission's role was restricted to investigation, persuasion and conciliation. Enforcement was left in the hands of individual complainants or the Attorney General. The latter could only file suit if he [sic] had 'reasonable cause' to believe that there was a 'pattern or practice of discrimination'. The Justice Department made little use of these powers and in 1972 a new Equal Opportunity Employment Act gave the Commission power to initiate civil action where conciliation failed and also provided for the transfer of the Attorney General's jurisdiction over 'pattern and practice' cases to the Commission two years later.[1]

In Britain, the return of a Labour government in 1974 brought the proposed 'new deal' on civil rights to the top of the political agenda. Those responsible for drafting the laws were able to draw on American experiments with administrative action, as well as considering the lessons to be drawn from the ineffectiveness of the Race Relations Board. Consequently, the two new Commissions created by the Sex Discrimination Act 1975 and the Race Relations Act 1976 were given wide-ranging duties and an impressive-looking set of powers. The Equal Opportunities Commission and the Commission for Racial Equality were required to work towards the elimination of discrimination, to promote equality of opportunity (and in the case of the CRE, good relations between racial groups) and to keep the legislation under review, submitting proposals for amending it as necessary. In order to accomplish these tasks, the Commissions were given power to conduct formal investigations, to subpoena witnesses and to issue non-discrimination notices. At the same time, to ensure that the new bodies could concentrate on a broad, strategic role, the link between them and individual complainants was weakened in a number of ways: individuals were allowed direct access to the tribunals and courts, the Commissions were given the discretion but not the duty to assist complainants and the conciliation function was transferred to ACAS.

These powers are by no means identical to those of the American EEOC. At one end of the procedural spectrum, the American agency retains responsibility for conciliation, whereas the British agencies do not. At the other end, the EEOC still has no power to issue a 'cease and desist order', which would be the equivalent of the British non-discrimination notice. Instead, once the Commission has collected evidence of discriminatory practices, it must take the employer to court, so that it is the judges who make the final decision and exact the appropriate penalty. It was this crucial difference which enabled Roy Jenkins to claim that the Sex Discrimination Bill presented to the House of Commons in 1975 was 'probably the most comprehensive Bill of its kind in the world' (Parliamentary Debates, House of Commons, Vol. 889, col. 512). It also precipitated a protest by Ian Gilmour on behalf of the Conservative opposition, a protest which was to foreshadow the legal quagmire which lay ahead. Referring to the EOC during the debate on the Sex Discrimination Bill, he described it as 'policewoman, prosecutor, judge, jury and even probation officer and after-care officer' rolled into one, and expressed strong reservations on the wisdom of giving such extensive powers to the Commission (ibid, col. 534).

In creating the EOC and the CRE, the legislators had produced an unusual form of the quasi-autonomous non-governmental organization, or 'quango'. A favourite tool of interventionist governments, the quango offers a number of advantages: 'hiving off' specialist tasks prevents overloading government departments and yet ultimate control is retained through ministerial supervision of funds and appointments; the semi-autonomous status of the quango serves to deflect criticism of controversial policies away from government, which is then free to pursue a number of contradictory policies simultaneously.

It was inevitable that the two equality Commissions, regardless of how they chose to interpret their duties and powers, would be criticized by groups at both ends of the political spectrum. Those on the right would consider almost any positive move by the Commissions as an unwarranted interference with market forces; those on the left would dismiss even their more radical efforts as an exercise in containment, which could never offer more than the appearance of equality.

Between these two extremes were many civil rights campaigners who refused to prejudge the issue, preferring to wait until the new quangos could be assessed on the basis of their achievements. Now that the Commissions have enjoyed a decade of existence, it is possible to offer such an assessment, an exercise made all the more illuminating because of the contrasting strategies adopted by the two bodies.

Mice in Manchester

Commentators are generally agreed that the Equal Opportunities Commission made an inauspicious start.[2] Much of the blame for this is laid at the door of the government for the casual way in which the Commission was established. The decision to locate it in Manchester (the original proposal was Bootle), away from the Houses of Parliament and government departments, was interpreted at best as a sign that the Home Office was not taking the legislation seriously and at worst as an attempt at sabotage. Despite the fanfare and self-congratulations, it looked as though Roy Jenkins preferred to settle for the appearance and not the reality of equality. The way in which members of the Commission were selected served to strengthen these suspicions.

The commissioners were not selected on the basis of their dedication to the cause of female equality, but in order to achieve political balance and ensure the representation of a number of interests. Betty Lockwood, ex-women's officer of the Labour Party, was appointed to chair the Commission and Elspeth Howe, a Bow group activist and wife of the Conservative Party shadow chancellor, was appointed her deputy.[3] These were the two full-time appointments; the rest of the commissioners were appointed on a part-time basis. The TUC and the CBI were each asked to nominate three commissioners and the Home Office, in consultation with other government departments, selected the remaining seven 'independent' commissioners. Women's organizations, who had played an active part in campaigning for the legislation, suggested candidates, but all of these were rejected. Although some of them could claim previous links with women's groups, none of the commissioners (apart from the TUC and CBI representatives) was directly answerable for their actions to a well-defined constituency.

Even before the full membership of the Commission had been decided, the two full-time commissioners took control, anxious to define an appropriate role and image for the Commission. Betty Lockwood announced that the EOC's emphasis would be on cooperation rather than coercion. She and Lady Howe embarked on a round of talks with employers and managers, in order to present a picture of moderation and common sense and to dissociate themselves from the strident voice of feminism. In February 1976, Lady Howe addressed a management conference at the Hilton Hotel. She reassured her audience that the commissioners would not approach their task as 'one-eyed egalitarians' and devoted much of her time to spelling out what the Sex Discrimination Act was *not* trying to do:

> It is *not* trying to turn men into women or vice versa . . . It is *not* trying to rewrite the English language (hence her and Betty Lockwood's insistence on the term chairman) . . . It is *not* trying to destroy the privacy of the family or the home . . . It is *not* trying to interfere with the employer's legitimate freedom. (EOC Press Notice, 23 February 1976, emphasis in the original)

When the commissioners arrived in Manchester to assume their duties at the beginning of 1976, they discovered a staffing structure created by the Home Office Planning Unit and almost 100 full-time staff already in post. With the Commission's enforcement powers very much in mind, civil servants with investigative skills had been seconded from such departments as Customs and Excise, the Inland Revenue and ACAS. However, when the commissioners decided to appoint a legal officer to take responsibility for law enforcement, they became embroiled in a three year wrangle with the Home Office over the appropriate grading for such an appointment. No effective law enforcement policy was developed and the civil servants returned to their departments having seen no active service. The rest of the staff included a high proportion of competent and committed people who had applied for jobs at the EOC because they wished to be part of the fight against discrimination. Once appointed, they became increasingly impatient with the lack of decisive direction from the commissioners.

The only formal investigation undertaken during 1976 was not concerned with employment, but with education. It was undertaken in response to allegations from parents that the Tameside education authority had discriminated against girls by providing more grammar school places for boys than for girls. On the surface, the issues seemed straightforward enough: a Tameside councillor had announced on television the council's intention to offer 60 percent of selective places to boys. There were, however, strong political undercurrents as the Labour government had already attempted (unsuccessfully) to have the Tameside decision to retain grammar schools declared illegal (Secretary of State for Education and Science v Tameside Metropolitan Borough Council [1976] All ER 665). These undercurrents were reflected within the EOC where Lady Howe, while agreeing to form part of the Tameside investigating team, asked that her opposition to the investigation be recorded in the minutes. The report, published in December 1977, can only be described as a damp squib. The investigating team made some useful comments on the educational provisions of the Sex Discrimination Act but were unable, on the basis of the available evidence, to make a finding of illegal discrimination.

In the field of employment, the EOC's softly-softly approach took the form of a detailed letter to 500 companies and organizations, outlining the provisions of the Sex Discrimination Act, including the role of the Commission, and requesting information with regard to their policies on equal opportunities for women. Clearly, the Commission had no intention of using its discretionary powers hastily:

> The very breadth of this discretion places upon the Commission the responsibility of choosing its priorities carefully ... Neither the public interest nor the cause of equality for women would be served by precipitate action or indiscriminate use of powers because these powers exist. (EOC *Annual Report* 1976: 4 and 5)

Inspiration for the first employment investigation came from Mr Justice Phillips, president of the EAT, who evidently had a much clearer grasp of the Commission's strategic role than the commissioners themselves. Dismissing the appeal of Electrolux against a successful equal pay claim by Ms Hutchinson, the judge acknowledged the limits of individual litigation. Aware that more than 200 other Electrolux employees had filed, or were intending to file, equal pay claims against the company, he pointed out that:

> it is unlikely that the individual answers put together can produce a coherent wage structure. That can only be done by negotiation, applying the current views and statutory prescriptions on equal pay and equal opportunities. It may be that the Equal Opportunities Commission could be of assistance in such an exercise. Certainly it lies beyond our competence and jurisdiction. (Electrolux v Hutchinson [1976] IRLR 410: 413)

When the EOC visited Luton, it found itself entering an industrial relations minefield. The seven women awarded equal pay by the Appeal Tribunal had been moved to different work, while the women replacing them were paid at the lower rate. The Commission prepared to embark on a job evaluation exercise as suggested by the judge, but this was strongly resisted by the trade unions, which feared that the skills of male workers would be downgraded in the process. The Commission therefore reluctantly adopted a quasi-legalistic approach and made a number of 'like work' comparisons between typical male and female jobs. After two and a half years, the equal pay aspects of the investigation were completed and the EOC issued its first non-discrimination notice. Electrolux protested that they did not deserve the stigma implied by such a notice, especially as they had already made the required changes. The Commission insisted that the notice was necessary so that the new pay structure could be monitored adequately, but agreed to drop the sex discrimination aspects of the investigation. Despite the considerable time and energy invested in this exercise, the crucial issues of job segregation and training opportunities for women therefore remained unresolved.

By the summer of 1977, a group of EOC staff had lost patience with the commissioners. They presented them with a series of proposals for action, involving a much wider use of the formal investigation procedure and threatening to resign unless they received a positive response (Mackie, *The Guardian*, 11 July 1977). Judging by the next press notice, the staff had scored a success:

> The Commission decided to increase the number of formal investigations into suspected sex discrimination and to place more emphasis on its law enforcement roles. The Commission is now in a position to use comprehensive information gained in case-work, visits to industry and its monitoring of the progress towards equal pay, to shift the emphasis towards direct law enforcement. (Press Notice, 12 July 1977)

There was certainly no shortage of potential targets: the names of several firms recurred with monotonous regularity in complaints made to the Commission and in tribunal applications. Although the final report of the survey of 500 large companies was not published until late in 1978, the Commission knew well before then how the various firms were responding. Most employers believed that improving job opportunities for women was less important than other business pressures; special policies for women arose only 'in response to labour supply needs' (EOC Second Annual Report: 9) and these occurred less frequently as unemployment rose. The majority of companies did not even analyse their workforce by sex; only 4 percent monitored progress on equality and a mere 2 percent had taken positive action to improve the position of women (EOC, October 1978, *Equality between the Sexes in Industry*). The Commission's enforcement powers were designed precisely for the purpose of combating such apathy: by means of a formal investigation, the Commission could require the company to produce the missing workforce statistics and could exert the pressure to ensure that equal opportunities did become a high priority.

Despite the firm tone of the July press notice, the Commission persisted in its kid glove policy and did not embark on any new formal investigations. Almost one year after they had put pressure on the commissioners to take a harder line, some of the staff tried again. Senior staff, invited to a commissioners' working weekend in a Yorkshire hotel, forced Betty Lockwood to abandon her agenda in order to discuss their grievances. These centred on the difficulties experienced by senior staff in carrying out their executive functions because of the way in which the full-time commissioners interfered in the day-to-day running of the Commission. As before, at least some of the commissioners appeared to respond positively to the staff complaints. The chief executive 'resigned' following the weekend hostilities and a golden opportunity presented itself to make a strong appointment. In the event, the commissioners played safe once again. The feminist candidate, shortlisted at the insistence of the firm of management consultants advising on the appointment, was not selected, although in the opinion of one commissioner: 'at the interview she was head and shoulders above everyone else'.

Not until it was relieved of the Electrolux burden did the Commission begin any new investigations. In 1979, four employment investigations were launched in quick succession. One concerned the membership conditions of a trade union, the Society of Graphical and Allied Trades (SOGAT), another was to look at the employment practices of the Leeds Permanent Building Society and the other two related to the recruitment and promotion policies at educational establishments, one a school and the other a college of further education.

Despite this apparent change in strategy, it is clear that the Commission still regarded the formal investigation as a weapon of last resort. The press statement on the SOGAT investigation ends with the sentence: 'After failing to solve the problem through discussion with SOGAT, the EOC decided to undertake a formal investigation' (Press Notice, 18 June 1979). The two London branches of SOGAT operated on a single sex basis and production jobs were advertised only within the all-male London Central branch, so that women were effectively excluded from all higher-grade positions. The discriminatory practices operated by the Leeds Permanent Building Society were equally blatant. There was evidence of direct discrimination in that no women were appointed as management trainees, although nearly a quarter of the applicants were women. There was also evidence of indirect discrimination; the requirement that managers be geographically mobile was presented in such a way that many women would be discouraged from applying. In practice, the requirement was operated flexibly so that women managers (if any were ever to be appointed) would have no difficulty in complying.

In 1980, the Commission made use of its general duty to promote equality of opportunity between men and women in order to launch a formal investigation which differed from all previous investigations, in that it contained no allegations of unlawful discrimination. It concerned the different redundancy terms offered to men and women employed at the British Steel Corporation works at Shotton. The report, produced within a year, was professional in style and confident in tone. Having identified the different statutory pension ages for men and women as the root cause of the problem, the findings were used to provide ammunition for the Commission's campaign to equalize the pension age.

The only new formal investigation undertaken in 1981 was not an employment investigation but concerned the Provincial Building Society's handling of mortgage applications (Press Notice, 10 February 1981). The Society applied to the High Court for an order stopping the investigation, on the grounds that the Commission had already made up its mind against the Society and had thereby violated the rules of natural justice. The tables were neatly turned on the Commission when it was issued with a subpoena, requiring it to produce internal documents and memoranda relating to the investigation. When these were produced in Court the judge agreed that they showed prejudice against the Society and that decisions had been taken on the basis of inadequate information. He severely reprimanded the Commission, which agreed to drop the investigation and pay the Building Society's legal costs (*Financial Times*, 29 April 1982).

The investigation was transformed into an informal, collaborative exercise. The ever-declining murmur of voices within the Commission in favour of an aggressive approach to law enforcement was effectively silenced and the policy of gentle persuasion reigned supreme. Almost four years were to elapse before the EOC plucked up courage to use its investigative powers again. In January 1986, an employment investigation at Dan Air Services was announced, but by this time, the usefulness of these powers had been severely curtailed by the courts (see below).

During its first decade of existence, the Commission attempted eight investigations which generated six reports and one non-discrimination notice. The four investigations started in 1979 became hopelessly entangled in technical difficulties. At the school, the Commission had been unable to find the necessary documentary evidence that would enable it to make a finding of discrimination, even though virtually all the senior posts at the school were occupied by men. Meanwhile, the college took objection to the appointment of an additional commissioner halfway through the investigation and threatened the Commission with judicial review. The matter was eventually settled out of court, but as a result of this delay, the investigation took five years from start to finish. The Leeds investigation took even longer; the draft report of the Commission's findings was available as early as 1981, but as a consequence of delaying tactics by the Society, the final report was not published until 1985. As the college and the building society both agreed to alter their employment practices in the light of the Commission's findings, the EOC decided not to issue non-discrimination notices.

The SOGAT investigation broke all records; the Commission sat on draft discrimination notices against the union and two London branches for more than two years, hoping that SOGAT would put its own house in order. In September 1986, after repeated assurances had been broken and numerous deadlines had passed, even the Commission's patience was exhausted and the non-discrimination notices were issued (EOC News Release, 16 September 1986).

In October 1986, the EOC issued a non-discrimination notice against Dan Air, thereby raising the total of organizations against whom such action had been taken to three (Electrolux, SOGAT and Dan Air). At the end of 1986, there were no formal investigations under way and no new investigations had been announced.

Incoherence in London
The timidity and indecision of the Commission in Manchester contrasts sharply with the almost frenzied activities of the Commission for Racial Equality in London. Commencing operations in June

1977, the CRE immediately involved itself in a variety of campaigns and projects, offering a high level of support for tribunal applicants and embarking on several formal investigations. Admittedly, the CRE had certain advantages: it had more staff and three times the budget available to the EOC; many of its staff were drawn from the old Race Relations Board and Community Relations Commission and therefore had some experience of race relations; it had a London headquarters and a regional support structure in the form of Community Relations Councils.

The CRE was not, however, without its problems or its critics. The choice of David Lane as the first chairperson of the Commission seemed unlikely to inspire confidence in the black people of Britain. An old Etonian and Conservative MP for Cambridge, Mr Lane believed that Britain could be at the forefront of racial harmony in the world, but only if it was able to reassure the white majority that 'immigration is being controlled at a manageably low level'. After two years as the head of the CRE, he was still expressing the hope that it would 'not be too long before I and my colleagues have worked ourselves out of a job'.[4] Before he could begin to establish racial harmony on a national scale, Mr Lane had to deal with a distinct lack of harmony within the Commission itself, where tensions existed between those members of staff recruited from the Race Relations Board and those from the Community Relations Commission, with the CRE itself being accused of racism.[5]

In contrast to the EOC, the initial impetus for action came from the commissioners rather than from the full-time staff. By the end of 1978, after only eighteen months of existence, the CRE had embarked on twenty-nine formal investigations. During 1979, ten more were started and in 1980 a further six. Belatedly, the Commission discovered that it had bitten off more than it could chew; beginning an investigation seemed simple enough, but seeing it through to a successful conclusion was a different matter altogether. When in 1981 the House of Commons Home Affairs Committee set up a sub-committee to examine the work of the CRE, the forty-five investigations had yielded only ten reports, eight of which had been accompanied by a non-discrimination notice. The fieldwork had been completed in a further fourteen investigations and four non-discrimination notices issued in relation to these. The Committee was not impressed. Far from commending the CRE for its vigorous policies, it saw the Commission as moving in too many directions at once, with no clearly defined priorities or objectives: 'The Commission's greatest defect is incoherence'.[6]

The ten published reports all dealt with small organizations. The Home Affairs Committee would have preferred to see a smaller number of investigations, concentrating on large organizations:

> Even one single completed investigation into the practices of a major employer or provider of services would have had a greater effect than the nailing of these small fry. (Home Affairs Committee, 1981: para 43)

The Committee was appalled by the CRE's 'failure to complete a single major investigation in the first four years of their existence' and condemned their investigative techniques as 'amateurish' (ibid, paras 45 and 46). During the enquiry, both commissioners and staff at the CRE had attempted to outline for the sub-committee some of the problems they had encountered in conducting formal investigations. The response was not particularly sympathetic.

One of the major problems faced by an investigating team is its reliance on information that can only be supplied by the respondent organization. Frequently, the respondents are unwilling or unable to supply it, or they produce it in a form which is difficult to use. If an organization proves to be obstructive and unhelpful and the Commission has to use its subpoena powers, the chances are that this move comes too late and that crucial evidence may already have been destroyed. The most cumbersome part of the procedure is contained in section 49(4) of the Race Relations Act 1976. It obliges the Commission, before embarking on investigations which allege discrimination by named persons, to inform those persons of its belief that unlawful acts may have been committed and to give them the opportunity to make oral and written representations. If, as a result of these representations, the terms of reference are altered, the whole procedure has to be repeated. A memorandum submitted to the sub-committee by the CRE staff side pointed out that comparable bodies, such as the Ombudsman, are not hampered by such obligations (Home Affairs Committee, 1981: Vol. II, 174–5).

Although the Committee agreed and recommended that section 49(4) be repealed, it did not accept that the removal of the offending section would make as much difference as the Commission claimed. It concluded that: 'Delays through the recalcitrance of respondents have seriously affected only a minority of the less significant investigations' and insisted that the Commission itself was the major culprit in perpetrating delays. It objected to the way in which the CRE left respondents 'on the rack' for long periods of time and urged it to develop a 'style of brisk and systematic investigation'. The Committee clearly believed that the delays in completing formal investigations could be attributed to the Commission's overzealousness in undertaking too many investigations at once, combined with lack of expertise in a new field.

Only a few of the early 'responsive' investigations into small operations were still outstanding and the Committee detected a welcome shift of emphasis. It referred to the British Leyland report, published in September 1981, as an example of the potential impact of the Commission's work when a well-known company was involved. (Subsequent developments at British Leyland, now Austin Rover, were outlined in Ch. 3.) The list of current investigations which the CRE supplied to the sub-committee showed a marked bias towards employment investigations and included a number of major manufacturing industries with household names. In general, the sub-committee approved the choice of priorities reflected in this list, including the spread across regions and different sectors of employment, although they did wonder how the housing, educational and services sections were spending their time.

In the final analysis, the MPs who investigated the CRE assumed that the chief source of its difficulties, and hence the solution to them, lay within the Commission itself. They argued that the CRE had been given 'the biggest powers in the Western World in relation to law enforcement' (Alex Lyon MP, Home Affairs Committee, 1981: Vol. II, 68); it had only to concentrate its resources on using these and it could not fail. The MPs refused to consider the possibility that Parliament, by building in so many safeguards to protect the rights of those against whom the Commission turned its great guns, had rendered those 'immense powers' virtually unusable.

What became of the 'biggest powers in the Western World'?
Far from developing a 'brisk and systematic' style of investigation, the CRE discovered that the larger organizations were even better equipped than the 'small fry' to take full advantage of the procedural complexities of the law and that the courts were either unable or unwilling to smooth the Commission's path. At the time of the Home Affairs Committee's investigation, these developments were as yet in their infancy and the Commission had faced only two applications for judicial review. The first opponent was none other than the Home Office itself, whose immigration procedures the Commission had decided to investigate. Against a general background of accusations of racism in immigration law and policy, the decision was precipitated by the allegation that an Indian woman arriving at Heathrow Airport in order to marry her fiancé had been subjected to a 'virginity test'.

The Home Office sought a declaration from the High Court that the Commission was exceeding its powers in proposing such an investigation. Mr Justice Woolf held that the CRE's duty to work towards 'the elimination of racial discrimination' was restricted to discrimination made unlawful by the Race Relations Act, which did not include immigration control. However, the Commission also had the duty to promote 'good relations between persons of different racial groups' and under this provision the investigation could be authorized.[7]

The CRE did go ahead with the investigation and four years later produced a report which made a number of recommendations for changing immigration procedures. There was of course no question of issuing a non-discrimination notice, as the Nationality and Immigration Acts were covered by the general exemption offered by section 41 of the Race Relations Act.[8] The Home Affairs Committee seemed unimpressed by the Commission's audacity in taking on its own paymaster and regarded the decision to tie up substantial resources in this enterprise as misguided, given the backlog of uncompleted investigations in other areas.

The second challenge to the CRE's use of its investigative powers came from the London Borough of Hillingdon. The Commission had decided to conduct a formal investigation into the way in which the Borough carried out its duty to provide accommodation for homeless persons. Once again, Heathrow Airport features in the proceedings, as it is situated in the Borough of Hillingdon, so that Hillingdon Council automatically becomes responsible for housing immigrant families arriving at Heathrow with nowhere to live. The Council believes that the government should help to shoulder this burden. In order to draw attention to this belief, an Asian family arriving from Kenya was dumped on the steps of the Foreign Office. A white Rhodesian family arriving at Heathrow during the same period was not accorded the same treatment and housing was provided for them. These were the actions which precipitated the CRE's involvement; the Commission's mistake, according to the Courts, was to draw the terms of reference for the investigation too widely. The Commission intended to investigate the Council's policy towards homeless people in general, whereas the original allegations had been directed specifically at the treatment of new immigrants arriving at Heathrow Airport and requiring housing accommodation. The High Court judgment implied that the investigation could go ahead under more tightly drawn terms of reference. The judge had been concerned here with the rules of natural justice and would not allow the Commission to 'throw the book' at Hillingdon; he recognized however that the Commission did have a basis for forming the belief that the Council might have discriminated.

When the case reached the House of Lords, Lord Diplock was clearly irritated at the 'Commission's insistence on pursuing this matter right up to your Lordships' House' at considerable public expense, when it could instead have resumed the investigation on the basis of amended terms of reference (R. v Commission for Racial Equality ex parte London Borough of Hillingdon [1982] IRLR 424). For the Commission, however, the judgment had implications beyond the Hillingdon case and it had presumably hoped that the House of Lords would offer a less restrictive interpretation of section 49. According to the editor of the *New Law Journal*, its failure to do so 'effectively defeated the spirit and intention of the CRE's powers under the Race Relations legislation'. Instead of supporting the CRE in ensuring that its purpose — 'to investigate and stamp out discriminatory practices' — is carried out, the courts have:

> signalled to those who may be thought to be discriminatory by the CRE that any small technical complaint will be sufficient to merit consideration and if upheld will enable them successfully to avoid investigation. (*New Law Journal*, 1 July 1982)

The editor of the *Industrial Relations Law Reports* was concerned to draw out the implications of the Hillingdon decision for employment. It would seem to rule out the possibility of launching an investigation into the general employment policies of a particular firm unless the Commission had evidence that those general policies were discriminatory. Otherwise, the investigation would have to confine itself to those particular features of the organization which the Commission believed at the outset to be suspect. He believes that 'Parliament may have so circumscribed the Commission's effectiveness as to undercut the practical use of formal investigations' (*October Highlights*, [1982] IRLR 393).

A perfect illustration of this limitation is provided by the EOC's investigation into the recruitment policy of Dan Air Services Ltd. Announcing the investigation, the EOC expressed its belief that 'the airline may unlawfully discriminate against male applicants in the appointment of their cabin staff' (Press Release, 22 January 1986). The investigation, carefully restricted to this particular aspect of recruitment policy, was completed within a year. A golden opportunity to tackle job segregation throughout the airline industry, including pilots and engineers, was lost, simply because the original complaint related only to the appointment of cabin staff.

The immediate consequence of the Hillingdon decision was to bring to a halt all those investigations into named persons where no unlawful discrimination was suspected. Such investigations were undertaken by the CRE as part of its general strategy for eliminating discrimination and promoting equality of opportunity. As they were not 'belief' investigations the Commission made no use of its subpoena powers, nor did it give the organizations the opportunity to make representations at the outset of the investigation. However, if the Commission in the course of its enquiries did uncover unlawful acts, it might well issue a non-discrimination notice. When therefore the Prestige Group was presented with a non-discrimination notice following such an investigation, it challenged the legality of this action in the light of the Hillingdon decision. The House of Lords confirmed that the CRE was not entitled to conduct an investigation into the activities of named persons (in this case the Prestige Group) unless it had reason to believe that unlawful discrimination might have occurred (R v Commission for Racial Equality ex parte Prestige Group plc, [1983] IRLR 408). The non-discrimination notice against Prestige was quashed and a number of other investigations were abandoned.

According to the White Paper on racial discrimination, which preceded the setting up of the CRE, there was to be a crucial difference between the new 'improved' Commission and the Race Relations Board which it was to replace. The CRE, unlike the Board, would not be:

> hampered by its dependence on receiving significant complaints in pursuing the crucial strategic role of identifying and dealing with discriminatory practices and encouraging positive action to secure equal opportunity. (*Racial Discrimination*, HMSO 1975: para 37)

It would therefore be free to conduct formal investigations into any organization for any purpose related to its functions. Similarly, the White Paper that preceded the Sex Discrimination Act saw the EOC as investigating discriminatory practices 'on its own initiative ... whether or not there had been individual complaints about the organization investigated' (*Equality for Women*, HMSO 1974: paras 110–11).

The judicial interpretation of section 49(4) has undermined this freedom and reduced the Commission to performing the old 'reactive' role of the Board. Blatant and specific discriminatory acts can be investigated; less tangible and more insidious practices, including those resulting in indirect, unintentional discrimination, cannot. The strategic role of the Commission, regarded by the Home Affairs Committee as the central rationale for its existence, was effectively destroyed.

Admittedly, s 49(4) had not formed part of the original Bill, nor had an equivalent section been included in the Sex Discrimination Act in 1975. The new provision was introduced as a House of Lords amendment which the government accepted and also extended to the Sex Discrimination Act.[9] The purpose of the amendment was to ensure that anyone who was the subject of a complaint had the right to be informed; it was not intended to create a straitjacket for the

Commission in the way that it has. Under the rules of interpretation, the judges do not look at Parliamentary Debates when interpreting statutory provisions. Even so, the way in which they have chosen to interpret s 49 makes an intelligent reading of the provisions taken as a whole virtually impossible.[10]

The Commission's powers in relation to non-discrimination notices have also proved fraught with difficulties. For example, one company on whom a notice was served wriggled out of its obligations by ceasing to trade under the name that appeared on the notice and resuming business under a new name. The Commission was powerless to take action against the new company. A further restriction is that a non-discrimination notice can only require the firm or organization to refrain from unlawful acts in the future; the Commission can make recommendations but it cannot insist that specific steps be taken, for example that a positive action programme be introduced (see Ch. 3, p. 54). Finally, the company has the right to appeal 'against any requirement of the notice' to an industrial tribunal, who may quash the requirement if it is 'unreasonable because it is based on an incorrect finding of fact or for any other reason' (s 59 of the Race Relations Act and s 68 of the Sex Discrimination Act).

In the case of the Commission for Racial Equality v Amari Plastics Ltd [1982] IRLR 252, the CRE argued that the employer's right of appeal was limited to an appeal against 'sentence' and not against 'conviction',[11] but the EAT and the Court of Appeal both agreed with Amari Plastics that all the issues of fact which formed the basis of the non-discrimination notice could be considered by the tribunal. According to Lord Denning:

> there must be a proper judicial inquiry as to whether those findings of fact are right. That means evidence of witnesses, with opportunity of cross-examination, and the like . . . in fairness to the company . . . (it) should be able to challenge the findings of fact which the Commission have already made: and to challenge them before the industrial tribunal which is the first impartial judicial tribunal to hear it. (p. 255)

Lord Denning admitted that the machinery was so elaborate and cumbersome that it was in danger of grinding to a halt. This was a far cry from the 'days of the Inquisition' analogy once considered appropriate by Lord Denning (see Ch. 5, p. 94), and he now extends his sympathy to the Commission:

> I am very sorry for the Commission, but they have been caught up in a spider's web spun by Parliament, from which there is very little hope of their escaping. (p. 255)

Lord Justice Griffiths suggested that if the procedures were proving to be unworkable, the Commission should consider proposing to the Secretary of State that the Act be amended (ibid, p. 254).

The Commission did precisely this in its *Review of the Race Relations Act*, published in July 1985. Its proposals for change in relation to formal investigation powers seek to repair the damage inflicted by the courts and to devise a method of enforcement which will be more difficult to sabotage. The Commission asks for the repeal of s 49(4) in order to reverse the effect of the Prestige judgment and so reinstate the Commission's power 'to conduct a formal investigation for any purpose connected with the carrying out of its duties'.[12] It cites the Home Affairs Committee's support for repeal of the offending section and also its view that the best safeguard for those investigated by the Commission lies in the right to seek judicial review.

Recognizing that the courts are hostile to the notion of entrusting all stages of the law enforcement process to one agency (the problem anticipated by Sir Ian Gilmour, quoted above on p. 109), the Commission asks to be relieved of part of its law enforcement function. If a formal investigation is allowed to run its course and then has to be followed by a detailed presentation of evidence and argument in court when the non-discrimination notice is challenged, an inordinate length of time and energy is expended on each investigation. In order to streamline the proceedings, the Commission proposes that 'an independent tribunal of fact' be brought in at an earlier stage. As soon as the Commission has obtained evidence of discrimination, whether during the course of a formal investigation or in some other way, it should be able to present this evidence to the tribunal who (after allowing full opportunity for cross-examination), would decide whether or not discrimination had occurred.

The tribunal and not the Commission would decide on the appropriate remedy in cases where discrimination was found. The Commission believes that only when such a separation of investigative and judicial functions has taken place will it become possible to strengthen the available remedies. The limitations of the non-discrimination notice could then be overcome by empowering the tribunal to order the discriminator to introduce specified changes, a remedy which the courts would find unacceptable in the hands of the Commission.

From the Commission's point of view, these proposed reforms seem to offer the best possible escape route out of the present impasse. They open up the possibility of speedier investigations, fewer complaints emanating from those investigated and a reduced level of judicial hostility directed at the Commission itself. They even create new, more powerful remedies, always assuming that the 'independent tribunal of fact' can be persuaded to make use of them; which brings us to the major flaw in the CRE's proposals. Given the appalling record of the tribunals and courts in the field of civil rights, any proposal that increases their involvement is a policy of desperation rather than genuine optimism.

There is an inescapable irony in the notion that the courts should be allowed to subject the Commissions to such close scrutiny in order to protect the rights of discriminators and that no-one should speak out on behalf of those for whom the law was created: the victims of discrimination themselves. If the judges are allowed to set the parameters of the debate, alternative routes to legislative reform will be closed off before they have been fully explored. Administrative law enforcement survives and even thrives in other jurisdictions and in other countries without necessarily encountering insuperable obstacles. What, then, is distinctive about the administrative framework erected by the anti-discrimination laws of the 1970s and how could it be improved?

There can be no doubt that the CRE and the EOC have interpreted their statutory duties and powers in very different ways. This in itself raises questions about the wisdom of creating such wide discretionary powers; how they are to be controlled and by whom? It also provides a unique opportunity to assess the relative merits and weaknesses of the different strategies, to look for the best practices in both and to assess the limits of the quango as an administrative form.

Notes

1. The US Commission on Civil Rights commented on the low level of activity from the Justice Department. Of the 115 cases referred to the Department by the EEOC from July 1968 to May 1970, only eight lawsuits were filed (US Commission on Civil Rights, 1970). Many of the cases it rejected subsequently came before the courts as private suits and in some of these the courts found patterns or practices of discrimination. See Hill (1977).

2. See for example Coussins (1976), Cameron (1977) and Coote (1978). Patricia Ashdown-Sharp recounts how Granada Television, whose studios are 350 yards from the Commission's headquarters, offered the EOC a weekly spot on its nightly news programme. The invitation was declined, on the grounds that there was no-one at the Commission to deal with such matters. See Ashdown-Sharp (1977). The phrase 'mice in Manchester' was coined by Ades and Stephens (1977).

3. When Sir Geoffrey Howe became Chancellor of the Exchequer in 1979, Lady Howe resigned from the EOC in order to avoid a possible conflict of interests.

4. Both these quotations are taken from Coote and Phillips (1979).

5. The case of Rasul v Commission for Racial Equality is discussed above, Ch. 5, p. 93. See also Coote and Phillips (1979) for further evidence of racial tensions within the Commission.

6. First Report from the Home Affairs Committee, Session 1981–2, Commission for Racial Equality, House of Commons 46, Vol. I para. 8, HMSO, 1981.

7. Home Office v Commission for Racial Equality [1982] 1 QB 385. If the EOC had decided to conduct a formal investigation into the sexually discriminatory aspects of immigration procedures, including the humiliating practice of requiring women to submit to an intimate physical examination, the Court would presumably have put a

stop to it. Although the duties of the EOC and the CRE are otherwise the same, there is no equivalent in the Sex Discrimination Act to the CRE's duty to 'promote good relations between persons of different racial groups'. See Applebey and Ellis (1984).

8. See Commission for Racial Equality, *Immigration Control Procedures: Report of a Formal Investigation*, CRE, February 1985. The general exemption for other legislation provided by s 41 of the Race Relations Act and s 51 of the Sex Discrimination Act is discussed in Chapter 8.

9. Schedule 4 of the Race Relations Act contains a list of amendments to the Sex Discrimination Act, including the insertion of a new section 58(3A) identical to section 49(4) of the Race Relations Act, which reads as follows:

(4) Where the terms of reference of the investigation confine it to activities of persons named in them and the Commission in the course of it propose to investigate any act made unlawful by this Act which they believe that a person so named may have done, the Commission shall —

(*a*) inform that person of their belief and of their proposal to investigate the act in question; and

(*b*) offer him an opportunity of making oral or written representations with regard to it (or both oral and written representations if he thinks fit);

and a person so named who avails himself of an opportunity under this subsection of making oral representations may be represented —

(i) by counsel or a solicitor; or

(ii) by some other person of his choice, not being a person to whom the Commission object on the ground that he is unsuitable.

10. Applebey and Ellis struggle valiantly to make sense of the provisions in the light of the House of Lords' judgment. They point out, inter alia, that if there can never be a general investigation into a named person, but only a 'belief' investigation, then the EOC's British Steel investigation was illegal. See Applebey and Ellis, 1984: 246–8 and 258–9.

11. This vivid description of the issues at stake is provided by Applebey and Ellis (1984), who also emphasize the importance of the Amari Plastics decision by pointing out that at the time of the litigation, every single employer against whom the CRE had issued a non-discrimination notice had lodged an appeal.

12. Race Relations Act 1976 s. 48: see Appendix 4). The Commission's proposals for reforming the formal investigation powers are to be found on pp. 18–24 of the report. A summary of the CRE's main proposals for amending the legislation is given in Appendix 5.

7 The administrative route to equality: who controls the quango?

Any administrative body that operates on the basis of wide-ranging discretionary powers and limited resources will almost certainly attract hostile criticisms from one quarter or another, whatever direction it takes. It may well tread warily at first and choose the middle path, hoping to achieve its aims on the basis of co-operation rather than confrontation. Only when this strategy fails will there be a re-evaluation, followed by a hardening of positions. Two studies of an American agency, the Massachusetts Commission Against Discrimination (MCAD), provide a vivid account of this process and also demonstrate the extent to which an agency's actions are influenced by the changing political climate.

Mayhew's evaluation of the work of the MCAD was published in 1968, when the Commission had been in existence for twenty-two years.[1] He saw the Commission as playing an integrative role by performing a balancing act between opponents of the legislation on one side and civil rights activists on the other. He recognized the danger that organizations can become so preoccupied with the conditions of their own survival that the original aims become compromised. He describes how in the sphere of employment, the MCAD was more concerned with avoiding confrontation and achieving a peaceful settlement than with enforcing the legislation. When its jurisdiction was extended to housing, where discriminatory practices were both more tangible and more blatant, such strategies were inappropriate: 'The activities of the civil rights groups thrust the Commission into active confrontation with more vigorous advocates and more determined opponents of equal opportunity' (Mayhew, 1968: 284).

Jowell's (1975) study of the MCAD covers approximately the same time period.[2] He characterizes the earlier, timid approach of the Commission as 'didactic'; it hoped to overcome discrimination through a process of education and persuasion. During the second phase, the 'tort' approach prevailed and priority was given to securing the rights of the complainant. Only during the late 1960s, with the growth of black militancy, did the commissioners begin to adopt an 'equal opportunity' approach, which concentrated on removing obstacles to progress and encouraging the growth of affirmative action programmes. It was the adoption of more aggressive strategies in regard to long-standing powers, rather than the acquisition of new powers, that characterized the changing outlook of the MCAD.

Jowell argues that it was necessary to allow the agency to develop in the way it did; such flexibility and adaptability were essential for its survival. For Jowell, the crucial determinant of 'whether and to what extent discretion can be limited' is the particular nature of the administrative task being considered. Having decided on balance that the discretionary powers of welfare agencies should be fettered, he reaches the opposite conclusion in the case of anti-discrimination agencies. He believes that any attempt to impose uniformity would be counter-productive and regressive and concludes that it is best to allow the agency plenty of scope to develop and elaborate the intention of the legislation and to employ whatever tactics it considers appropriate. These may involve 'subtle threats and cajolement, and selective enforcement rather than the bludgeon blow of strict enforcement according to defined rights and firm obligations' (Jowell, 1975: 197).

On the one hand, Jowell recognizes that it is the abuses of the discretionary system which have prompted welfare rights groups to demand more precise rules and formal procedures. On the other hand, he assumes that those who administer civil rights laws do not require the same level of scrutiny as welfare officers. Presumably they can be trusted to use their discretionary powers to obtain maximum benefits for the victims of discrimination. He also assumes that the scope for action will increase as the laws become more acceptable with the passing of time; a rule-based system would then become rapidly outdated.

Unfortunately, the British civil rights agencies have not spent their first decade of existence expanding their wings in an increasingly favourable political environment and show no signs of being able to progress in a unilinear fashion through the didactic, tort and equal opportunity approaches.

Co-operation or confrontation?
The Equal Opportunities Commission has made no secret of its preference for co-operation and has consistently used its formal investigation powers only as a last resort. On the few occasions when the powers have been used, a finding of illegal discrimination is not automatically followed by a non-discrimination notice. For example, the Leeds Building Society had agreed to change its practices and

procedures as a result of the EOC's investigation, so the Commission decided it would be inappropriate to issue a non-discrimination notice.[3] In the case of the school, the investigators had found no conclusive evidence of discrimination. The EOC confined itself to recommending a tightening-up of the procedure for making appointments and promotions at the school and suggesting that the male teachers should desist from making derogatory remarks about their female colleagues.[4] In the case of the college, the Commission found that the promotion policy had resulted in unlawful discrimination against women in the business studies department. During the course of the investigation, the college authorities introduced a number of changes to the appointment and promotion procedures throughout the college so that, once again, a non-discrimination notice was considered unnecessary.[5]

The Commission would argue that such a strategy should be judged in terms of its end results and that a non-discrimination notice directed solely at the business studies department and imposed on a resentful and hostile authority would be less effective in improving the position of the women lecturers than the wider-ranging reforms achieved with a measure of agreement. Hence the Commission's enthusiasm for a joint exercise with Debenhams. A formal investigation had been planned originally, but when Debenhams suggested a joint review, the Commission acquiesced on the grounds that the 'spin-off for the credit industry' would be the same and achieved more rapidly (Press Notice, 19 June 1979). The same technique was employed to persuade a secondary school to allow girls and boys equal access to craft subjects and this time the Commission intended to 'monitor the situation' (Press Notice, 15 January 1980). By the time Barclays Bank offered to co-operate on a voluntary basis if the Commission would drop its proposed investigation into recruitment polices at the Bank, the EOC had developed a sophisticated understanding of what such a 'voluntary' agreement should entail.[6]

Some degree of co-operation is obviously desirable: the question is how far the Commissions should be prepared to compromise in order to secure such co-operation. Coote and Phillips (1979) give an account of how the CRE's investigation into Massey Ferguson almost became an informal exercise. Massey Ferguson argued that the CRE's action constituted a threat to Britain's export drive and that an important contract with Pakistan would be placed in jeopardy if there were any suggestion of racism within the company. The Head of the CRE and the director of its Equal Opportunities Division were both persuaded by these arguments, but the commissioners would have none of it and insisted that the formal investigation go ahead. Coote and Phillips are quite scathing about 'the CRE's determination to stay on cosy terms with the people it is investigating' and contrast this approach with the one adopted by investigators working for the Ombudsman, who are instructed to confine themselves to taking statements and collecting documents.[7] Coote and Phillips have no patience at all with a friendly, persuasive approach which in their view simply causes delays and blurs the lines of conflict.

In 1979, when Coote and Phillips offered this assessment of the CRE's work, no-one could have anticipated that the Commission would find itself on a legal collision course during which its enforcement powers would be progressively undermined by the courts. By 1984, the CRE was being advised that on occasion, it might be best to follow the example of the EOC after all, and instead of issuing a non-discrimination notice, 'rely simply on the publication of the report and its attendant publicity, which may well cause embarrassment to those named in it' (Applebey and Ellis, 1984: 254).

When the Prestige decision cut the legal ground from under the CRE's feet, a number of ongoing investigations could only be completed with the co-operation of the respondent. At first glance, an EOC-style joint exercise does appear to offer a number of advantages. There is no problem of access to records, paperwork and employees within the organization, so that results are produced more quickly, in a matter of months rather than years. Also, the recommendations can be broadly based, transcending the question of whether or not the previous mode of operation was unlawful. From the point of view of the organization itself, implementing the recommendations could prove to be a useful public relations exercise, in contrast to the possible commercial damage that could follow from a formal investigation and a non-discrimination notice.

Such a strategy does, however, suffer from an insuperable disadvantage. If during the course of a joint exercise, the EOC or CRE staff discover evidence of serious discrimination which the organization is unwilling to acknowledge or rectify, the quango is placed in an impossible position. On the one hand, it has the statutory duty to work towards the elimination of discrimination. On the other hand, it has restricted its own freedom of action; any attempt to use its enforcement powers at this stage would invite the accusation that it has proceeded unfairly. Publicity is the Commission's only remaining weapon, always assuming that during the course of the negotiations it has not also compromised its freedom to publish.

A vivid illustration of the 'avoidance tactics' available to a hostile employer is provided by Vera Sacks. She describes how an important institution responded to the EOC's overtures by indulging in a 'pincer' movement:

> On the one hand they agreed to co-operate with the Commission on new recruitment practices while on the other their legal advisers insisted on further clarification of the Commission's findings and threatened judicial review. Either the Commission continued the investigation or settled. It chose the latter course, although wisely only agreed to suspend the investigation pending monitoring. (Sacks, 1986: 584)

The EOC has chosen to keep its 'big guns' in reserve and to use them as little as possible. On the one occasion when it was faced with a court action, it retreated at the first sign of judicial anger. Now that the CRE's confrontational approach has given the game away, it is not so easy to convince employers who discriminate that a terrible fate awaits them if they refuse to co-operate. In the long run however, the EOC may well be grateful to the CRE for having the courage to put its powers to the test, so that any re-evaluation of the legislation can be based on experience rather than on speculation.

Other legal powers
In addition to the power to undertake formal investigations, the Commissions have a number of other law enforcement powers. They can bring proceedings in relation to discriminatory advertisements and in cases where someone has been instructed or induced to discriminate. They can also take action where an individual or organization already found to have discriminated, whether as a result of a tribunal or court hearing or a formal investigation, seems likely to break the law again. They may also initiate proceedings in cases of persistent or continuing discrimination, but only in the area of employment. In using any of these additional powers, the Commissions are responsible for assembling and presenting the evidence, leaving the final verdict to the tribunals or courts.

In relation to discriminatory advertisements, both Commissions have adopted a strategy of education and persuasion. The CRE has apparently kept advertisers in line without resorting to the law at all; the EOC brought one successful case against a company that advertised in a discriminatory fashion over a period of time; a case which gave greater legal weight to its *Guidance on Advertising Practice* (1977). The EOC believes that the advertising industry has settled down to a high level of compliance in this area, but the CRE has discovered an interesting new twist: it reports a jump in complaints concerning job advertisements from twenty-nine in 1984 to seventy-one in 1985. This is not a resurgence of overt discrimination against racial minorites, but an upsurge of interest in the positive action provisions and a genuine attempt to encourage job applications from disadvantaged groups. Many of the complaints were without foundation and originated from people who took objection to the positive action provisions; others arose because advertisers did overstep the legal mark and the CRE has consequently issued guidelines intended to reduce these difficulties.[8]

Concerning its powers with regard to 'instructions and pressure to discriminate', the CRE reports a steady stream of cases each year, mostly involving employment agencies or careers services, instructed by employers not to send them black applicants. Again, there was a significant increase in complaints in 1985, with forty-three reports made against employers, compared with fifteen the previous year. This increase is almost entirely due to a new policy initiative in the West Midlands, involving the Manpower Services Commission and the Careers Service. Many of the culprits were employers refusing to take black trainees on work placements under the Youth Training Scheme. The CRE recognizes that the cases it is able to resolve through tribunal proceedings or settlements are merely the tip of an iceberg. It is clear that discriminatory pressure is not being adequately identified and reported by agencies outside the West Midlands, 'either because they may be unaware of the law, or because they fear the loss of a work placement' (CRE, 1985 *Annual Report*, June 1986: 13).

The EOC's experience of the 'instructions to discriminate' provisions is similar, although the Commission has only recently instigated full legal proceedings under these provisions.[9] Reports from employment agencies receiving discriminatory instructions from employers are usually dealt with informally; if necessary, a signed undertaking is obtained from the employer. However, the Commission does point out that its ability to take legal action is hampered by an EAT ruling in a case under the Race Relations Act, which held that 'a course of prior dealing between the agency and the employer had to be established' (EOC, October 1986: 28).

The case to which the Commission refers is CRE v Imperial Society of Teachers of Dancing [1983] ICR 473. The EOC considers that this judgment 'represents a dilution of the principle of non-discriminatory recruitment' and asks that the legislation be amended to make it clear that 'no client using a recruitment agency may express gender preferences (unless these are permitted by virtue of the lawful exceptions)' (EOC, October 1986: 28–9).

Dealing with persistent discrimination using the law as it stands at present is also easier said than done. The provisions are complicated and time-consuming; the Commission must first seek a declaration from an industrial tribunal that discrimination has occurred. Only when the tribunal's finding has become final (when time limits for appeal have expired), is the Commission able to apply for a county court injunction to stop any further discrimination. The CRE in particular is unhappy with the provision and in its consultative draft on changing the law (July 1983) recommended that the relevant sections be repealed. Initially, the EOC seemed more enthusiastic and announced its intention of following up successful tribunal applications, particularly those involving job segregation, in order to identify cases of persistent discrimination (EOC, *Second Annual Report*, April 1978: 19–20).

Not until 1983 did the Commission hit on a suitable subject and curiously, it arose from a tribunal case involving an organization which the Commission was already investigating: the print union SOGAT. There can be no doubt that the case involved discrimination of a most blatant and persistent kind. When Ms Turnbull, a cleaner and a member of SOGAT, applied for promotion to a more highly-paid job, the male members of her union dissolved the chapel and established a new one. They excluded women cleaners from the new chapel and so prevented Ms Turnbull from proceeding with her application for promotion. The EOC assisted Ms Turnbull in her proceedings and also used its persistent discrimination powers against SOGAT on behalf of other women (EOC Press Release, 25 November 1983). The EOC seemed well pleased with its excursion into unknown legal territory but has not as yet repeated the experiment.

Both Commissions have played an important role in assisting individuals wishing to file discrimination complaints. The Commissions have a wide discretion in this area; they can offer a range of assistance, from giving advice to providing legal representation, and they can offer it in a variety of circumstances. They can intervene if the case raises a question of principle, or if it would be unreasonable to expect the applicant to deal with the case unaided, or 'by reason of any other special consideration' (Sex Discrimination Act 1975 s 75, Race Relations Act 1976 s 66: see Appendix 4). Once again, the higher level of activity has come from the CRE, which has managed to provide some kind of assistance for roughly 80 percent of those requesting help, despite the steadily rising tide of requests, currently running at some 1,200 annually. Recognizing that in the absence of legal aid, the majority of tribunal applicants have nowhere to turn except to the Commission, the CRE attempts to offer some kind of support to all those with a justifiable grievance, despite an appallingly low success rate. As a consequence of this high profile, in 1983 the CRE was able to claim that of the 106 successful tribunal cases heard since the Act came into force, it had provided support in 76 cases.

The EOC receives fewer formal requests for assistance each year than the CRE. Initially, this was because it did not treat every enquiry as a potential request for assistance and was much more

selective than the CRE in inviting people to make a formal application. Those who did so were more likely to be turned away, as the
EOC decided from the beginning to give priority to 'the second
stage'; in other words, to cases which were the subject of an appeal
before the Employment Appeal Tribunal and beyond (see EOC,
First Annual Report, May 1977: 21). The EOC's involvement in such
cases has proved invaluable. It has broadened the concept of equal
pay by insisting that the Equal Pay Act be read in the context of
Community Law and has consequently scored a number of successes
in the European Court; it has also played a leading role in the
development of case law on both direct and indirect discrimination.
However, the process of shopping around for the perfect case, and
then dropping it if difficulties arise, is an unnecessarily ruthless and
restrictive interpretation of the Commission's role. The evidence
presented in Chapter 4 demonstrated that for the majority of applicants, the offer of support at the appeal stage comes far too late,
when considerable damage has already been sustained. Fortunately,
there are signs of a shift in emphasis at the Commission. As doors
have closed in other areas of law enforcement, the EOC has taken
steps to encourage more applications for assistance and has begun to
provide a greater degree of support at the early stages. The number
of requests, which had hovered between 150 and 250 for a number of
years, rose in 1985 to reach the 500 mark and the EOC offered its
services in three-quarters of these cases, mostly at the tribunal stage
(EOC, *Tenth Annual Report*, 1986: 50).

Promotional work
Both the EOC and the CRE devote a large percentage of their
resources to promotional work and have tended to see this as an
addition rather than an adjunct to their law enforcement role. In
other words, they use techniques of education and persuasion to
heighten awareness of discrimination and to encourage the spread of
non-discriminatory practices, without reference to their legal powers. There would seem to be some statutory justification for this, as
the duties of the two Commissions are much more broadly defined
than their powers (see SDA s 53(1) and RRA s 43(1), reproduced in
Appendix 4), but the Home Affairs Committee was not at all pleased
with the way in which the CRE went about its promotional role. The
Committee condemned the Commission for allowing its priorities to
be determined by outside pressures and attempting to do far more
than 'a small statutory body' could hope to accomplish. The Committee believed that promotional work should be used to publicise the
results of law enforcement, thereby creating a 'ripple effect'. Without such a link, the CRE's 'promotional arm has no ammunition and

is reduced to firing paper bullets at random' (Home Affairs Committee, 1981: paras. 11–15). As the results of the Commission's formal investigations became available, the relationship between enforcement work and promotional work did tighten up considerably. The report into the allocation of council housing in the London Borough of Hackey provided the basis for a promotional drive into housing allocation in other local authority areas.[10] Then an enquiry into the recruitment policies of Kirklees local authority precipitated a series of visits to authorities in other multi-racial areas. Similarly, an investigation into St Chad's Hospital in West Birmingham prompted a review of employment practices throughout the National Health Service.[11]

Clearly, the Commissions should be encouraged to obtain maximum possible advantage from any successes in the law enforcement field. However, the Home Affairs Committe did adopt a particularly restrictive view of the Commission's role. It also insisted that, as a law enforcement body, the Commission should remain scrupulously impartial and avoid making 'partisan interventions in political debate' (ibid, paras 18–19). By way of illustration, the Committee referred to the CRE's support for the Inner London Education Authority when it was threatened with abolition and also its outspoken attack on the Nationality Bill.[12] In the same vein, the Committee objected to the Commission's attempts to pose as a representative organ for ethnic minority groups and believed that it should relinquish its ties with local communities and devolve such responsibilities elsewhere. It insisted that 'the task of promoting good race relations lies mainly with the government and local government' (para. 11), but did not indicate how the Commission could be expected to operate effectively when government had abdicated its responsibility.

The difficulty with the Committee's image of an impartial body, standing aloof from grass roots activities and political controversy, is that the two Commissions were set up in order to further a particular cause: the abolition of discrimination and the promotion of equal opportunity. This is not a marginal activity, but strikes at the heart of social organization within both the public and private sectors. It is not possible to tackle the problem of institutionalized discrimination without becoming involved in political debate and taking up positions on a wide range of issues. Both Commissions are well aware of the dilemma that this situation poses, although they have responded to it rather differently.

Although the EOC has disassociated itself from the women's movement and shown little interest in developing community links, it has not hesitated to take a stand on a range of policy issues affecting women. Nor has it allowed itself to be gagged merely because such issues were excluded from the scope of the Sex Discrimination Act. During its first decade of existence, the EOC has accumulated an impressive stock of research evidence on a range of issues of crucial importance in the battle for sex equality. It has issued guidelines on areas such as child-care provision, sex bias in education, job segregation, job evaluation schemes and positive action. By casting its net widely, the Commission has demonstrated the fallacy of attempting to draw a line between the public and the private spheres in the way that the white paper *Equality for Women* had attempted to do. The white paper had insisted that 'The government does not and should not seek to intervene in the private relationships of citizens' (HMSO, 1974). In practice, however, the two spheres are inextricably linked and the effects of government measures impinge equally on both.

The Commission has been prepared to challenge government policy on specific issues such as nationality, maternity provision, parental leave, taxation, unemployment benefit, social security and pension provision. It has also reprimanded the government on a number of occasions for its general lack of commitment to sex equality. In its second annual report, the Commission reminded the government of its special responsibility to provide a lead. It registered its 'sense of disappointment at the apparently low priority given to this issue by the departments of a government responsible for introducing the Sex Discrimination Act in the first place' (EOC, *Second Annual Report*, April 1978: 1).

The following year, the Commission criticized the government for introducing new discriminatory legislation after passing the Sex Discrimination Act and pointed out that unless it had the 'active co-operation' of government and both sides of industry, the Commission's achievements would be limited (EOC, *Third Annual Report*, May 1979: 4). As it became clear that such co-operation was not forthcoming, an atmosphere of despondency set in, so that after five years of existence, the Commission was moved to remark:

> It can fairly be said that in the entire post-war era, there has not been a five-year period more unhelpful and less propitious in which to embark on the task of promoting equal opportunities for women. (EOC, *Fifth Annual Report*, June 1981: 1)

At the beginning of 1981, the EOC proposed a number of amendments to the Equal Pay and Sex Discrimination Acts but the government made no effort to implement them. Had it done so, the Commission would not have had to witness the sorry spectacle of the British government being taken to the European Court of Justice on two separate occasions.[13] Since Lady Platt took over as Head of the Commission in 1983, the annual reports have been somewhat blander in tone, although murmurings of discontent still surface occasionally, on such issues as the compexity of the equal value regulations, the government's negative attitude towards Community law and inadequate funding for the Commission's work. The EOC also reacted strongly to the government white paper *Building Businesses ... Not Barriers* (1986), objecting specifically to the proposed reduction in maternity rights (Press Release, 16 July 1986) and the proposal to charge tribunal applicants a £25 fee (Press Release, 7 November 1986). The Commission has also made strenuous efforts to persuade the government to withdraw its opposition to the EEC draft Directive on Parental Leave. It has enumerated the advantages to both employers and families to be derived from parental leave and has produced costings to show that it would not be an expensive exercise (Press Release, 25 March 1985 and 22 May 1986).

The CRE has also adopted a broad view of its role and become involved in a range of issues of vital importance to black people. Specific projects or campaigns have often developed into broader policy commitments. For example, participation in the campaign for the repeal of 'sus' law gradually evolved into a concern to monitor racism throughout the criminal justice system.[14] Two research projects into the employment prospects of Asian and West Indian school-leavers provided the foundation for a broader concern with the problems of black youth, which intensified as the inner city areas were starved of funds and unemployment rates rose.

Like the EOC, the CRE did not hesitate to lay the blame at the door of government. In the very first annual report the government was reminded of its 'unredeemed commitment', made in the 1975 white paper, *Racial Discrimination*, to develop a major strategy for combating racial disadvantage. It was also chastised for the 'frenzied atmosphere in which the debate on immigration has been conducted' and reprimanded for its use of section 41 of the Race Relations Act to exempt discriminatory government activities from scrutiny (see CRE, *First Annual Report*, July 1978: 34–5, and below, Ch. 8). Two years later, the Commission reminded the government that 'expressions of good intent are not sufficient' and called for the reform of the Nationality law and the Public Order Act. It urged the government to become an equal opportunity employer and also to increase its financial support for race relations work (CRE, *Annual Report*, June 1980). One year later, the CRE complained that the Civil Service still had no effective equal opportunity policy and that the government had taken no action to monitor compliance with the equal opportunities clause in government contracts. 'Home Office ministers have made excellent speeches about the government's commitment to good race relations, but these words have not been matched by government action' (CRE, *Annual Report*, July 1981: 2). In subsequent reports the CRE continued to demand a much greater commitment from central government on issues such as education and contract compliance; also from local government, where the abolition of the GLC and the six Metropolitan County Councils had left a policy vacuum. The Commission insisted that it was doing its best but that 'the scale of what is required is beyond the resources of a single agency' (CRE, *Annual Report*, June 1986: 1).

Immobilizing the quango
This curious spectacle of the two Commissions firing 'paper bullets' at the government year after year and obtaining no positive response merely serves to demonstrate what a curious creature is the quango. Its 'quasi-autonomy' becomes a double-edged weapon in the hands of an unsympathetic government: because it is independent, it can be ignored; because it is not independent, it can be subdued through government control of funds and appointments. The use of this weapon has had a particularly stultifying effect on the work of the EOC, where the commissioners have never succeeded in pulling together to formulate decisive policies. For the CRE, the problem has been less acute, partly because the Home Office did appoint some commissioners with a track record in the field of race relations, whereas in the case of the EOC, it was considered sufficient to appoint a number of women, regardless of background. Even so, CRE appointments have not been entirely free of controversy. The Home Affairs Committee received a number of complaints about the way in which five of the commissioners had been replaced in 1980. It was, however, unable to decide whether or not the failure to reappoint certain commissioners was a consequence of their more radical and aggressive approach to the work of the Commission (Home Affairs Committee, 1981: para. 22).

A second important difference between the two Commissions is that the TUC and CBI each has two nominees on the CRE in contrast to the three that they demanded, with Department of Employment backing, on the EOC (see Ch. 4, note 1). Instead of using their position as commissioners to educate their respective organizations on the merits of equal opportunity, they have used their position as TUC and CBI representatives to ensure that the Commissions' work does not threaten the industrial status quo. Meehan tells us that despite the obsession with confidentiality which has led to the sacking of EOC staff, the TUC and CBI representatives routinely refer Commission discussion documents to their 'parent' organizations. An early intervention by the TUC prevented the Commission from embarking on a survey of trade unions, because trade unionists were 'reluctant to let the EOC into territory traditionally occupied by the TUC'.[15] When one of the TUC commissioners, Ethel Chipchase, stepped out of line and signed the EOC's protective legislation report, although the other TUC commissioners had refused to do so, she was removed from the EOC and also lost her job as TUC Women's Officer (Meehan, 1985: 143).

Similarly, the CBI commissioners were able to ensure that the EOC was not allowed to rush headlong into using the provision which allowed it to issue codes of practice on employment, following consultations with appropriate organizations (see Ch. 3, p. 55). When the EOC decided to issue guidelines as the first step in this process, rather than to publish a draft code, one of the CBI commissioners wrote to his CBI colleagues: 'I am glad to be able to tell you that this is to a great extent due to CBI influence on the EOC' (Mackie, *The Guardian*, 11 July 1977, quoted in Meehan, 1985: 143). The EOC subsequently issued two consultative draft codes, in 1981 and again in 1982. The consultation process took so long that the final codes of practice were not approved by Parliament until April 1985. By then, the CRE codes had been operative for fifteen months and had already been used in a number of tribunal cases and settlements (CRE, *Annual Report*, June 1986: 14).

The issue of protective legislation is one of the few areas of EOC policy on which the TUC and CBI commissioners have not been in agreement. Determined to ensure that the Commission does nothing to rock the boat in the field of industrial relations, this group of six regards decision making in areas relating to manufacturing industry as its exclusive prerogative. They have combined on a number of occasions to block initiatives from the staff and other commissioners. During an interview, one commissioner related a classic example of this occurring, when the Commission was asked to consider a proposal to undertake a formal investigation into a small manufacturing firm in the North-West of England. The activities of this particular company had initially come to the attention of the Commission as a result of the discriminatory way in which the firm advertised job vacancies. The Commission decided that further information was needed before a decision could be reached. For reasons of geographical convenience, the two commissioners chosen for this exploratory work did not include any of the TUC or CBI representatives. At a subsequent meeting, the two commissioners reported back with a strong recommendation that the investigation should go ahead. Although the company was small, it provided an excellent example of job segregation based on sex and the findings would have had far-reaching implications for similar firms. Even so, the proposal was thrown out, following the united opposition of the TUC and CBI representatives, some of whom had discussed the matter during their customary joint perusal of the agenda on the train journey from London. One of the CBI representatives was the Engineering Employers' Federation nominee; in its dealings with the Commission, the firm was represented by the Federation.

It is theoretically possible for the 'independent' commissioners on the EOC to combine forces against the TUC/CBI contingent, but this rarely happens. There are several reasons for this: the other commissioners are not answerable to a constituency in the same sense that the six 'industrial' commissioners are; this latter group, nominated by their organizations to ensure that EOC policy takes on an acceptable shape, is expected to spend time and energy on Commission business, such as drafting suitable wording for policy documents. The other part-time commissioners, by contrast, must make time outside other commitments in order to carry out their duties. As Home Office appointees, they will only serve for a limited period of time, whereas TUC and CBI nominees can continue as commissioners indefinitely. Over the years, they are able to accumulate a level of knowledge and expertise with which new appointees cannot hope to compete.

There is no particular reason why the remaining commissioners should share a unified outlook, which would enable them to combine forces against the industrial block. On the contrary, the commissioners reflect such a wide range of viewpoints that it is impossible for them to act in unison. As a former member of the EOC's senior staff astutely observed: 'The political mix which exists means that consensus is the order of the day and a consensus between such diverse interests does not produce courageous or dynamic action' (Jackson, 1984: 193). One Home Office appointee made such strong 'anti-feminist waves' (to quote a phrase coined by a fellow commissioner), that it was difficult to understand the rationale for her appointment at all. It is as though the late Ronald Bell were to have been appointed to the CRE.[16]

When his term of office came to an end, one part-time commissioner gave vent to his dissatisfaction with the way in which appointments were made:

> Most commissioners have been minor figures with dubious credentials for the job. It has been a huge mistake, and it was clearly a deliberate decision, not to include in the membership of the Commission some credible leaders of the women's movement(s) who had some depth of knowledge and understanding of the issues. . . . The effect of the weakness of the appointments to the Commission has been the worse because the Commissioners (other than the nominees of the CBI and TUC) have been given no guidance and have not been held accountable to anyone,

formally or informally. This has enabled the CBI and TUC to exercise disproportionate influence which has generally been cautious, defensive and at times destructive.[17]

Appointments to quangos are generally made from the government list of 'the great and the good': prominent people are thereby rewarded for their contributions to political parties and to different areas of public life. The same ex-commissioner insists that: 'Appointments from the list of the great and the good are indefensible if the appointments are not great and good for the purpose'. He stresses the need to recognize that specific jobs require people with specific interests, expertise and commitment and suggests that ministers nominating members to quangos should be required to set out the qualifications and reasons for appointing those nominated. He also suggests that:

> The dead hand of the CBI and TUC should be relaxed by either reducing their representation or by increasing the other members or by persuading the CBI and TUC to nominate people with more commitment to making the Commission work even at the cost of occasionally embarrassing employers and unions.

Inevitably, the situation that has just been described has had a direct effect on members of staff, particularly as the EOC commissioners have been less willing than the CRE commissioners to permit staff involvement in the decision-making processes. On a number of occasions, the EOC commissioners have suffered embarrassment at the hands of their more committed and dynamic members of staff (see above, Ch. 6). In response to this situation they have tended to replace staff who leave with people who appear to be less militant. As one commissioner put it: 'There are too many people who are committed to the women's cause, so they can't think straight' (quoted in Coote, 1978: 735). The minority view has been expressed most forcefully by one ex-commissioner, who has witnessed the steady decline in the proportion of women among the senior staff of the Commission. He believes that the Commission's recruitment and promotion policies constitute unlawful indirect discrimination against women: the Commission will not appoint women committed to the cause of female equality and women are generally more committed than men.

In 1985, when the chief executive of the Commission retired, members of staff were not at all surprised when a man was appointed to replace her. Two well-qualified women, who were not even short-listed for the post, filed tribunal applications accusing the Commission of sex discrimination. One of them was a university professor who was herself a commissioner; she lost her case. The other, a senior member of staff at the Commission, withdrew her case after the tribunal pre-hearing.

For the staff at the CRE, the major cause for concern is the way in which the Home Office intervenes in senior staff appointments. In its submission to the Home Affairs sub-committee, the CRE staff side expressed the fear that Home Office 'advice' would prevent the appointment of anyone who might pressurize the Commission 'to assume a more radical, forward-looking stance' (Home Affairs Committee, 1981: Vol. II, 171). The Committee disagreed with this line of analysis, on the grounds that it was based on a 'fundamental misunderstanding of the purposes of management' and merely confirmed its view that the Home Office was right to insist on consultation over the appointment of senior staff.

The Committee then launched its own attack on the CRE staff, based on evidence it had received concerning administrative inefficiency and lack of professional competence. The Committee noted that 51 percent of the staff throughout the executive grades were of African, Asian or Caribbean origin. While it is careful not to make a causal connection between these two pieces of information, the report does remind the Commission that it is a professional body and that any system of ethnic quotas would be 'self-destructive and unlawful'. It suggests that an interchange of staff between the Commission and the Civil Service would prove valuable; it would strengthen rather than dilute the Commission by providing it with some administrative expertise.

Yet again, the Committee refused to recognize the significance of the CRE staff submission, or to acknowledge the extent to which the quango is at the mercy of government. Byrne and Lovenduski (1978) have pointed out that attempts to alter parts of the social structure using people who are firmly embedded in that structure will result in immobilism. Institutions cannot be changed without damaging vested interests; in order to be effective, the quango would have to disassociate itself from these interests. While the government remains apathetic or hostile towards the aims of a particular quango, it is unlikely to tolerate the appointment of radical and imaginative people in the key positions. The only room for manoeuvre lies in those appointments over which the government has no direct control, such as the CBI and TUC nominees. Ironically, as the EOC experience demonstrates, this is precisely the group that can prove most obstructive to change. It is of course always possible that the tables could be turned in the future. On the one hand, Home Office appointees are becoming increasingly conservative; one former commissioner believes that the second EOC Chairperson 'was appointed for her conservative views and the fact that she was anti-feminist' (see

Applebey and Ellis, 1984: 271). On the other hand, anti-sexist and anti-racist policies within the trade union movement may develop to the point at which such negative attitudes towards equality legislation become unacceptable.[18]

Accountability

Since their creation some ten years ago, there has been little official interest in the work of the two equality Commissions. The Home Office comment that the EOC has used its powers 'sensibly' and that neither Commission has 'caused too much trouble' speaks volumes (Applebey and Ellis, 1984: 272). The Labour Home Secretary Merlin Rees visited the EOC in 1977 and demanded more action (Ashdown-Sharp, 1977); since then the Commission has been almost totally ignored. At least the CRE has had some attention, which has forced it to take stock of its own procedures and policies. A number of changes were introduced following the scrutiny by the Home Affairs Committee and there is now a minister at the Home Office with special responsibility for racial affairs.

In the early years, both Commissions experienced some confusion over the respective roles of commissioners and senior management. At the CRE, there was a tendency for the commissioners to become involved in decisions which were better left to management and, paradoxically, to retreat from making decisions in areas which were clearly their prerogative (Home Affairs Committee, 1981: Vol. II, 192). The Committee concluded that the existence of two separate posts, one a full-time chairperson and the other a chief executive, constituted an obstacle to effective operation and recommended that these two posts be combined (Vol. I, para. 21). In 1983, this recommendation was adopted with the appointment of Peter Newsam as Executive Chairperson of the CRE and the abolition of the post of chief executive.

At the EOC, similar problems were allowed to remain unresolved. In her review of the work of the Commission at the end of its first decade of existence, Vera Sacks reported that the commissioners were still providing no effective leadership. They appeared to be 'supervising very closely rather than delegating within an agreed policy framework ... they are neither determining strategy nor directing policy' (Sacks, 1986: 563–4). Lady Platt confined her activities to public relations and negotiations with the government, thereby leaving a leadership vacuum. If the Commission were to be made accountable to a select committee for its actions, or were to be taken under the wing of a sympathetic department of government, such a situation would not be permitted to continue. It is essential that this exclusion zone surrounding the EOC and its activities be stripped away in its entirety without delay. It is the height of irresponsibility for the government to create such an organization, entrust it with a mammoth task and then leave it to its own devices.

In the meantime, there is no reason at all why the Commissions should conduct their affairs in a veil of secrecy. Such a situation merely invites sloppy procedures and leaves them isolated and vulnerable when the chips are down. The humiliation suffered by the EOC at the hands of the Provincial Building Society provides a vivid illustration of the consequences of secrecy. If the EOC's decision-making procedures had been open to scrutiny, it might have conducted its preliminary enquiries in a more professional manner and not been open to such a hammering from the judge.

Decisions taken behind closed doors are regarded with suspicion, even if inspired by the best of motives. The Commissions' powers to assist individual complainants are very broad but there is a requirement to act rationally. This means that assistance cannot be given or withheld on an intuitive or idiosyncratic basis, so that there must be a checklist of criteria and priority areas against which each application is examined. Not only should this information be made public, but applicants whose requests are turned down are entitled to some feedback. Does a rejection mean that the case has no merits, or that the Commission is already involved in a similar case, or even that the applicant is expected to win without Commission support?

If support is offered and then abruptly withdrawn at a crucial stage without explanation, the distress will be even greater. When the mother of a twelve-year-old girl complained to the EOC that her daughter was not allowed to study woodwork and metalwork at school as an alternative to cooking and needlework, the Commission decided to support a test case in the county court. Before the case could be heard, the EOC changed its mind and withdrew its support, whereupon the mother applied for judicial review of this decision. Apparently, no explanation for this change of heart was offered to the parent, but in its *Fourth Annual Report* the Commission gives as its reasons the belief that the plaintiff no longer had any reasonable prospect of success and that 'there was a serious risk that the case would result in a narrowly restrictive interpretation . . . of the Act' (EOC, *Fourth Annual Report*, June 1980: 9). This assessment proved correct; the plaintiff lost her case against the school and dropped her case against the Commission. The judge expressed the view that cooking and needlework were generally more advantageous to girls than woodwork and metalwork and that the girl had been 'used as a weapon . . . in her mother's campaign for women's rights'.[19] The way in which the EOC attempted to swop horses in midstream was both unethical and counterproductive; it reinforced the image of the Commission as timid and indecisive without preventing the development of bad case law.

Like the EOC, the CRE gives no details of its deliberations to the people whose applications for assistance it rejects, but in other ways it has been much more receptive to enquiries from journalists and researchers. Even after the unsympathetic report from the Home Affairs Committee, it did not retreat into its shell, but attempted to respond positively to the more constructive criticisms. The EOC, by contrast, adopted an extremely defensive stance in response to early criticisms and has steadfastly refused to allow access to any materials or meetings regarded as confidential. When in 1983 two academic lawyers were not even granted the courtesy of an interview, matters came to a head. The researchers recorded their dissatisfaction with this situation and insisted:

> There can be no question of secrecy being required, as in the case of certain government departments, in the interests of national security, and the public have a genuine right to know how the Commission spends the taxpayers' money. (Applebey and Ellis, 1984: 236).

Following the publication of this article, the Commissioners reconsidered their position and when Vera Sacks was commissioned by the *Modern Law Review* to write an article on the EOC, the staff were instructed to co-operate fully. It is to be hoped that the critical comments in her report will not provoke an ostrich-like response. Ms Sacks makes a number of constructive suggestions which the Commission would do well to heed. For example, she shows how the EOC could make more effective use of its own research findings and casework in order to develop a coherent enforcement strategy (Sacks, 1986).

The government's own obsession with secrecy has done nothing to facilitate public scrutiny of the quangos and their activities. A Freedom of Information Act would do much to alleviate these difficulties. Even if the government continued to ignore the Commissions, at least the people affected by their decisions would no longer be kept in the dark. However, while the threat of judicial review continues to be the only way in which decisions can be challenged, it is likely that the Commissions will respond defensively and waste a great deal of time and resources in covering their tracks.

It should go without saying that the two Commissions must be able to demonstrate that their own employment practices are beyond reproach. They have no right to expect a positive response from other employers unless they are prepared to set an example. Both Commissions have been dogged by industrial relations problems in the past and both have been criticized for the way in which staff appointments are made. In its 1983 *Annual Report*, the CRE led the way by providing the kind of statistical breakdown of its own staff that is the prerequisite for an effective equal opportunities policy. Two years later, the EOC followed suit. Although both Commissions claim that their policies cover race, sex and disability, a perusal of their work-force statistics shows that there is plenty of scope for improvement. In 1985 the CRE had only one employee registered as disabled and the EOC had two. In the same year, 53 percent of the CRE's staff were of African, Asian or Afro-Caribbean origin and were well distributed throughout the different grades and departments. The EOC reports a grand total of six staff of non-European origin, representing 3 percent of the total workforce, only one of whom holds a senior position.

The distribution of women within both organizations tends to follow the traditional pattern of female employment, so that men are over-represented at the higher grades. This is more pronounced within the CRE, mainly because half its staff are female, in contrast to the EOC's figure of almost 80 percent. There are five posts above the grade of principal in both organizations; in 1985 men occupied four of these posts at the EOC and all five at the CRE. Forty-three of the fifty-five CRE posts at senior executive officer level and above were held by men, whereas the EOC divided its twenty-eight appointments at these grades equally between men and women.[20]

Perhaps it is time for the two Commissions to scrutinize each other's employment practices; or perhaps they should be amalgamated and instructed to build on the best practices of both (although see the arguments against amalgamation, presented in Ch. 8). Whatever organizational changes are made, it is imperative that those entrusted with the task of working towards eliminating discrimination are not ignored. Unless they receive constant encouragement, support and recognition for their endeavours, and are held publicly accountable for their actions, they cannot be expected to make much of an impact.

Notes

1. Mayhew (1968). The Commission began life in 1946 as the Massachusetts Fair Employment Commission and became the MCAD in 1950 when its jurisdiction was extended to include housing discrimination.

2. Jowell (1975). Despite its later publication date, this book covers three different administrative agencies, so that the fieldwork on the MCAD was conducted during 1966.

3. EOC (February 1985). *Formal Investigation Report: Leeds Building Society.* See also EOC, *Ninth Annual Report*, June 1985, HMSO: 10.

4. EOC (July 1983) *Formal Investigation Report: Sidney Stringer School and Community College.* It is interesting to remember that absence of documentary

evidence had also been the stumbling block in a previous investigation involving schools: see the discussion of the Tameside investigation in Chapter 6.

5. EOC (October 1984) *Formal Investigation Report: Ebbw Vale College of Further Education.*

6. See Chapter 3, p. 59. The legally binding agreement between the EOC and Barclays Bank is given in full in *Equal Opportunities Review*, No. 4, November/December 1985: 18.

7. Coote and Phillips, 1979: 52. However, even the Ombudsman's department does not spurn the idea of co-operation altogether. According to de Smith, the Parliamentary Commissioner 'has placed a very high priority on cultivating good relations with heads of departments, so as to obtain their co-operation in his investigations' (de Smith, 1974: 632).

8. CRE, June 1985. Some employers also use the 'genuine occupational qualification' (GOQ) exemption in the RRA to increase job opportunities for racial minorities (see RRA s 5). Local authorities who wish to appoint ethnic minority social workers make use of the exemption for employees who provide 'personal services promoting the welfare' of particular racial groups (s 5(2) (d)). The equivalent provision in the Sex Discrimination Act (s 7(2) (e)) has proved less controversial, although criticism has been levelled against other parts of section 7, seen as reflecting outmoded concepts of gender and undermining the principle of equal treatment (see Pannick, 1985: Ch. 9).

9. The first case occurred in February 1987, when the EOC successfully took British Car Auctions of Preston to the tribunal for refusing to employ men as drivers. The company preferred to recruit attractive women for this work and had instructed the jobcentre accordingly (EOC Press Release, 10 February 1987).

10. CRE (January 1984) *Hackney Housing Investigated.* The investigation found extensive direct discrimination in the allocation of housing to black families and issued a non-discrimination notice against Hackney. Ironically, it was a strategic investigation, not begun on the basis of any suspicion that unlawful acts were being committed. Despite its considerable value and widespread implications, it was, according to the Prestige decision, outside the Commissioner's powers (see CRE, July 1985: 21).

11. See CRE, *Annual Report*, June 1985: 14, 15 and 19. However, as we have seen, a number of local authorities and health authorities have been slow to respond to the CRE's efforts (see Ch. 3).

12. The Labour Party members of the Home Affairs sub-committee appear to have endorsed the general criticism but attempted (unsuccessfully) to have these particular examples deleted from the report (Home Affairs Committee, 1981: Vol. I, p. 1).

13. See the introductory remarks to the Sixth and Seventh *Annual Reports*. On the first occasion, the British Equal Pay Act was found not to meet the requirements of Community Law (see Introduction, note 8). In the second, the Sex Discrimination Act was similarly found wanting (see Ch. 1, note 8).

14. See CRE, *First Annual Report*: 33, and *Third Annual Report*: 7. In subsequent reports, the CRE has included a review of the work of the police, the courts and the prison service in relation to racial minorities. 'Sus' is a reference to the provisions of section 4 of the Vagrancy Act 1824, which empowered the police to arrest anyone suspected of loitering with intent to commit a criminal offence. 'Sus' was repealed in 1981, following a sustained campaign by a number of organizations and a growing body of evidence that it was being used to harass black people (Gordon, 1983: Ch. 2).

15. Meehan, 1985: 142, quoting from an article by Anna Coote in *The Guardian*, 17 December 1976.

16. Ronald Bell was one of a small group of MPs vociferously opposed to the sex and race discrimination legislation when it was debated in Parliament.

17. Eric Robinson served as a part-time commissioner on the EOC from 1976 until 1980. Although he was nominated by the Secretary of State for Education to represent the interests of education on the Commission, he was at no stage required to give an account of himself, either to the Department of Education or to the Home Office. The quotations are taken from a memo which he sent to Alf Dubs MP on completing his term of office (Mr Dubs was a member of the civil liberties group of backbench Labour MPs). The memo conveys a deep sense of disappointment, both with the Commission for its lack of achievements and with the Labour Party for its apparent indifference to this failure.

18. The appointment of Pat Turner from GMBATU as a TUC nominee in May 1985 was an important step in the right direction.

19. Whitfield v London Borough of Croydon (unreported). A crucial weakness in the case was that the school had subsequently allowed the daughter to 'opt in' to the boys' class as a special concession, but the mother and daughter turned it down as a gesture which failed to address the problem of 'less favourable treatment'. In addition to the information contained in the EOC's *Fourth Annual Report*, accounts of this case are to be found in Coote, 1978, and in Coote and Campbell, 1982: 121–2.

20. As there are so few men employed at the EOC, numerical equality at this level means that a higher proportion of the total male staff are employed in these exalted positions in comparison with the female staff (36 percent compared with 10 percent). A comparison between the two Commissions also suggests that the EOC has a strong case for asking the Home Office to increase the number of senior appointments it can make. In 1985, the authorized staffing complement of the CRE was 226 posts and that of the EOC 166.5 posts.

8 Achieving equality through legislation: a strategy for the future

The limits of legal reform

Since the beginning of the twentieth century there has been a steady growth in the range and intensity of government intervention in British society. A similar increase in legislative and administrative activity has occurred throughout western democratic societies, as each has responded to political pressures from less advantaged groups. The ideology of laissez-faire, which held that the forces of the market would accomplish the well-being of everyone without the need for governments to intervene, fell into disfavour. The welfare ideology which replaced it sought initially to guarantee an acceptable minimum standard of living for all members of society, and subsequently to remove some of the obstacles which obstructed the routes to equal opportunity for certain groups. Anti-discrimination legislation marks the high point in the development of welfarism: ideologically, it offers the ultimate test of commitment to the principle of equality; historically, it may prove to be a watershed, as the social democratic consensus, always fragile, begins to collapse and the philosophy of laissez-faire stages a comeback.

The British anti-discrimination laws of the mid–1970s were heralded by their sponsors as a great leap forward. They epitomized the values of social democracy by insisting that all citizens, regardless of sex or race, should be able to participate in the benefits and opportunities created by welfare capitalism. Yet even as the new laws reached the statute book, the fragile political consensus, and the mood of optimism which had accompanied it, was beginning to evaporate. Caught between the two imperatives of political legitimation and economic accumulation (Habermas, 1976), politicians were becoming increasingly preoccupied with the latter. As the economy moved into recession, the principles of equality and participation sank to the bottom of the political agenda. Those involved in implementing the new provisions unexpectedly found themselves swimming against the tide, so that their efforts were not rewarded, but frequently dismissed as irrelevant and even utopian. With the replacement of a Labour government by a Conservative government in May 1979, these hostile forces grew in strength and number. The tension between the ideology of equality that had inspired the civil rights legislation and the renewed insistence on a return to 'free market forces' and individual initiative became increasingly evident.

Socialist analyses of these developments have veered between two extremes. On the one hand, the welfare state has been welcomed as a major victory for the working class in achieving a significant reallocation of resources. On the other, it has been dismissed as a capitalist plot which ensures the reproduction of the working class while 'buying off' political opposition. Each interpretation on its own is simplistic and ignores the contradictory nature of welfare capitalism. If working-class initiatives are necessarily co-opted and transformed in order to fit the requirements of the state, political activism is redundant. Such a conclusion is theoretically unsound, because it assumes the existence of an omnipotent and omniscient ruling class; it is politically absurd because it implies that socialists should redirect their energies to dismantling the welfare state. So, too, while legislative reforms which purport to give legal rights to employees may not be the panacea for the evils of industrial capitalism, they cannot be dismissed as a ruling class conspiracy to divide and weaken the workforce.

The tragic irony of the last decade is that social reformers have found themselves spending a great deal of energy fighting a rearguard action to prevent the dismantling of welfare provisions formerly regarded as 'functional' for capitalism and therefore secure from attack. Such a radical shift in the political ground has made it difficult to develop a critique of the welfare state without appearing to be either utopian or subversive. Without such a critique, however, politicians committed to the principles of welfare will merely replicate past errors. They should not be surprised to find that people who have experienced the welfare system as humiliating, alienating and discriminatory are less than enthusiastic in their support.

The history of welfare legislation demonstrates that it is not enough to campaign on the basis of broad principles of social policy. Rather, it is essential to learn from past disappointments and plan the mechanisms for implementing new policies with some care. This is equally the case whether the reforms are being wrenched from a hostile government that will implement them with 'hesitation', 'repugnance' and 'bad faith',[1] or whether the legislators are genuinely inspired by an egalitarian zeal.

The rapid growth of government departments and administrative agencies that accompanied the creation of the welfare state brought in its wake a number of problems not anticipated by its founders. It is becoming increasingly evident that there are no easy answers. Administrative structures do not necessarily operate in the best interests of the people they are created to serve. Nor can the courts be relied on to safeguard these interests. They may sometimes intervene to 'protect' individuals from abuses of state power, but they do so on the basis of an individualistic ideology which contradicts and undermines the aims of much social legislation.

This clash of ideologies is particularly acute in relation to civil rights laws. If administrators do not use their powers effectively or are slapped down by the courts for being too effective, a rights-based system seems to offer an attractive alternative. Yet the notion of tackling institutionalized discrimination by giving legal rights to individuals does not sound promising, nor is it any less dependent on a sympathetic judiciary to make it effective than the administrative route.

Judicial reform

At first glance, the division of power between democratically elected members of a government and those who preside over the judicial system seems straightforward enough: parliament makes the legislation and the courts interpret it. However, an examination of the development of case law in almost any area of social legislation demonstrates that such a statement of the relationship between the political and the legal systems is misleading in its simplicity. Judges often see themselves as preserving the principles of freedom, justice and the rule of law against encroachment, even by elected representatives implementing policies which they consider to be in the public interest and for which there is widespread support. Such members of the judiciary have sought to curtail the excesses of interventionist governments by reference to constitutional freedoms and common law precedents. They insist that without such boldness, abuses of power by the executive would multiply unchecked (Denning, 1980). Others are critical of the judges, and consider that the judicial view of the 'public interest' is equally partial. Thus Griffith believes that the judicial system, far from protecting the governed from the excesses of government, functions to uphold 'conventions, established and settled interests' (Griffith, 1977: 213).

Our examination of the civil rights case law during the last ten years has provided ample evidence to support the views expressed by Griffith. Many of the legislative amendments proposed by the Commissions would not be required if the judiciary had responded more sympathetically to the aims of the legislation, or had followed the lead set by the small number of more 'enlightened' judges.[2] Nor would the Commissions have to expend so much time and energy devising strategies for using their formal investigative powers had the judges not created such a legal minefield for them.

Although certain members of the judiciary have fallen over themselves to protect employers from the 'draconian' powers of the two Commissions, only rarely has the same protection been extended to tribunal applicants, who are necessarily challenging employers from a position of relative weakness. If the courts had been concerned to correct this imbalance, they would not have made such heavy weather of the burden of proof issue. In formal terms, as we have seen, the burden of proof in direct discrimination cases rests with the applicant. In practice, as a small number of judges have recognized, at some stage in the presentation of a case, the burden has to shift to the employer, otherwise it can never be discharged.

This was the position adopted by Mr Justice Browne-Wilkinson in the case of Khanna v the Ministry of Defence (see Ch. 5) and also by the Northern Ireland Court of Appeal, which reasoned that: 'If discrimination could not be inferred from the circumstances, the object of the legislation would be largely defeated'. In the particular case which inspired these comments, the Court of Appeal considered that as the successful candidate for an appointment was a man and the unsuccessful but better qualified candidate was a woman, they had prima facie evidence of discrimination on grounds of sex, so that the burden of proof shifted to the employer (Wallace v South Eastern Education and Library Board [1980] IRLR 193). Unfortunately, very few tribunals and courts have adopted this common-sense approach and best practices have not become generalized through the development of case law. An amendment is therefore needed to make it quite clear that once less favourable treatment has been established, the person responsible for that treatment will be called to account (see CRE, July 1985: 13–14; EOC, October 1986: 35).

It is difficult to know how much can be achieved by tinkering with the wording of the legislation in this way. If the tribunals and courts remain out of step with the fundamental aims of the equality laws, new loopholes and escape routes will open up as fast as the old ones are closed. At the end of the day, the understanding and attitudes of the people who adjudicate is more important than devising a new form of words.

In recognition of this problem, the Commissions have suggested ways in which the quality of decisions made in discrimination cases might be improved. Their central target, however, is not the appeal courts where case law is developed, but the industrial tribunals and county courts who hear the cases in the first instance. The CRE refers to the tendency of tribunal members to regard complainants as:

trouble-makers, as over-sensitive, or mistaken when the truth is that they
have been treated less favourably on account of their race. (CRE, July
1985: 15)

In a similar vein, the EOC identifies an unwillingness on the part of
the tribunals and courts 'to recognize a single act of discrimination as
an issue of significance' (EOC, October 1986: 31) and comments on
the research of Leonard (discussed in Ch. 4), which exposed serious
deficiencies in the way in which tribunals handled discrimination
cases.

Both Commissions believe that the solution lies in a greater degree
of specialization and training for the people who adjudicate in discrimination cases; the CRE goes so far as to advocate a separate
'discrimination division' within the tribunal system, to hear race and
sex discrimination cases. The problem of how to improve the level of
expertise in the county courts requires a different approach, given the
small number of cases.[3] The EOC and the CRE would resolve this
problem by abolishing the present split between cases of employment
discrimination, which are heard by industrial tribunals, and cases of
discrimination in other areas, currently dealt with by the county
courts. The Commissions would like to see county court jurisdiction
transferred to the industrial tribunal system, where adjudicators
would be trained to handle all complaints of discrimination, whether
related to employment or not.

The Commissions have indicated the path down which we must
travel in order to improve the quality of decisions in discrimination
cases. There is, however, much further to travel than they have
suggested. The flaws in the present system are by no means confined
to the lower courts and tribunals, and yet the Commissions have
adopted a more restrained approach towards senior members of the
judiciary. Perhaps the boldest comment comes from the Northern
Ireland EOC, when it refers to 'the immense significance of the
shifting sands of judicial interpretation in the area of discrimination
law' (EOC, NI, March 1983: 6). Other practitioners have expressed
their criticisms of the judiciary even more forcibly; Bindman (1985),
for example, does not mince his words:

> A number of very senior judges have displayed both ignorance and racial
> hostility. Judges who are unable to control their prejudices should not be
> allowed to sit in race cases. (Bindman, 1985: 1138)

The CRE's proposals for a specialist division to hear discrimination cases offers no more than a partial solution to the problem. In the
longer term, what is required is a fundamental overhaul of the
methods by which all adjudicators, from tribunal members through
to the most senior judges, are selected and trained. Only then will it
be possible to:

develop a younger, more professional judiciary, with the qualities which people expect from their judges: openmindedness, humanity, fairness and the necessary expertise. (Gifford, 1986: 33)

It will require nothing less than a vigorously enforced and carefully monitored programme of positive action throughout the legal profession before the monopoly of elderly, white men from privileged backgrounds can be broken and confidence in the integrity and representativeness of the judicial system be assured.

Administrative reform

If the relationship between the parliamentary system and the judicial system is sometimes misunderstood, the role of the quango is even more obscure. It is a hybrid, an administrative body with some judicial characteristics. It is quasi-autonomous: a creature of government and yet retaining a degree of independence. In theory, these hybrid qualities could be a recipe for flexible and dynamic action; in practice, as we have seen, they can lead to near-paralysis. Under attack from all quarters, the quango is then unable to move decisively in any direction.

Since 1979, the murmur of voices from the political right, demanding a drastic reduction in the numbers and powers of these administrative bodies, has become a strident, persistent chorus. The quangos have been left largely undefended from such attacks, because those political groups that favour interventionist policies have their own reservations about this particular form of implementation. The people it is established to serve frequently experience the quango as a remote and alien body which appears to make arbitrary decisions that cannot easily be challenged.

Although the government can capitalize on the current hostility towards quangos when it wishes to curtail or terminate the activities of particular organizations, an attack on quangos in general is more difficult to sustain. The government may choose to reduce its involvement in a number of areas, but that is not the same as ceasing to manage the corporate economy altogether; the quango remains an extremely useful political tool. The 'great quango hunt' launched by the Conservative government in 1979 produced only a modest haul (Barker, 1982b: 225–31). In keeping with the philosophy of non-interventionism, a number of bodies were abolished or merged and others, stripped of their powers, were reduced to an advisory role. At the same time, the government discreetly created several new ones.[4] Significantly, the Commission for Racial Equality and the Equal Opportunities Commission have so far not appeared on the government's 'hit list'.

The cynical explanation as to why this should be so is that their existence conveniently symbolizes a commitment to equality without requiring any major shift in policy or resources (see Coote, 1978; Coote and Phillips, 1979). So long as the Commissions are relatively harmless and ineffectual, their abolition could prove to be an unnecessary embarrassment. In view of the disturbances that have occurred since 1981 in a number of inner city areas, in which unemployed black youth featured prominently, it might be seen as politically expedient to retain the body which is positively committed to improving race relations. A somewhat different set of pressures may be protecting the CRE's sister Commission at the present time; dismantling the EOC could well precipitate a further deterioration in the government's already fraught relationship with the European Economic Community. While the future of the Commissions is dependent on such contingent considerations, rather than on an unwavering commitment to the principle of equality, then they must be regarded as vulnerable.

It is interesting that both the women who have headed up the Equal Opportunities Commission have employed similar metaphors to describe their dilemma. In 1979, Betty Lockwood referred to her membership of the Commission as constantly walking:

> a tightrope between the demands of the long-standing campaigners for women's equality . . . and the majority of the population who are fearful . . . of busybodying. (EOC Press Notice, 8 February 1979)

Four years later, Lady Platt used even more graphic terminology:

> There are going to be the male chauvinists on one side, the militant feminists on the other and me on a high wire in the middle. (*Daily Telegraph*, 12 January 1983)

The tightrope imagery is particularly apposite, as the Commission has been accused of 'floating above' the problems of sex discrimination and inequality and failing to establish a political ground from which it could influence society as a whole (Barker, 1982a: 20). Vera Sacks believes with Blumrosen that:

> it is essential for administrators to involve participants from the beneficiary class in order to counteract pressures from the group to be regulated and tendencies towards a debilitating bland neutrality (Blumrosen, 1977, quoted in Sacks, 1986: 591)

She urges the EOC to 'go public' and 'lay siege to the political citadel' (Sacks, 1986: 592).

By comparison with the EOC, the Commission for Racial Equality has made greater efforts to forge links with the groups whose interests it was created to promote; and yet it was severely reprimanded by the Home Affairs Select Committee for so doing. It is difficult to see how the Commissions can perform their promotional role satisfactorily unless they do establish links with both the perpetrators and the victims of discrimination, yet it is precisely these links which are seen to compromise their judicial role.

Whatever they do, the Commissions will never be able to please all of the people all of the time. They are, however, in desperate need of friends and allies and would do well to heed the advice to 'go public', in the broader sense of 'making the administrative process accessible to those it affects and providing a window through which it can be seen' (Law Reform Commission of Canada, 1985). Such openness would help to disperse the cloud of hostility and suspicion which inevitably accompanies decision-making processes that are shrouded in secrecy. The decisions will be no less controversial, but if they are clearly derived from a known set of policies and priorities, they can no longer be dismissed as arbitrary, intuitive or incoherent. If the Commissions also establish and publicize internal rules of procedure, they will be able to reassure employers and judges that they are proceeding fairly; giving adequate (but not excessive) notice of their intentions, allowing access to information and the right to be heard.

To recommend such a course of action in the political climate of 1987 may seem like a recipe for suicide. Yet it is surely preferable to the alternative of burying one's head in the sand. A Commission that produces no results is doomed in any event. A Commission penalized merely for striving to fulfil its statutory duties at least retains its integrity. Incidentally, it also ensures that it is difficult for the government to conceal the real political purpose behind any interference with the Commission's work.

Judging on past performance, the EOC seems unlikely to adopt such an aggressive stance. The CRE, subjected to an intense political scrutiny by politicians and judges, has shown greater courage and tenacity. However, if the record of the EOC is an indictment of the system of patronage by which appointments to quangos are made, the record of the CRE does not cancel this indictment. Rather, it illustrates a point made by the Law Reform Commission of Canada (LRC):

> The many excellent appointees that currently occupy office do so in spite of the system, not because of it. The atmosphere does not stimulate achievement, nor does it invite regeneration. (LRC Canada, 1985: 77)

In Canada, as in Britain, appointments to administrative agencies are 'matters of political prerogative influenced significantly by partisan considerations'. The Law Reform Commission recognizes the need for a more open system of selection, in order to ensure a consistently high standard of performance and to restore public confidence in the system (LRC Canada, 1985: 77–8). The same considerations apply in Britain, where the problem has been identified as how to 'restrain the Executive from using the patronage system as a means of reward or appeasement for "baronial henchmen"' (Davies, 1982: 179). Not only is the system anachronistic, given that appointments to the Civil Service have been based on open competition for more than 100 years, it is also a system which consistently under-represents certain sections of the population. Davies points out that 'women, people under forty and those from outside the London and South East region' are conspicuous by their absence from the list of 'the great and the good' from which appointments are made (see Davies, 1982: 172); she might well have added manual workers and racial minorities to the list of under-represented groups.

It is time to throw away the list of 'the great and the good' and to invite applications from as wide a range of people as possible. Candidates submitted by such groups as the TUC and the CBI could then be considered on their merits, alongside other applicants. The expertise of the EOC and CRE staff could be used to establish non-discriminatory procedures for each stage of the selection process. Finally, the system of remuneration would need to be reviewed, to ensure that no suitably qualified person was excluded for financial reasons.[5]

Closing the gap between individual and collective solutions

Over the years, members of staff at the EOC and CRE have acquired an impressive body of expertise in identifying discriminatory practices and prescribing appropriate remedies. As we have seen, a great deal of this expertise is squandered through a combination of indecisive action and unhelpful judicial interventions. The reforms proposed so far would help to restore the credibility and authority of the two Commissions and make it possible to harness the energies of the staff more effectively. Implementing some of the legislative changes requested by the Commissions would help to accelerate this process.

The present law recognizes two forms of discrimination: first, isolated acts against individuals and second, systematic discrimination, which affects an entire class or group. Only the concept of indirect discrimination provides a bridge between the two. The major procedural device for challenging the first form is individual litigation, whereas the second is to be unmasked by means of the formal investigation. The Commissions have recommended that the gap between individual proceedings on the one hand and the full panoply of the formal investigation on the other be closed, by empowering them to bring proceedings against anyone suspected of unlawful discrimination. Not only would they be able to take action on behalf of individuals not wishing to bring their own proceedings, but they would also be able to present evidence of discrimination to a tribunal at any stage during a formal investigation (EOC, October 1986: 27–8). Remedies would also need to be co-ordinated, so that the Commissions and tribunals could deal with issues as they arose, whether they concerned individual compensation or broader questions of discriminatory employment practices. If an individual case revealed widespread discrimination, appropriate action could be taken. Alternatively, individual victims of discrimination, identified during the course of a wider investigation, could be compensated (CRE, July 1985: 24–5).

The Commissions are asking to play a much more active role in the collection and presentation of evidence necessary to identify discriminatory practices. As we have seen, the Commissions do provide legal representation for some tribunal applicants. They have also been permitted to appear as a type of *amicus curiae*, or friend of the court, in a small number of cases where they wished to bring wider issues to the attention of the judges.[6] The CRE proposes that this arrangement be placed on a more regular footing, enabling it to join in proceedings whenever people other than the complainants might be affected by the alleged discrimination (CRE, July 1985: 24–25). This would, in effect, be a way of smuggling a form of class action into British discrimination law. The CRE would identify the discriminated class and take legal action on its behalf. The tribunal could be empowered to award remedies on a group basis and, in partnership with the Commission, take steps to ensure that discriminatory practices cease.

Given the resources and expert knowledge of the Commissions, and assuming a well-trained and receptive judiciary, this form of class action could become an effective weapon in the battle against discrimination. It does, however, have two disadvantages. First, it is paternalistic; it would be for the Commissions to select the cases they wished to pursue, leaving other groups with no collective remedy. Second, its application would be restricted to cases of discrimination; it would not be available to consumer groups and others, where the arguments for some form of class action are equally compelling.

In the United States, the class action is by no means free of problems (see Ch. 2). In Britain, similar difficulties would arise. In addition, class litigation could prove to be an expensive and risky venture, as plaintiffs involved in an unsuccessful action would face lawyers' fees and a bill for costs. This does not occur in the United States, where different costs rules prevail and where the contingent fee system means that lawyers collect no fee in unsuccessful cases.

Evidently then, 'the American concept of the class action cannot simply be transplanted into English procedure' (Pannick, 1985: 297); far-reaching changes would be necessary, including the extension of legal aid to tribunal applicants.

In the short run, it would be useful to give the Commissions the powers they seek, so that the tribunals and judges become more receptive to the concept of systemic discrimination and more willing to prescribe appropriate remedies. In the long run, however, it would be most unwise to rule out the possibility of removing the obstacles which prevent the introduction of a more general form of class action in Britain. In a society in which people are becoming more aware of collective entitlements, a legal system which cannot recognize and respond to such entitlements is increasingly unacceptable (see Hepple, 1983: 85).

The importance of political will
The single most important change required to breathe new life into the sex and race equality laws is a massive change of heart on the part of the British government. If the current rhetoric of non-interventionism were to be replaced by a major act of commitment to seek out and destroy discriminatory practices, such a transformation would be worth 100 minor legislative amendments. Instead of allowing itself to be backed into a corner by the European Court and to be cast in the role of the villain in a succession of tribunal cases, the government would begin to take the lead in establishing exemplary employment practices. Encouraged by this example, industrial and commercial organizations would begin to treat the civil rights laws seriously, especially if the government made full use of its purchasing power to ensure the compliance of all employers holding government contracts. No longer marginalized and ostracized, the two Commissions could be brought in from the cold and given a major role in developing and monitoring equal opportunity programmes in both the public and private sectors. Organizational and structural changes would be required to ensure that the expression of commitment was genuinely reflected in employment patterns and policy formulation in all areas of government and that it could not easily be displaced by other considerations.

One way in which such a radical shift of policy could be implemented would be through the creation of a new government department exclusively concerned with the development and co-ordination of policies on equality. A recent policy document produced by the Labour Party provides a useful model, although it is confined to the issue of sex equality. The plan is to establish a Ministry for Women and to make it effective and responsive to the needs of women. The Minister is to be given a seat in the Cabinet, full ministerial support, a team of advisers and a committed staff. All government departments are to establish women's units and be required to produce equality reviews twice annually. The Equal Opportunities Commission is to retain its independence, be made more accountable to women and given additional powers and a strong regional structure. The new Ministry is also to establish regional units and explore new forms of consultation in order to 'reach women who cannot normally make known their views to government' (Labour Party, 1986: 14). In their efforts to ensure that the new Ministry does not become marginalized, the authors of the policy document have attempted to learn from similar experiments elsewhere. Unfortunately, the inescapable conclusion to be drawn from such experiments is that, in the absence of political will, little can be achieved.[7]

Although the Labour Party document refers to the dual oppression faced by ethnic minority women and expresses a commitment to anti-racist policies in general, it makes no comment on the relationship between the Equal Opportunities Commission and the Commission for Racial Equality, or the extent to which it might be possible to develop structures within government which would deal simultaneously with issues of sex and race discrimination. Among the various groups currently considering these issues, it seems that the Social Democratic Party is alone in favouring the idea of establishing a Human Rights Commission to replace the two existing bodies and to tackle discrimination in all its manifestations (Social Democratic Party, 1986). Those supporters of anti-discrimination policies who shy away from this idea fear that it would in practice lead to fewer resources and less decisive action; that amalgamation necessarily implies both a cost-cutting exercise and a process of dilution, during the course of which the more aggressive voices within the Commissions would be silenced.

Once again, the question of political will is crucial in resolving this dilemma. It would be perfectly possible to create a Human Rights Commission that was unimaginatively staffed, politically marginalized and starved of resources. With the wholehearted support of the government of the day, it would be equally possible to equip such a Commission with appropriate personnel, adequate powers and generous funding, so that it was able to make substantial progress in dismantling a wide range of discriminatory practices. Even so, there are strong arguments for keeping two separate bodies, in order to ensure that the different structures of disadvantage which underpin sexual and racial inequality are adequately identified and explored. At the same time, both Commissions would benefit from a much greater degree of co-operation and exchange of information in areas of mutual concern. The aim should be to obtain maximum advantage from any positive achievements and to generalize best practices wherever possible.

Removing exemptions and generalizing best practices
A government that was genuinely committed to the eradication of discrimination would be acutely embarrassed by the provisions in the present law which allow it to be treated more leniently than organizations within the private sector. For example, the House of Lords has decided, by a majority of three to two, that the expression 'provision of goods, facilities and services' in s 20 of the Race Relations Act and s 29 of the Sex Discrimination Act applies only to 'market-place activities' and so excludes a wide range of government activities. The judgment was given in a case involving a woman subjected to discriminatory treatment by an entry clearance officer applying immigration rules (R v Entry Clearance Officer ex parte Amin [1983] 2 All ER 864). As a result, the government is free to discriminate in such areas as immigration control, the prison system and policing. The CRE and the EOC have both asked that the laws be amended to reverse the effect of the House of Lords' decision (CRE, July 1985: 8; EOC, October 1986: 24).

If this particular exemption was a creative aberration on the part of the House of Lords, the same cannot be said of other exemptions, notably s 41 of the Race Relations Act and s 51 of the Sex Discrimination Act (see Appendix 4). These sections were quite explicitly designed to release government departments from the burden of scrutinizing a wide range of legislation for possible discrimination. Section 51 of the SDA offers a general exemption for all Acts passed before the SDA came into force and for statutory instruments made or approved under such Acts, including instruments made since 1975. The main purpose of this provision was evidently to exclude areas of law whose inclusion would have involved considerable financial outlay, such as taxation and social security. When introducing the legislation in 1975, Roy Jenkins had admitted that: 'although this is an important Bill, it is not a money-spending Bill' (Parliamentary Debates, House of Commons, Vol. 889, col. 516). Section 6(4) of the SDA, which excluded 'provisions in relation to death and retirement' from the scope of the Act, was also devised for financial reasons.

The impetus for reducing the number and scope of exemptions permitted under the SDA has come not from the British government, but from Europe. As a result of the EEC Social Security Directive, a number of changes have been made to Britain's social security legislation.[8] Similarly, the Sex Discrimination Act 1986 is a hodgepodge of measures required (with the exception of those parts which repeal the protective laws – see Ch. 1) to bring us into line with the Equal Treatment Directive. The government has adopted a 'minimalist' position, making the smallest number of changes necessary to comply with European law. As a result of the decision of the European Court of Justice in November 1983 (see Ch. 1, note 8), the exemption enjoyed by firms of five or fewer employees is removed and the exemption for private households is modified. Discriminatory collective agreements are declared illegal, but there is no machinery for enforcing this provision. Following Ms Marshall's victory at the European Court, compulsory retirement of men and women at different ages is to cease (Marshall v Southampton Area Health Authority [1986] IRLR 140). However, section 6(4) of the 1975 Act is modified rather than repealed, which means that women over sixty are not entitled to redundancy payments and discriminatory pension schemes are still permitted.

Although the EEC Commissioners have expressed some concern over the all-encompassing wording of s 51, this section has not as yet been denounced by the European Court. The government insists that most of the laws affected have nothing to do with employment and are therefore beyond the scope of the Equal Treatment Directive (see ROW Europe, 1983: 76). The only tribunal case in which s 51 has proved decisive in preventing a successful outcome centred on a GLC prohibition on women wrestlers. The industrial tribunal had found the prohibition to be discriminatory, but the EAT reversed the decision on the grounds that local authorities were entitled to impose restrictions on wrestling licences under the Local Government Act 1963 and were therefore covered by s 51 of the SDA (Greater London Council v Farrar [1980] ICR 266). In order to appease the Commissioners, the government included a section in the 1986 Act, so that no public entertainment licence can include a requirement which would constitute unlawful employment discrimination. Apart from this minor amendment, the offending section remains intact.

Section 41 of the Race Relations Act is even broader in scope, providing a blanket exemption for all legislation and subordinate legislation, past, present and future. In relation to nationality and residence, circulars and other ministerial pronouncements are also exempt. The effect of this provision is to place the most serious manifestations of institutionalized discrimination, including nationality and immigration law, beyond reach. The CRE points out that ordinary constitutional principles would not give priority over Acts of Parliament to lesser forms of law-making, some of which receive little or no parliamentary scrutiny (CRE, July 1985: 9). Both Commissions have asked for the repeal of the offending sections

(CRE, July 1985: 9; EOC, October 1986: 23). Statutes would then take priority over subordinate legislation and more recent statutes would prevail over earlier ones. Any government minister wishing to discriminate would find the back-door route sealed off and any proposed discriminatory measures would have to be discussed openly and justified to Parliament.

Once central government had demonstrated its willingness to launch a frontal attack on institutionalized discrimination, local authorities and other public bodies could be invited to take up the challenge. Section 71 of the Race Relations Act requires local authorities to have regard to the need to eliminate racial discrimination and to promote equality of opportunity between persons of different racial groups (see Appendix 4). There is no equivalent provision in the Sex Discrimination Act. In practice, s 71 has proved useful in shielding local authorities that have taken positive steps to promote racial equality, but the present wording is too vague to enable action to be taken against authorities who have done nothing. The CRE suggests a new form of words which would give local authorities a specific duty to combat discrimination and would require them to produce annual programmes and reports so that progress could be measured. The Commission would like to see the same duty extended to all public bodies and not restricted to local authorities, as at present (CRE, July 1985: 35–6). The EOC endorses these suggestions and asks that the provisions of s 71, as amended by the CRE, be added to the Sex Discrimination Act (EOC, October 1986: 38–9).

For any government with a genuine commitment to civil rights issues, the Commissions' proposed amendments provide an essential starting point. On the basis of a decade of experience, the CRE and the EOC are well situated to identify the major weaknesses in the legislation and to suggest how these might be rectified. Not surprisingly, however, they have chosen to stay very much within the framework of the existing laws. They offer, as the EOC puts it, 'a practitioner's view of the problems' (EOC, October 1986: 1). Their concern is 'to make the present Act(s) work better', not to question 'the structure and general thrust' of the law, with which they have no quarrel (CRE, July 1985: (x)). The question that the two Commissions do not address is whether it would be better to adopt a radically different model of equality.

There can be no doubt that women rather than men were intended to be the main beneficiaries of the equal pay and sex discrimination laws, and that the Race Relations Acts were directed at alleviating the oppression suffered by certain racial groups. Yet the legislation is drafted in neutral language, so that members of either sex or any racial group can make a complaint of discrimination. Indeed, there is evidence that a number of men have benefited from the sex equality laws[9] and that white people have been able to assert their rights as members of a racial group (see for example the case of the Hackney gardening apprentices, discussed in Ch. 3, p. 53).

From a civil libertarian standpoint, it is difficult to see how it could be otherwise; it cannot be acceptable to destroy the rights of one individual or group in the process of creating rights for another. Yet, as we have seen, a purely formal model of equality is inadequate; it can be used to increase the mobility of individuals within existing structures, but cannot be used to challenge the structures themselves. The chief significance of the 1970s civil rights legislation lies in its partial recognition of this limitation and its tentative efforts to overcome it by experimenting with the concepts indirect discrimination and positive action. Ten years on, with the structures of inequality still intact, it is time to review the position.

Positive discrimination or positive action?
The notion of employing special measures in order to overcome historical and structural disadvantage is not in itself new to Britain. Indeed, it is precisely the identification of specific groups with particular needs, and the development of a legislative and administrative apparatus to service them, that distinguished welfare capitalism from its harsher, laissez-faire version. During the 1960s, phrases such as 'educational priority areas' and 'community development projects' became an everyday feature of social democratic vocabulary. The Plowden Committee, intent on solving the problem of educational deprivation, did not beat about the bush:

> We ask for 'positive discrimination' in favour of ... schools [in areas of social disadvantage] and the children in them, going well beyond an attempt to equalise resources ... The first step must be to raise the schools with low standards to the national average; the second, quite deliberately to make them better ... The schools must supply a compensating environment. (Central Advisory Council for Education (1967) (Plowden Report): para. 151)

The discovery that so many people were failing to be swept along by the rising tide of post-war prosperity was a matter of some concern and regret for politicians. Although puzzled by the persistence of deprivation however, they did not regard it as evidence of a fundamental flaw in the system of distribution and exchange. Inevitably then, they responded to each new 'pocket' of deprivation with a series of ad hoc remedies, involving only minor and temporary shifts in resource allocation. When community workers employed by the Community Development Projects rejected the self-help ideology which inspired the projects and embarked on a much more radical analysis of urban problems, many of the projects were deprived of funds and closed down prematurely (see CDP, 1977; Cockburn, 1977).

In the harsher economic and political climate of the 1980s, attempts to divert resources to the needy are less ambitious, but it is no less difficult to ensure that even modest remedial programmes will produce the results intended, without employing some form of positive discrimination. For example, the government's recent 'task force' initiative is designed to provide work in areas of high unemployment; without some form of local labour contract compliance, however, there is no way of ensuring that the target group will derive full benefit from the programme.[10]

A major weakness of many of these experiments in positive discrimination is the absence of any goals or targets by which the success of the schemes can be measured. One way of remedying this situation is to establish a system of quotas, whereby a specified percentage of the available positions is reserved for members of the disadvantaged group. As far as the labour market is concerned, experiments with quotas began and ended with the Disabled Persons (Employment) Act; in this case the existence of quotas merely enabled us to measure precisely the extent to which the legislation had failed (see Ch. 3).

In theory, it would be possible to devise a system of quotas that was effectively enforced and produced rapid results. In practice, as we have seen (Ch. 3, pp. 65–6), there are a number of objections to proceeding down this path. Furthermore, it has been argued that employment quotas are essentially conservative. They allow employers to slot people into existing patterns of employment, without having to consider how these patterns might be changed to meet the needs of potential employees (see Jackson, 1984). Positive action programmes, on the other hand, can only be effective if they begin to dismantle the barriers which prevent women and racial minority groups from competing on equal terms with white men. In order to ensure that this is done, employers will have to be required to set targets, devise timetables and produce progress reports.

The objections which have been raised to the use of employment quotas carry less weight in the area of political representation. There, too, women and black people are initially co-opted into white male structures, but once inside they can begin to alter the structures and shift the priorities of the organization. In a number of European countries, the results of political quotas are impressive: for example, in Norway in 1986 of eighteen Cabinet Ministers eight were women, including the Prime Minister. Women occupied 27 percent of the seats in Parliament and 28 percent of the seats on public bodies (Halsaa, 1986).[11] This contrasts dramatically with Britain, where in

1986 the Prime Minister was the only woman in the Cabinet and the House of Commons was entirely white and overwhelmingly male (there were 27 women in a House of 650 members). It is vital that women and racial minorities be represented adequately on decision-making bodies in all areas of public life and it may prove necessary to accomplish this by using quotas. The trade union movement has created a small space within which the voices of its female membership are beginning to be heard, partly through the use of reserved seats. Similar measures may prove necessary in order to secure the representation of black workers.

When the needs of all workers are given equal consideration, it becomes increasingly apparent that the present structure of the labour market is unsatisfactory in a number of ways. A full working day with continuity of employment over several years is regarded as the norm and part-time employment is treated as second best. Annual leave is taken as a block and working parents who stay at home when their children are sick are labelled as irresponsible (see Novarra, 1980: Ch. 1). Workers who wish to return to their countries of origin to visit relatives are frequently denied a period of extended leave and so are compelled to surrender their jobs (see Brown, 1984: 156). A much more flexible set of arrangements is required, which would allow variations in working hours and periods of leave for child care and other purposes, and would provide retraining as and when required.

In an era of high unemployment and technological change, traditional patterns of work are increasingly outmoded and a major restructuring of the labour market seems inevitable. The trade union movement is presented with a golden opportunity to influence these developments and so help to create a society which believes in 'taking rights seriously' (Dworkin, 1977) and in which all forms of discrimination become legally, politically and morally unacceptable.

Postscript

At the general election in June 1987, a Conservative government was returned to office for a third term. As a result of the election, the representation of women in the House of Commons has improved slightly, with the return of 41 women MPs. For the first time, the House contains a small number of black MPs: there are three, one of whom is a women. Apart from this small step in the right direction, the current political agenda contains little to gladden the hearts of those committed to improving the life chances of women and racial minority groups in Britain. On the contrary, in 1987 the immediate future looked extremely bleak, as the government returned with renewed vigour to the tasks of 'lifting the burden' on employers, reducing employment rights and clipping the wings of trade unions and local authorities.

The government has expressed no commitment to equal opportunities policies, and is only moving forward on these issues in response to external pressure. To some extent, the pressures already identified (see p. 154) continue to operate. In recognition of the potential time-bomb created by social deprivation and high unemployment, the government is investing in inner cities as 'enterprise zones' and thereby introducing a form of 'contract compliance' through the back door (see p. 154). In stark contrast, the Local Government (No. 2) Bill 1987, if enacted in its present form, will make it virtually impossible for local authorities to pursue contract compliance at all. Not only will they be required to put out to private tender many of the services they currently provide themselves (such as cleaning, catering and refuse collection), they will also be prevented from imposing 'non-commercial' conditions on contractors. They will therefore be precluded from interfering in any way with the contractors' terms and conditions of employment, the composition of the workforce or methods of selection, training and promotion. There is a narrow exclusion to cover s 71 of the Race Relations Act, but local authorities will be advised to possess clear evidence of unlawful racial discrimination before invoking this exemption. Contract compliance in relation to racial groups will be severely curtailed and in relation to women it will become illegal.

In the past, the European Economic Community has provided a useful impetus to progress in the field of sex equality, although there is no guarantee that this beneficial influence will continue (see Hoskyns, 1985, 1986). For the moment, however, European law is the only hope for many women currently caught up in the legal quagmire created by the equal value regulations. It could be years rather than months before the European Court comes to grips with these issues. By then, as the pressures towards privatization and sub-contracting gather momentum, many women will no longer work for the same employer as their better-paid male colleagues and their claims will cease to be valid (see Gregory and Stoddart, 1987).

In the absence of any commitment on the part of the government to come to grips with the problems of racial and sexual disadvantage, to derive hope from certain aspects of inner city policy and from EEC law is merely to clutch at straws. A major new initiative against discriminatory practices is long overdue; unfortunately, it seems that we will have to wait a little longer.

Notes

1. These terms were used by Marx to describe the way in which the ruling classes implemented the factory and workshop legislation of 1867. See Marx, 1974: Vol 1, 464, quoted in Corrigan, 1977: 89.

2. Examples of amendments required merely to ensure that the original aims of the legislation are not frustrated are those concerned with direct discrimination (see Ch. 2, p. 35 and note 5), indirect discrimination (see Ch. 2, p. 43) and instructions to discriminate (see Ch. 7, p. 131).

3. The CRE reports a grand total of fifteen complaints of racial discrimination using the county court procedure in 1982 and eighteen in 1983 (CRE, July 1985: 15). The EOC informs us that 'only a handful of the thousands of complaints in the fields of education and consumer services have reached the county courts' and points to the procedural complexities, delays and expense involved in bringing a county court case (EOC, October 1986: 32).

4. Cawson (1982) refers to the establishment of new quangos for the development of the London and Liverpool dockland areas, at the same time that the government was 'launching an ideological offensive' against the quango. When the Greater London Council and the six Metropolitan authorities were abolished in 1985, several new quangos were created to take over some of the functions of the defunct councils.

5. The vast majority of quango appointments are part-time and involve the payment of an honorarium or fees on a sessional basis. Some members, such as trade union officials, may waive the payments. In 1985, the remuneration paid to the twenty-two CRE Commissioners totalled some £57,500, almost two-thirds of which went to the full-time Chairperson; the Commissioners received another £22,000 in expenses (CRE, *Annual Report*, June 1986: 42). In the same year, the fourteen EOC Commissioners shared just under £69,000 in remuneration; their expense claims are not shown separately from those of the staff (EOC, *Annual Report*, July 1986: 42).

6. Both Commissions were permitted to present evidence on this basis in the 'discovery' cases, SRC v Nasse and Vyas v Leyland Cars, discussed in Chapter 6. The EOC has appeared in a similar capacity in an equal pay case (Shields v Coomes [1977] IRLR 131) and a sex discrimination case (Page v Freight Hire [1981] IRLR 13). In the United States, *amicus curiae* briefs are a common occurrence. Individuals and organizations who are not parties to the case but have an interest in its outcome may submit evidence relevant to the issues before the court.

7. Appendices at the end of the Labour Party document give information about other countries, particularly Australia and France. In Australia, the Women's Affairs section flourished while it was located within the department of the Prime Minister and the Cabinet in the mid–1970s, was cast into the wilderness in the late 1970s by the Fraser government, but has prospered since under the Hawke administration. In France, the Ministry for Women's Rights created by the Socialist government in 1982 was abolished by Prime Minister Chirac within a few days of taking office in 1986.

8. See Appendix 2 for the full text of the Directive on Social Security. See also ROW Europe, 1983: Ch. 7. The Social Security Act 1980 and subsequent regulations issued under this Act have removed some of the more blatantly discriminatory features of the social security system. Some of the changes are largely cosmetic, as in the replacement of the 'male breadwinner' by the 'nominated breadwinner' concept; others, such as the Severe Disablement Allowance, achieve equality on the basis of 'levelling down'. Married and cohabiting women continued to be barred from claiming Invalid Care Allowance until the victory of Ms Drake at the European Court of Justice (Drake v Department of Health and Social Security [1986] 3, *Common Market Law*

Reports 43). See Land and Ward (1986) on the extent to which the 1986 Social Security Act represents a step backwards for women.

9. Hutton (1984) argues that men are using the Sex Discrimination Act to break into female dominated areas of employment, rather than vice versa, and that it is men rather than women who complain of sex discrimination when making job applications. His presentation does tend to overstate the case, however, as he neglects to mention that three times as many women as men file tribunal applications under the SDA. In numerical terms, relatively few men use the law and when they do, their chances of success are no higher than for women. Interestingly, for tribunal applicants using the Race Relations Act, the sex ratio is reversed; three-quarters of the applications are filed by men.

10. I am indebted to Harriet Harman MP for this particular example of positive discrimination.

11. Halsaa admits that Norway has traditionally been a very closed white society and has failed to address the problem of racial discrimination. She believes that this situation is about to change. Ironically, the rapid improvement in the position of women in the Norwegian labour force during the 1980s is largely due to the policy of replacing foreign workers with Norwegians (see Moore and Wybrow, 1984).

Appendix I
Policy documents from the Trades Union Congress

A. Charter on equality for women within trade unions

Commended by the General Council of the Trades Union Congress to all union executives and committees. (Endorsed by Congress, 1979)

1. The National Executive Committee of the union should publicly declare to all its members the commitment of the union to involving women members in the activities of the union at all levels.

2. The structure of the union should be examined to see whether it prevents women from reaching the decision-making bodies.

3. Where there are large women's memberships but no women on the decision-making bodies special provision should be made to ensure that women's views are represented, either through the creation of additional seats or by co-option.

4. The National Executive Committee of each union should consider the desirability of setting up advisory committees within its constitutional machinery to ensure that the special interests of its women members are protected.

5. Similar committees at regional, divisional and district level could also assist by encouraging the active involvement of women in the general activities of the union.

6. Efforts should be made to include in collective agreements provision for time off without loss of pay to attend branch meetings during working hours where that is practicable.

7. Where it is not practicable to hold meetings during working hours every effort should be made to provide child-care facilities for use by either parent.

8. Child-care facilities, for use by either parent, should be provided at all district, divisional and regional meetings and particularly at the union's annual conference, and for training courses organised by the union.

9. Although it may be open to any members of either sex to go to union training courses, special encouragement should be given to women to attend.

10. The content of journals and other union publications should be presented in non-sexist terms.

B. Black workers: a charter for equality of opportunity

Equal opportunities within trade unions

Trade unions cannot just talk about equal opportunity, they must be seen to be taking active steps to make it a reality. As a first step, they should examine their own structures and procedures. The following checklist is commended to unions to improve equal opportunities within their own organisations and activities.

Trade union organisation

The National Executive Committee of the union should declare publicly to all its members the commitment of the union to involving black workers in the activities of the union at all levels.

The structure of the union should be examined to ensure the removal of barriers which can prevent black workers from reaching union office and decision-making bodies (e.g. shop stewards, branch officials, regional and national committees, national officials etc.).

The National Executive Committee should consider the possibility of setting up an advisory committee within its constitutional machinery to ensure that the issue of equal opportunities is actively pursued.

Similar committees at regional, divisional and district level could also assist by encouraging the active involvement of black workers in the general activities of the union.

Trade union recruitment

When trade unions are seen to be fighting for the rights of their black members, this will encourage other black workers to join and become active in the trade union movement. To assist trade union organisers and to attract black workers, unions should consider the production of recruitment material and sections of membership cards in the appropriate ethnic minority languages.

Trade union education

Trade unions should examine their educational provision to ensure that the issues of equal opportunities and racialism are adequately covered. In certain areas of the country, it could be beneficial to develop courses in basic trade unionism aimed specifically at ethnic minorities, and where possible, presented in ethnic minority languages.

Trade union publications

The content of journals and other union publications should ensure that they reflect the multi-racial nature of their membership and consider matters of relevance to ethnic minorities.

Grievance procedure

Trade unions are urged to ensure that officials at all levels deal particularly vigorously and effectively with any employment grievances concerning racial discrimination which are brought to them by their members.

Trade union representatives

Trade unionists who act in a representative position in the trade union movement on public bodies should ensure that the cause of equal opportunities is pursued by those organisations.

Racialists at work

Trade unions should review their rules and policies in order to ensure that trade union members are not allowed to use the trade union movement as a means of disseminating racialist propaganda and ideas. Unions should also ensure that the myths and propaganda of racialists are countered, and the positive contribution ethnic minorities have given to industry and services is publicised.

Trade unions and social activities

Ethnic minority members should be encouraged to attend any social club or social activity organised by or for workers to help them to integrate into the working community.

Equality at work

Trade unionists know from past experience that the best means of eliminating disadvantages or discrimination in the workplace is through collective bargaining. The recommendations below are framed to ensure equal opportunities for black workers and are commended to union negotiators as collective bargaining objectives.

Equal opportunities clause

An important initial step should be to negotiate an equal opportunities clause in appropriate collective agreements or as an agreement in itself. The TUC model clause is printed on the back of this Charter [see C below]. Such a clause should be published and distributed throughout those areas covered by the agreement.

Reviewing and implementing an equal opportunities policy

Once an agreement on an equal opportunities policy has been reached, trade unions and management should regularly review employment practices and the structure of the workforce to see that there is no direct discrimination against ethnic minorities in the areas of recruitment, promotion and training opportunities.

Similarly a joint review should be carried out to ensure that indirect discrimination is not occurring in these fields. For example, are qualifications or English tests being applied which give advantages to one race over another, but are not really necessary for the job in question; or do recruitment methods prevent ethnic minorities from becoming aware of vacancies?

If either direct or indirect discrimination practices are discovered, steps must be taken to eliminate them immediately.

Personnel procedures

An important step for eliminating both direct and indirect discrimination is to ensure personnel procedures for recruitment, promotion, etc., are clearly laid down for all to follow and understand. Action along these lines can remove informal arrangements which may lend themselves to malpractice.

Health and safety

Trade union representatives in the workplace should ensure that ethnic minority workers fully understand all health and safety regulations and that, where necessary, these are translated into the relevant ethnic languages.

Overcoming disadvantage

Because of past discrimination many black workers are still unable to compete for jobs equally with white workers. To counteract these effects and to tackle the specific disadvantages faced by members of ethnic minority groups, unions should press for:

Industrial language training for ethnic minority workers who speak little English.
Recruitment material designed to encourage applications by ethnic minorities and displayed or publicised where ethnic groups will see such material.
The development of basic training courses by employers and Industrial Training Boards, open to all unqualified black workers to counteract disadvantage, improve their status and ability, and provide the appropriate industrial qualifications.

C. TUC model equal opportunities clause

The parties to this agreement are committed to the development of positive policies to promote equal opportunity in employment regardless of workers' sex, marital status, creed, colour, race or ethnic origins. This principle will apply in respect of all conditions of work including pay, hours of work, holiday entitlement, overtime and shift-work, work allocation, guaranteed earnings, sick pay, pensions, recruitment, training, promotion and redundancy.

The management undertake to draw opportunities for training and promotion to the attention of all eligible employees, and to inform all employees of this agreement on equal opportunity. The parties agree that they will revise from time to time, through their joint machinery, the operation of this equal opportunity policy. If any employee considers that he or she is suffering from unequal treatment on grounds of sex, marital status, creed, colour, race or ethnic origins, he or she may make a complaint which will be dealt with through the agreed procedures for dealing with grievances.

Appendix 2
European Community law: the key provisions

Article 119 of the Treaty of Rome 1957 (signed by Britain in 1973)
Each Member State shall during the first stage ensure and subsequently maintain the application of the principle that men and women should receive equal pay for equal work.

For the purpose of this Article, 'pay' means the ordinary basic or minimum wage or salary and any other consideration, whether in cash or in kind, which the worker receives, directly or indirectly, in respect of his employment from his employer. Equal pay without discrimination based on sex means:
   (a) that pay for the same work at piece rates shall be calculated on the basis of the same unit of measurement;
   (b) that pay for work at time rates shall be the same for the same job.

Council Directive 75/117 of 10 February 1975
Approximation of Laws relating to equal pay for men and women

Article 1
The principle of equal pay for men and women outlined in Article 119 of the Treaty, hereinafter called 'principle of equal pay', means, for the same work or for work to which equal value is attributed, the elimination of all discrimination on grounds of sex with regard to all aspects and conditions of remuneration.

In particular, where a job classification system is used for determining pay, it must be based on the same criteria for both men and women and so drawn up as to exclude any discrimination on grounds of sex.

Article 2
Member States shall introduce into their national legal systems such measures as are necessary to enable all employees who consider themselves wronged by failure to apply the principle of equal pay to pursue their claims by judicial process after possible recourse to other competent authorities.

Article 3
Member States shall abolish all discrimination between men and women arising from laws, regulations or administrative provisions which is contrary to the principle of equal pay.

Article 4

Member States shall take the necessary measures to ensure that provisions appearing in collective agreements, wage scales, wage agreements or individual contracts of employment which are contrary to the principle of equal pay shall be, or may be declared, null and void or may be amended.

Article 5

Member States shall take the necessary measures to protect employees against dismissal by the employer as a reaction to a complaint within the undertaking or to any legal proceedings aimed at enforcing compliance with the principle of equal pay.

Article 6

Member States shall, in accordance with their national circumstances and legal systems, take the measures necessary to ensure that the principle of equal pay is applied. They shall see that effective means are available to take care that this principle is observed.

Article 7

Member States shall take care that the provisions adopted pursuant to this Directive, together with the relevant provisions already in force, are brought to the attention of employees by all appropriate means, for example at their place of employment.

Article 8

1. Member States shall put into force the laws, regulations and administrative provisions necessary to comply with this Directive within one year of its notification and shall immediately inform the Commission thereof.

2. Member States shall communicate to the Commission the texts of the laws, regulations and administrative provisions which they adopt in the field covered by this Directive.

Article 9

Within two years of the expiry of the one-year period referred to in Article 8, Member States shall forward all necessary information to the Commission to enable it to draw up a report on the application of this Directive for submission to the Council.

Article 10

This Directive is addressed to the Member States.
Done at Brussels, 10 February 1975.

Council Directive 76/207 of 9 February 1976
On the implementation of the principle of equal treatment for men and women as regards access to employment, vocational training and promotion, and working conditions

Article 1

1. The purpose of this Directive is to put into effect in the Member States the principle of equal treatment for men and women as regards access to employment, including

promotion, and to vocational training and as regards working conditions and, on the conditions referred to in paragraph 2, social security. This principle is hereinafter referred to as 'the principle of equal treatment'.

2. With a view to ensuring the progressive implementation of the principle of equal treatment in matters of social security, the Council, acting on a proposal from the Commission, will adopt provisions defining its substance, its scope and the arrangements for its application.

Article 2

1. For the purposes of the following provisions, the principle of equal treatment shall mean that there shall be no discrimination whatsoever on grounds of sex either directly or indirectly by reference in particular to marital or family status.

2. This Directive shall be without prejudice to the right of Member States to exclude from its field of application those occupational activities and, where appropriate, the training leading thereto, for which, by reason of their nature or the context in which they are carried out, the sex of the worker constitutes a determining factor.

3. This Directive shall be without prejudice to provisions concerning the protection of women, particularly as regards pregnancy and maternity.

4. This Directive shall be without prejudice to measures to promote equal opportunity for men and women, in particular by removing existing inequalities which affect women's opportunities in the areas referred to in Article 1(1).

Article 3

1. Application of the principle of equal treatment means that there shall be no discrimination whatsoever on grounds of sex in the conditions, including selection criteria, for access to all jobs or posts, whatever the sector or branch of activity, and to all levels of the occupational hierarchy.

2. To this end, Member States shall take the measures necessary to ensure that:

(a) any laws, regulations and administrative provisions contrary to the principle of equal treatment shall be abolished;
(b) any provisions contrary to the principle of equal treatment which are included in collective agreements, individual contracts of employment, internal rules of undertakings or in rules governing the independent occupations and professions shall be, or may be declared, null and void or may be amended;
(c) those laws, regulations and administrative provisions contrary to the principle of equal treatment when the concern for protection which originally inspired them is no longer well founded shall be revised; and that where similar provisions are included in collective agreements labour and management shall be requested to undertake the desired revision.

Article 4

Application of the principle of equal treatment with regard to access to all types and to all levels, of vocational guidance, vocational training, advanced vocational training and retraining, means that Member States shall take all necessary measures to ensure that:

(a) any laws, regulations and administrative provisions contrary to the principle of equal treatment shall be abolished;

(b) any provisions contrary to the principle of equal treatment which are included in collective agreements, individual contracts of employment, internal rules of undertakings or in rules governing the independent occupations and professions shall be, or may be declared, null and void or may be amended.

(c) without prejudice to the freedom granted in certain Member States to certain private training establishments, vocational guidance, vocational training, advanced vocational training and retraining shall be accessible on the basis of the same criteria and at the same levels without any discrimination on grounds of sex.

Article 5

1. Application of the principle of equal treatment with regard to working conditions, including the conditions governing dismissal, means that men and women shall be guaranteed the same conditions without discrimination on grounds of sex.

2. To this end, Member States shall take the measures necessary to ensure that:

(a) any laws, regulations and administrative provisions contrary to the principle of equal treatment shall be abolished;

(b) any provisions contrary to the principle of equal treatment which are included in collective agreements, individual contracts of employment, internal rules of undertakings or in rules governing the independent occupations and professions shall be, or may be declared, null and void or may be amended;

(c) those laws, regulations and administrative provisions contrary to the principle of equal treatment when the concern for protection which originally inspired them is no longer well founded shall be revised; and that where similar provisions are included in collective agreements labour and management shall be requested to undertake the desired revision.

Article 6

Member States shall introduce into their national legal systems such measures as are necessary to enable all persons who consider themselves wronged by failure to apply to them the principle of equal treatment within the meaning of Articles 3, 4 and 5 to pursue their claims by judicial process after possible recourse to other competent authorities.

Article 7

Member States shall take the necessary measures to protect employees against dismissal by the employer as a reaction to a complaint within the undertaking or to any legal proceedings aimed at enforcing compliance with the principle of equal treatment.

Article 8

Member States shall take care that the provisions adopted pursuant to this Directive, together with the relevant provisions already in force, are brought to the attention of employees by all appropriate means, for example at their place of employment.

Article 9

1. Member States shall put into force the laws, regulations and administrative provisions necessary in order to comply with this Directive within 30 months of its notification and shall immediately inform the Commission thereof. However, as regards the first part of Article 3(2)(c) and the first part of Article 5(2)(c), Member States shall

carry out a first examination and if necessary a first revision of the laws, regulations and administrative provisions referred to therein within four years of notification of this Directive.

2. Member States shall periodically assess the occupational activities referred to in Article 2(2) in order to decide, in the light of social developments, whether there is justification for maintaining the exclusions concerned. They shall notify the Commission of the results of this assessment.

3. Member States shall also communicate to the Commission the texts of laws, regulations and administrative provisions which they adopt in the field covered by this Directive.

Article 10
Within two years following expiry of the 30-month period laid down in the first sub-paragraph of Article 9(1), Member States shall forward all necessary information to the Commission to enable it to draw up a report on the application of this Directive for submission to the Council.

Article 11
This Directive is addressed to the Member States.
Done at Brussels, 9 February 1976.

Council Directive 79/7 of 19 December 1978
On the progressive implementation of the principle of equal treatment for men and women in matters of social security

Article 1
The purpose of this Directive is the progressive implementation, in the field of social security and other elements of social protection provided for in Article 3, of the principle of equal treatment for men and women in matters of social security, hereinafter referred to as 'the principle of equal treatment'.

Article 2
This Directive shall apply to the working population — including self-employed persons, workers and self-employed persons whose activity is interrupted by illness, accident or involuntary unemployment and persons seeking employment — and to retired or invalided workers and self-employed persons.

Article 3
1. This Directive shall apply to:
   (a) statutory schemes which provide protection against the following risks:
   — sickness,
   — invalidity,
   — old age,
   — accidents at work and occupational diseases,
   — unemployment;
   (b) social assistance, in so far as it is intended to supplement or replace the schemes referred to in (a).

2. This Directive shall not apply to the provisions concerning survivors' benefits nor to those concerning family benefits except in the case of family benefits granted by way of increases of benefits due in respect of the risks referred to in paragraph 1(a).

3. With a view to ensuring implementation of the principle of equal treatment in occupational schemes, the Council, acting on a proposal from the Commission, will adopt provisions defining its substance, its scope and the arrangements for its application.

Article 4

1. The principle of equal treatment means that there shall be no discrimination whatsoever on grounds of sex either directly, or indirectly by reference in particular to marital or family status, in particular as concerns:

— the scope of the schemes and the condition of access thereto,
— the obligation to contribute and the calculation of contributions,
— the calculation of benefits including increases due in respect of a spouse and for dependants and the conditions governing the duration and retention of entitlement to benefits.

2. The principle of equal treatment shall be without prejudice to the provisions relating to the protection of women on the grounds of maternity.

Article 5

Member States shall take the measures necessary to ensure that any laws, regulations and administrative provisions contrary to the principle of equal treatment are abolished.

Article 6

Member States shall introduce into their national legal systems such measures as are necessary to enable all persons who consider themselves wronged by failure to apply the principle of equal treatment to pursue their claims by judicial process, possibly after recourse to other competent authorities.

Article 7

1. This Directive shall be without prejudice to the right of Member States to exclude from its scope:

(a) the determination of pensionable age for the purposes of granting old-age and retirement pensions and the possible consequences thereof for other benefits;
(b) advantages in respect of old-age pension schemes granted to persons who have brought up children; the acquisition of benefit entitlements following periods of interruption of employment due to the bringing up of children;
(c) the granting of old-age or invalidity benefit entitlements by virtue of the derived entitlements of a wife;
(d) the granting of increases of long-term invalidity, old-age, accidents at work and occupational disease benefits for a dependent wife;
(e) the consequences of the exercise, before the adoption of this Directive, of a right of option not to acquire rights or incur obligations under a statutory scheme.

2. Member States shall periodically examine matters excluded under paragraph 1 in order to ascertain, in the light of social developments in the matter concerned, whether there is justification for maintaining the exclusions concerned.

Article 8

1. Member States shall bring into force the laws, regulations and administrative provisions necessary to comply with this Directive within six years of its notification. They shall immediately inform the Commission thereof.

2. Member States shall communicate to the Commission the text of laws, regulations and administrative provisions which they adopt in the field covered by this Directive, including measures adopted pursuant to Article 7(2).

They shall inform the Commission of their reasons for maintaining the existing provisions on the matters referred to in Article 7(1) and of the possibilities for reviewing them at a later date.

Article 9

Within seven years of notification of this Directive, Member States shall forward all information necessary to the Commission to enable it to draw up a report on the application of this Directive for submission to the Council and to propose further measures as may be required for the implementation of the principle of equal treatment.

Article 10

This Directive is addressed to the Member States.
Done at Brussels, 19 December 1978.

Appendix 3
Equal pay legislation: a selection from the key provisions

A Sex Discrimination Act 1975, Schedule 1

SCHEDULE 1

EQUAL PAY ACT 1970

PART II

ACT AS AMENDED

1970 CHAPTER 41

An Act to preven* discrimination, as regards terms and conditions of employment, between men and women. [29th May 1970]

BE IT ENACTED by the Queen's Most Excellent Majesty, by and with the advice and consent of the Lords Spiritual and Temporal, and Commons, in this present Parliament assembled, and by the authority of the same, as follows:—

1.—(1) If the terms of a contract under which a woman is employed at an establishment in Great Britain do not include (directly or by reference to a collective agreement or otherwise) an equality clause they shall be deemed to include one.

(2) An equality clause is a provision which relates to terms (whether concerned with pay or not) of a contract under which a woman is employed (the "woman's contract"), and has the effect that—

> (a) where the woman is employed on like work with a man in the same employment—

>> (i) if (apart from the equality clause) any term of the woman's contract is or becomes less favourable to the woman than a term of a similar kind in the contract under which that man is employed, that term of the woman's contract shall be treated as so modified as not to be less favourable, and

>> (ii) if (apart from the equality clause) at any time the woman's contract does not include a term corresponding to a term benefiting that man included in the contract under which he is employed, the woman's contract shall be treated as including such a term;

(*b*) where the woman is employed on work rated as equivalent with that of a man in the same employment—

(i) if (apart from the equality clause) any term of the woman's contract determined by the rating of the work is or becomes less favourable to the woman than a term of a similar kind in the contract under which that man is employed, that term of the woman's contract shall be treated as so modified as not to be less favourable, and

(ii) if (apart from the equality clause) at any time the woman's contract does not include a term corresponding to a term benefiting that man included in the contract under which he is employed and determined by the rating of the work, the woman's contract shall be treated as including such a term.

(3) An equality clause shall not operate in relation to a variation between the woman's contract and the man's contract if the employer proves that the variation is genuinely due to a material difference (other than the difference of sex) between her case and his.

(4) A woman is to be regarded as employed on like work with men if, but only if, her work and theirs is of the same or a broadly similar nature, and the differences (if any) between the things she does and the things they do are not of practical importance in relation to terms and conditions of employment ; and accordingly in comparing her work with theirs regard shall be had to the frequency or otherwise with which any such differences occur in practice as well as to the nature and extent of the differences.

(5) A woman is to be regarded as employed on work rated as equivalent with that of any men if, but only if, her job and their job have been given an equal value, in terms of the demand made on a worker under various headings (for instance effort, skill, decision), on a study undertaken with a view to evaluating in those terms the jobs to be done by all or any of the employees in an undertaking or group of undertakings, or would have been given an equal value but for the evaluation being made on a system setting different values for men and women on the same demand under any heading.

B   Equal Pay (Amendment) Regulations 1983

STATUTORY INSTRUMENTS

1983 No. 1794

SEX DISCRIMINATION

The Equal Pay (Amendment) Regulations 1983

Laid before Parliament in draft

Made - - - -	6*th December* 1983
Coming into operation	1*st January* 1984

New form of equality clause

2.—(1) In subsection (2) of section 1 of the Equal Pay Act 1970 (c) (equality clauses to be implied into contracts of employment), after paragraph *(b)* there shall be inserted the following paragraph:—

"*(c)* where a woman is employed on work which, not being work in relation to which paragraph *(a)* or *(b)* above applies, is, in terms of the demands made on her (for instance under such headings as effort, skill and decision), of equal value to that of a man in the same employment—

(i) if (apart from the equality clause) any term of the woman's contract is or becomes less favourable to the woman than a term of a similar kind in the contract under which that man is employed, that term of the woman's contract shall be treated as so modified as not to be less favourable, and

(ii) if (apart from the equality clause) at any time the woman's contract does not include a term corresponding to a term benefiting that man included in the contract under which he is employed, the woman's contract shall be treated as including such a term.".

(2) For subsection (3) of the said section 1 (defence of genuine material difference) there shall be substituted the following subsection:—

"(3) An equality clause shall not operate in relation to a variation between the woman's contract and the man's contract if the employer proves that the variation is genuinely due to a material factor which is not the difference of sex and that factor—

(a) in the case of an equality clause falling within subsection (2)*(a)* or *(b)* above, must be a material difference between the woman's case and the man's; and

(b) in the case of an equality clause falling within subsection (2)*(c)* above, may be such a material difference.".

Appendix 4
Sex and Race Discrimination laws: some key provisions

The Race Relations Act 1976 was closely modelled on the Sex Discrimination Act passed the previous year. The parallel presentation which follows is designed to highlight the similarities and differences between the Acts. For reasons of space it has only been possible to include the most important sections of the Acts and it has been necessary to transfer section 47 of the Race Relations Act to the final page of the Appendix.

Sex Discrimination Act 1975

1975 CHAPTER 65

An Act to render unlawful certain kinds of sex discrimination and discrimination on the ground of marriage, and establish a Commission with the function of working towards the elimination of such discrimination and promoting equality of opportunity between men and women generally; and for related purposes.
[12th November 1975]

DISCRIMINATION TO WHICH ACT APPLIES

Sex discrimination against women. **1.**—(1) A person discriminates against a woman in any circumstances relevant for the purposes of any provision of this Act if—

> (a) on the ground of her sex he treats her less favourably than he treats or would treat a man, or

> (b) he applies to her a requirement or condition which he applies or would apply equally to a man but—

>> (i) which is such that the proportion of women who can comply with it is considerably smaller than the proportion of men who can comply with it, and

>> (ii) which he cannot show to be justifiable irrespective of the sex of the person to whom it is applied, and

>> (iii) which is to her detriment because she cannot comply with it.

(2) If a person treats or would treat a man differently according to the man's marital status, his treatment of a woman is for the purposes of subsection (1)(a) to be compared to his treatment of a man having the like marital status.

Sex discrimination against men. **2.**—(1) Section 1, and the provisions of Parts II and III relating to sex discrimination against women, are to be read as applying equally to the treatment of men, and for that purpose shall have effect with such modifications as are requisite.

(2) In the application of subsection (1) no account shall be taken of special treatment afforded to women in connection with pregnancy or childbirth.

Discrimination against married persons in employment field. **3.**—(1) A person discriminates against a married person of either sex in any circumstances relevant for the purposes of any provision of Part II if—

> (a) on the ground of his or her marital status he treats that person less favourably than he treats or would treat an unmarried person of the same sex, or

Race Relations Act 1976

1976 CHAPTER 74

An Act to make fresh provision with respect to discrimination on racial grounds and relations between people of different racial groups; and to make in the Sex Discrimination Act 1975 amendments for bringing provisions in that Act relating to its administration and enforcement into conformity with the corresponding provisions in this Act.   [22nd November 1976]

DISCRIMINATION TO WHICH ACT APPLIES

1.—(1) A person discriminates against another in any circumstances relevant for the purposes of any provision of this Act if— *(Racial discrimination.)*

    (a) on racial grounds he treats that other less favourably than he treats or would treat other persons ; or

    (b) he applies to that other a requirement or condition which he applies or would apply equally to persons not of the same racial group as that other but—

        (i) which is such that the proportion of persons of the same racial group as that other who can comply with it is considerably smaller than the proportion of persons not of that racial group who can comply with it ; and

        (ii) which he cannot show to be justifiable irrespective of the colour, race, nationality or ethnic or national origins of the person to whom it is applied ; and

        (iii) which is to the detriment of that other because he cannot comply with it.

(2) It is hereby declared that, for the purposes of this Act, segregating a person from other persons on racial grounds is treating him less favourably than they are treated.

(b) he applies to that person a requirement or condition which he applies or would apply equally to an unmarried person but—

> (i) which is such that the proportion of married persons who can comply with it is considerably smaller than the proportion of unmarried persons of the same sex who can comply with it, and

> (ii) which he cannot show to be justifiable irrespective of the marital status of the person to whom it is applied, and

> (iii) which is to that person's detriment because he cannot comply with it.

(2) For the purposes of subsection (1), a provision of Part II framed with reference to discrimination against women shall be treated as applying equally to the treatment of men, and for that purpose shall have effect with such modifications as are requisite.

Discrimination by way of victimisation. **4.**—(1) A person (" the discriminator ") discriminates against another person (" the person victimised ") in any circumstances relevant for the purposes of any provision of this Act if he treats the person victimised less favourably than in those circumstances he treats or would treat other persons, and does so by reason that the person victimised has—

(a) brought proceedings against the discriminator or any other person under this Act or the Equal Pay Act 1970, or

(b) given evidence or information in connection with proceedings brought by any person against the discriminator or any other person under this Act or the Equal Pay Act 1970, or

(c) otherwise done anything under or by reference to this Act or the Equal Pay Act 1970 in relation to the discriminator or any other person, or

(d) alleged that the discriminator or any other person has committed an act which (whether or not the allegation so states) would amount to a contravention of this Act or give rise to a claim under the Equal Pay Act 1970,

or by reason that the discriminator knows the person victimised intends to do any of those things, or suspects the person victimised has done, or intends to do, any of them.

(2) Subsection (1) does not apply to treatment of a person by reason of any allegation made by him if the allegation was false and not made in good faith.

2.—(1) A person (" the discriminator ") discriminates against another person (" the person victimised ") in any circumstances relevant for the purposes of any provision of this Act if he treats the person victimised less favourably than in those circumstances he treats or would treat other persons, and does so by reason that the person victimised has—

Discrimination by way of victimisation.

(a) brought proceedings against the discriminator or any other person under this Act ; or

(b) given evidence or information in connection with proceedings brought by any person against the discriminator or any other person under this Act ; or

(c) otherwise done anything under or by reference to this Act in relation to the discriminator or any other person ; or

(d) alleged that the discriminator or any other person has committed an act which (whether or not the allegation so states) would amount to a contravention of this Act,

or by reason that the discriminator knows that the person victimised intends to do any of those things, or suspects that the person victimised has done, or intends to do, any of them.

(2) Subsection (1) does not apply to treatment of a person by reason of any allegation made by him if the allegation was false and not made in good faith.

3.—(1) In this Act, unless the context otherwise requires—

Meaning of " racial grounds " " racial group," etc.

" racial grounds " means any of the following grounds, namely colour, race, nationality or ethnic or national origins ;

" racial group " means a group of persons defined by reference to colour, race, nationality or ethnic or national origins, and references to a person's racial group refer to any racial group into which he falls.

(2) The fact that a racial group comprises two or more distinct racial groups does not prevent it from constituting a particular racial group for the purposes of this Act.

DISCRIMINATION IN THE EMPLOYMENT FIELD
Discrimination by employers

Discrimination against applicants and employees.

6.—(1) It is unlawful for a person, in relation to employment by him at an establishment in Great Britain, to discriminate against a woman—

> (*a*) in the arrangements he makes for the purpose of determining who should be offered that employment, or
>
> (*b*) in the terms on which he offers her that employment, or
>
> (*c*) by refusing or deliberately omitting to offer her that employment.

(2) It is unlawful for a person, in the case of a woman employed by him at an establishment in Great Britain, to discriminate against her—

> (*a*) in the way he affords her access to opportunities for promotion, transfer or training, or to any other benefits, facilities or services, or by refusing or deliberately omitting to afford her access to them, or
>
> (*b*) by dismissing her, or subjecting her to any other detriment.

Discriminatory training by certain bodies.

47.—(1) Nothing in Parts II to IV shall render unlawful any act done in relation to particular work by a training body in, or in connection with—

> (*a*) affording women only, or men only, access to facilities for training which would help to fit them for that work, or
>
> (*b*) encouraging women only, or men only, to take advantage of opportunities for doing that work,

where it appears to the training body that at any time within the 12 months immediately preceding the doing of the act there were no persons of the sex in question doing that work in Great Britain, or the number of persons of that sex doing the work in Great Britain was comparatively small.

(2) Where in relation to particular work it appears to a training body that although the condition for the operation of subsection (1) is not met for the whole of Great Britain it is met for an area within Great Britain, nothing in Parts II to IV shall render unlawful any act done by the training body in, or in connection with—

> (*a*) affording persons who are of the sex in question, and who appear likely to take up that work in that area, access to facilities for training which would help to fit them for that work, or
>
> (*b*) encouraging persons of that sex to take advantage of opportunities in the area for doing that work.

[*Note*: This section was amended by the Sex Discrimination Act 1986. (See p. 67, note 4.)]

DISCRIMINATION IN THE EMPLOYMENT FIELD

Discrimination by employers

4.—(1) It is unlawful for a person, in relation to employment by him at an establishment in Great Britain, to discriminate against another—

    (*a*) in the arrangements he makes for the purpose of determining who should be offered that employment ; or

    (*b*) in the terms on which he offers him that employment ; or

    (*c*) by refusing or deliberately omitting to offer him that employment.

(2) It is unlawful for a person, in the case of a person employed by him at an establishment in Great Britain, to discriminate against that employee—

    (*a*) in the terms of employment which he affords him ; or

    (*b*) in the way he affords him access to opportunities for promotion, transfer or training, or to any other benefits, facilities or services, or by refusing or deliberately omitting to afford him access to them ; or

    (*c*) by dismissing him, or subjecting him to any other detriment.

Discrimination against applicants and employees.

37.—(1) Nothing in Parts II to IV shall render unlawful any act done in relation to particular work by a training body in or in connection with—

    (*a*) affording only persons of a particular racial group access to facilities for training which would help to fit them for that work ; or

    (*b*) encouraging only persons of a particular racial group to take advantage of opportunities for doing that work,

where it appears to the training body that at any time within the twelve months immediately preceding the doing of the act—

    (i) there were no persons of that group among those doing that work in Great Britain ; or

    (ii) the proportion of persons of that group among those doing that work in Great Britain was small in comparison with the proportion of persons of that group among the population of Great Britain.

(2) Where in relation to particular work it appears to a training body that although the condition for the operation of subsection (1) is not met for the whole of Great Britain it is met for an area within Great Britain, nothing in Parts II to IV shall render unlawful any act done by the training body in or in connection with—

    (*a*) affording persons who are of the racial group in question, and who appear likely to take up that work in that area, access to facilities for training which would help to fit them for that work ; or

    (*b*) encouraging persons of that group to take advantage of opportunities in the area for doing that work.

Discriminatory training by certain bodies.

(3) Nothing in Parts II to IV shall render unlawful any act done by a training body in, or in connection with, affording persons access to facilities for training which would help to fit them for employment, where it appears to the training body that those persons are in special need of training by reason of the period for which they have been discharging domestic or family responsibilities to the exclusion of regular full time employment.

The discrimination in relation to which this subsection applies may result from confining the training to persons who have been discharging domestic or family responsibilities, or from the way persons are selected for training, or both.

Other discriminatory training etc.

48.—(1) Nothing in Parts II to IV shall render unlawful any act done by an employer in relation to particular work in his employment, being an act done in, or in connection with,—

    (a) affording his female employees only, or his male employees only, access to facilities for training which would help to fit them for that work, or

    (b) encouraging women only, or men only, to take advantage of opportunities for doing that work,

where at any time within the twelve months immediately preceding the doing of the act there were no persons of the sex in question among those doing that work or the number of persons of that sex doing the work was comparatively small.

38.—(1) Nothing in Parts II to IV shall render unlawful any act done by an employer in relation to particular work in his employment at a particular establishment in Great Britain, being an act done in or in connection with—

Other discriminatory training etc.

(a) affording only those of his employees working at that establishment who are of a particular racial group access to facilities for training which would help to fit them for that work ; or

(b) encouraging only persons of a particular racial group to take advantage of opportunities for doing that work at that establishment,

where any of the conditions in subsection (2) was satisfied at any time within the twelve months immediately preceding the doing of the act.

(2) Those conditions are—

(a) that there are no persons of the racial group in question among those doing that work at that establishment ; or

(b) that the proportion of persons of that group among those doing that work at that establishment is small in comparison with the proportion of persons of that group—

(i) among all those employed by that employer there ; or

(ii) among the population of the area from which that employer normally recruits persons for work in his employment at that establishment.

**Acts done
under statutory
authority.**

51.—(1) Nothing in Parts II to IV shall render unlawful any act done by a person if it was necessary for him to do it in order to comply with a requirement—

    (a) of an Act passed before this Act ; or

    (b) of an instrument made or approved (whether before or after the passing of this Act) by or under an Act passed before this Act.

(2) Where an Act passed after this Act re-enacts (with or without modification) a provision of an Act passed before this Act, subsection (1) shall apply to that provision as re-enacted as if it continued to be contained in an Act passed before this Act.

EQUAL OPPORTUNITIES
COMMISSION

**Establishment
and duties of
Commission.**

53.—(1) There shall be a body of Commissioners named the Equal Opportunities Commission, consisting of at least eight but not more than fifteen individuals each appointed by the Secretary of State on a full-time or part-time basis, which shall have the following duties—

    (a) to work towards the elimination of discrimination,

    (b) to promote equality of opportunity between men and women generally, and

    (c) to keep under review the working of this Act and the Equal Pay Act 1970 and, when they are so required by the Secretary of State or otherwise think it necessary, draw up and submit to the Secretary of State proposals for amending them.

41.—(1) Nothing in Parts II to IV shall render unlawful any act of discrimination done—

Acts done under statutory authority etc.

    (*a*) in pursuance of any enactment or Order in Council ; or

    (*b*) in pursuance of any instrument made under any enactment by a Minister of the Crown ; or

    (*c*) in order to comply with any condition or requirement imposed by a Minister of the Crown (whether before or after the passing of this Act) by virtue of any enactment.

References in this subsection to an enactment, Order in Council or instrument include an enactment, Order in Council or instrument passed or made after the passing of this Act.

(2) Nothing in Parts II to IV shall render unlawful any act whereby a person discriminates against another on the basis of that other's nationality or place of ordinary residence or the length of time for which he has been present or resident in or outside the United Kingdom or an area within the United Kingdom, if that act is done—

    (*a*) in pursuance of any arrangements made (whether before or after the passing of this Act) by or with the approval of, or for the time being approved by, a Minister of the Crown ; or

    (*b*) in order to comply with any condition imposed (whether before or after the passing of this Act) by a Minister of the Crown.

The Commission for Racial Equality

General

43.—(1) There shall be a body of Commissioners named the Commission for Racial Equality consisting of at least eight but not more than fifteen individuals each appointed by the Secretary of State on a full-time or part-time basis, which shall have the following duties—

Establishment and duties of Commission.

    (*a*) to work towards the elimination of discrimination ;

    (*b*) to promote equality of opportunity, and good relations, between persons of different racial groups generally ; and

    (*c*) to keep under review the working of this Act and, when they are so required by the Secretary of State or otherwise think it necessary, draw up and submit to the Secretary of State proposals for amending it.

47.—*Codes of Practice*
    [*see page 196 below*]

Investigations

Power to conduct formal investigations.

57.—(1) Without prejudice to their general power to do anything requisite for the performance of their duties under section 53(1), the Commission may if they think fit, and shall if required by the Secretary of State, conduct a formal investigation for any purpose connected with the carrying out of those duties.

Assistance by Commission.

75.—(1) Where, in relation to proceedings or prospective proceedings either under this Act or in respect of an equality clause, an individual who is an actual or prospective complainant or claimant applies to the Commission for assistance under this section, the Commission shall consider the application and may grant it if they think fit to do so on the ground that—

    (a) the case raises a question of principle, or

    (b) it is unreasonable, having regard to the complexity of the case or the applicant's position in relation to the respondent or another person involved or any other matter, to expect the applicant to deal with the case unaided,

or by reason of any other special consideration.

(2) Assistance by the Commission under this section may include—

    (a) giving advice ;

    (b) procuring or attempting to procure the settlement of any matter in dispute ;

    (c) arranging for the giving of advice or assistance by a solicitor or counsel ;

    (d) arranging for representation by any person including all such assistance as is usually given by a solicitor or counsel in the steps preliminary or incidental to any proceedings, or in arriving at or giving effect to a compromise to avoid or bring to an end any proceedings,

    (e) any other form of assistance which the Commission may consider appropriate,

Investigations

48.—(1) Without prejudice to their general power to do anything requisite for the performance of their duties under section 43(1), the Commission may if they think fit, and shall if required by the Secretary of State, conduct a formal investigation for any purpose connected with the carrying out of those duties.

Power to conduct formal investigations.

66.—(1) Where, in relation to proceedings or prospective proceedings under this Act, an individual who is an actual or prospective complainant or claimant applies to the Commission for assistance under this section, the Commission shall consider the application and may grant it if they think fit to do so—

Assistance by Commission.

    (*a*) on the ground that the case raises a question of principle ; or

    (*b*) on the ground that it is unreasonable, having regard to the complexity of the case, or to the applicant's position in relation to the respondent or another person involved, or to any other matter, to expect the applicant to deal with the case unaided ; or

    (*c*) by reason of any other special consideration.

(2) Assistance by the Commission under this section may include—

    (*a*) giving advice ;

    (*b*) procuring or attempting to procure the settlement of any matter in dispute ;

    (*c*) arranging for the giving of advice or assistance by a solicitor or counsel ;

    (*d*) arranging for representation by any person, including all such assistance as is usually given by a solicitor or counsel in the steps preliminary or incidental to any proceedings, or in arriving at or giving effect to a compromise to avoid or bring to an end any proceedings ;

    (*e*) any other form of assistance which the Commission may consider appropriate,

SUPPLEMENTAL

71. Without prejudice to their obligation to comply with any other provision of this Act, it shall be the duty of every local authority to make appropriate arrangements with a view to securing that their various functions are carried out with due regard to the need—

Local authorities: general statutory duty.

    (*a*) to eliminate unlawful racial discrimination ; and

    (*b*) to promote equality of opportunity, and good relations, between persons of different racial groups.

Codes of practice

47.—(1) The Commission may issue codes of practice containing such practical guidance as the Commission think fit for either or both of the following purposes, namely—

   (*a*) the elimination of discrimination in the field of employment;

   (*b*) the promotion of equality of opportunity in that field between persons of different racial groups.

(2) When the Commission propose to issue a code of practice, they shall prepare and publish a draft of that code, shall consider any representations made to them about the draft and may modify the draft accordingly.

(3) In the course of preparing any draft code of practice for eventual publication under subsection (2) the Commission shall consult with—

   (*a*) such organisations or associations of organisations representative of employers or of workers; and

   (*b*) such other organisations, or bodies,

as appear to the Commission to be appropriate.

(4) If the Commission determine to proceed with the draft, they shall transmit the draft to the Secretary of State who shall—

   (*a*) if he approves of it, lay it before both Houses of Parliament; and

   (*b*) if he does not approve of it, publish details of his reasons for withholding approval.

(5) If, within the period of forty days beginning with the day on which a copy of a draft code of practice is laid before each House of Parliament, or, if such copies are laid on different days, with the later of the two days, either House so resolves, no further proceedings shall be taken thereon, but without prejudice to the laying before Parliament of a new draft.

(6) In reckoning the period of forty days referred to in subsection (5), no account shall be taken of any period during which Parliament is dissolved or prorogued or during which both Houses are adjourned for more than four days.

(7) If no such resolution is passed as is referred to in subsection (5), the Commission shall issue the code in the form of the draft and the code shall come into effect on such day as the Secretary of State may by order appoint.

(8) Without prejudice to section 74(3), an order under subsection (7) may contain such transitional provisions or savings as appear to the Secretary of State to be necessary or expedient in connection with the code of practice thereby brought into operation.

(9) The Commission may from time to time revise the whole or any part of a code of practice issued under this section and issue that revised code, and subsections (2) to (8) shall apply (with appropriate modifications) to such a revised code as they apply to the first issue of a code.

(10) A failure on the part of any person to observe any provision of a code of practice shall not of itself render him liable to any proceedings; but in any proceedings under this Act before an industrial tribunal any code of practice issued under this section shall be admissible in evidence, and if any provision of such a code appears to the tribunal to be relevant to any question arising in the proceedings it shall be taken into account in determining that question.

(11) Without prejudice to subsection (1), a code of practice issued under this section may include such practical guidance as the Commission think fit as to what steps it is reasonably practicable for employers to take for the purpose of preventing their employees from doing in the course of their employment acts made unlawful by this Act.

Appendix 5
Amending the equality laws: summaries of the Commission's proposals

A. The Commission for Racial Equality: Review of the Race Relations Act 1976: Proposals for Change

Discrimination and the Scope of the Act

1. (i)   Either by direct statement or by use of illustration as to what is meant by 'on racial grounds', the Act (without the need for reference to case-law) should make the position clear that *direct discrimination* does not necessarily involve a racial motive.

(ii)   A new definition of *indirect discrimination* is required making unlawful any practice, policy or situation which is continued, allowed, or introduced and which has a *significant adverse impact* on a particular racial group and which cannot be *demonstrated to be necessary*.

(iii)   The legislation should exemplify the meaning of *significant adverse impact*, for example by an illustration in which a 20 percent difference in impact between racial groups is treated as significant.

(iv)   The legislation should exemplify the test of what is *necessary* with illustrative formulations for each of the various fields in which the Act applies. For example, in a matter involving employment it will need to be shown that what is having the adverse impact is necessary to ensure that the functions of the job are carried out safely and competently and that the same end cannot be achieved in a less discriminatory manner.

2. Protection against victimisation for invoking the Act is at present incomplete. The remedy for victimisation should be redefined so that there is protection against a person's suffering any detriment whatever as a result of his or her doing any of the acts listed in section 2 1(a)-(d) (involvement in allegations, proceedings, etc. under the Act).

3. At present the Act covers discrimination on the grounds of colour, race, nationality or ethnic or national origins. The question whether religious discrimination should be made unlawful and, if so, in what circumstances needs to be considered but in a wider context than that of an amendment to the Race Relations Act.

Exemptions from the Act

4. At present a wide range of actions, governmental in nature, are outside the ambit of the Act. The definition relating to the provision of 'goods, facilities and services' in the Act should make it clear that it extends to all areas of governmental and regulatory activity whether central or local such as acts in the course of immigration control, the prison and police services, and planning control.

5. The Race Relations Act is by its own terms subordinated to a wide range of rules existing or future with which it conflicts. The basic legislation making discrimination unlawful should be superior to earlier Acts and all subordinate legislation or other forms of rule-making. Where Government requires as a matter of policy that discrimination should be permitted on grounds of birth, nationality, descent or residence, this should be provided for expressly by statute.

6. Work experience trainees are not regarded as 'employed' and therefore not covered by the main provisions of the Act. They should be brought directly within the protection of the Act as though they were employees and not continue to rely on the more limited and little known protection given by designation under section 13.

7. The present exemption for seamen recruited abroad in section 9 of the Act should be repealed by use of the special power provided for that purpose in section 73 of the Act. Section 8 of the Act should be amended so that the Act applies to employment onboard a ship registered at a port of registry in Great Britain wherever the work takes place and not as at present if the work is wholly outside Great Britain. Corresponding provision should be made for employment on aircraft and hovercraft.

Proving Discrimination and Adjudication

8. The burden of proof in direct discrimination cases should build on the established case-law and be set out in the statute. The person against whom discrimination is alleged, in circumstances consistent with less favourable treatment on racial grounds, should be required to establish non-racial grounds for that treatment since he or she is the person best able to show the grounds for his or her own actions.

9. Where a respondent deliberately and without reasonable excuse either omits to reply, or gives an evasive or equivocal reply, to a questionnaire pursuant to section 65 of the Act, there should be a duty, rather than a discretion on the part of the tribunal of fact to draw the inference that it considers just.

10. A discrimination division within the industrial tribunal system should be established to hear both employment and non-employment race and sex discrimination cases. The County Court jurisdiction for non-employment cases should go. The discrimination division should be able to call upon the services of High Court Judges for more complex cases and should have full remedial powers. Personnel of the division should be available to hear other types of industrial tribunal cases when not sitting in the division.

11. In accordance with the recommendations of the Royal Commissions on Legal Services, legal aid should be extended to cover racial discrimination cases in tribunals.

Formal Investigations and Law Enforcement

12. Subsection 49(4) of the Act should be repealed. This would mean that the effect of the *Prestige* case would be reversed and the Commission's powers 'to conduct a formal investigation for any purpose connected with the carrying out of' its duties (s.48) would thereby be clearly established.

13. The Commission's non-discrimination notices issued as a consequence of formal investigations, are subject to appeal. In their place, the Commission should have the power to take evidence of discrimination directly to an independent tribunal of fact seeking a finding that discrimination has occurred and appropriate remedies. This access to the tribunal should not be conditional upon a formal investigation having taken place, though in practice this would often be the case.

14. A non-discrimination notice is a remedy in the hands of the Commission but such a notice cannot prescribe particular changes in practice. If the remedy was instead placed in the hands of an independent tribunal, the tribunal should be able to order particular changes in practice.

Remedies

15. (i) The remedy referred to in Proposal 14 should be a remedy generally available to the independent tribunal of fact to deal with potential future discrimination. The tribunal of fact should be under a duty to consider whether such a remedy is appropriate in any case where discrimination is proved.

(ii) The Commission should have the power to join in any proceedings in which discrimination is alleged to draw the attention of the tribunal of fact to the potential for future discrimination in the situation.

(iii) In any case brought by the Commission — see Proposal 13 — the tribunal of fact should have the power to award compensation to any person it finds to have suffered unlawful discrimination either named or otherwise sufficiently identified provided that any such person joins the proceedings within a specified time and seeks the compensation.

16. Non-monetary remedies. In addition to the remedies now available a full range of mandatory orders should be available to the tribunal of fact.

(i) A preventive remedy should be available where a person has stated a directly discriminatory intention to avoid that intention being put into practice.

(ii) The tribunal of fact should have the power, in appropriate cases where discrimination is proved, to order those positive action measures such as special training or encouragement of members of particular racial groups which are at present permitted as voluntary measures in the circumstances set out in the Act.

(iii) The remedy referred to in Proposals 14 and 15(i) should apply also to the whole area of education. Instead of Secretary of State having powers under section 19(2) and (3) of the Act, the tribunal of fact should have the power to order changes in practice to deal with potential future discrimination.

(iv) In employment cases interim relief should be available to preserve a complainant's position pending a hearing provided that the relief is sought promptly and the remedy appears appropriate to the tribunal of fact.

(v)   In employment cases it should be possible for the tribunal of fact to order appointment, promotion, reinstatement or re-engagement where it appears appropriate to do so.

17. Monetary remedies. The provision of compensation should be improved as follows:

(a)   There should be a prescribed norm figure by way of compensation for injury to feelings.

(b)   Compensation should be payable where indirect discrimination is proved and the present exception in s.57(3) removed.

(c)   The tribunal of fact should be able to award continuing payments of compensation until a stipulated event such as promotion or engagement occurs.

(d)   The statutory limit to compensation in employment cases set out in section 56(2) of the Act should be removed.

18. The special defence provided under section 32(3) of the Act should be removed. It covers the case where an employer can show that he or she took 'such steps as were reasonably practicable to prevent the employee from doing that act, or from doing in the course of his employment acts of that description'.

Mechanisms for Bringing about Change

19. The Commission's code-making power under section 47 should not be restricted to the field of employment, but should be extended to include other areas.

20. The Secretary of State should be given powers to prescribe ethnic record-keeping of (i) employees in different grades and applicants for employment and (ii) recipients of housing or other service provision by public bodies. The orders prescribing the keeping of records should be capable of limitation by (i) area of the country (ii) types of activity (iii) duration of the record-keeping. There should be a power in the Commission to require returns to be made where record-keeping has been prescribed. Safeguards against abuse of the information should be enacted.

21. Where there is agreement between the Commission and a body on specific practices to be adopted, the Commission should have the power to accept legally-binding and enforceable undertakings by that body to adopt those practices. The undertakings should be recorded in a public register.

22. (i)   The general statutory duty imposed on local authorities by section 71 of the Act should be amended to conform to those imposed on the Commission by section 43(1)(a) and (b) with regard to each of the various functions of the authorities. Those duties are 'to work towards the elimination of discrimination and to promote equality of opportunity and good relations between persons of different racial groups generally'.

(ii)   This duty should be extended to all bodies carrying on a service or undertaking of a public nature (for a definition see section 75(5) of the Act).

(iii)   Public bodies as above should be required by law to publish, in their annual reports or separately, annual programmes and reports to enable the public to evaluate their work in the field of race.

23. (i)   An employer should be permitted to give special training to persons of particular racial groups, whether or not they are his or her employees, where there is under-representation in the work-force as defined in section 38; and section 38 should be widened accordingly so that the training aspect of the provision covers non-employees. An employer would then not need to rely upon designation under section 37. Training schemes for young people such as apprenticeships should be explicitly covered by such a provision.

(ii)   An employer should be entitled where there is under-representation of a particular racial group in the work-force (as defined in section 38) to carry out a policy of preferring a member of that group for employment in the narrowly confined situation where competing applicants for employment are equally well qualified to carry out the job in question.

B.   The Equal Opportunities Commission: Legislating for Change? — Review of the Sex Discrimination Legislation: a Consultative Document

The Commission would particularly welcome comments on its four main proposals:

1. Consolidation

The basis of sex discrimination law is found in two Acts of Parliament, the Sex Discrimination Act 1975 and the Equal Pay Act 1970 (as amended). It has also been much affected by European law based on the EEC Treaty and Council Directives. The Commission proposes that the existing statutes be repealed and re-enacted in a single consolidating statute for easier reference and consistent procedures and that this statute should incorporate the requirements of European law.

2. Remedies

Compensation awards for sex discrimination are currently very low, failing to reflect the seriousness of discrimination for the individual. Many complainants consider the awards are even derisory. It is, therefore, proposed that there should be a statutory minimum award of compensation, possibly specified in the SDA rather than in other legislation. The Commission proposes in relation to formal investigations, while recognising that the investigatee must have an opportunity to state his/her case within the investigation, the repeal of the right to make pre-investigation representations and representations against a Non-Discrimination Notice. The right of appeal against a Notice would remain. The Commission also proposes that there should be a power under a non-discrimination notice to order changes to practice or procedure and that the Commission should have greater powers to bring discriminators before the Courts.

Amendments are also proposed in relation to tribunal and county court jurisdictions, levels of awards of compensation and the procedure for enforcing awards.

3. Positive action

The Commission proposes that the existing law about single sex training be extended to include the training of apprentices. It adheres to the general principles that all recruitment must be non-discriminatory but recognises that this may prevent action which a responsible employer may wish to take. It will welcome comments for and against any extensions of the Acts and provisions in this field of employment and also as to whether changes are required to provide for special activities for women which are intended to raise their self-confidence or enable them to gain experience in traditionally male dominated fields.

4. *Pregnancy*

The Commission regards this issue as being of major importance for equality of opportunity for women in employment. Under current legislation a pregnant woman is protected from unfair dismissal and given the right to return to work under the Employment Protection (Consolidation) Act if she has at least two years' continuous employment with the same employer. Under the SDA, the situation is less clear in that it has been argued that a pregnant woman has no male comparator and cannot, therefore, claim that she is treated differently from a man in the same circumstances. More recent case law has accepted that an appropriate comparison is with a sick man, but this can be misleading because pregnancy is not a sickness and many pregnant women remain in good health.

The Commission proposes that the Employment Protection (Consolidation) Act should provide protection against dismissal on the grounds of pregnancy, irrespective of length of service. The Commission also seeks views as to whether the SDA should make it explicit that it is unlawful to discriminate against a woman because she is pregnant.

Other issues

In addition to the issues on which the Commission is particularly seeking comment, changes are proposed to many other aspects of the legislation. These include:

- redefinition of indirect discrimination;
- extending the law to cover private members clubs which have members of both sexes;
- the repeal of an exemption relating to the use of actuarial data in insurance;
- the amendment or repeal of some of the genuine occupational qualifications recognised under the Act;
- an amendment to allow boys and girls of primary school age to compete with each other in sporting events;
- imposing a duty on all public bodies to work towards eliminating discrimination and to promote equality of opportunity generally.

The Commission intends to make firm proposals after consolidating comments on the consultative document.

List of cases

References

Official publications

Advisory, Conciliation and Arbitration Service (1979) *Conciliation in Complaints by Individuals to Industrial Tribunals: the ACAS Role*. London: ACAS.

Central Advisory Council for Education (1967) *Children and their Primary Schools* (Plowden Report). London: HMSO.

Central Arbitration Committee (1983) *1982 Annual Report*. London: CAC.

Department of Employment, *Employment Gazette* (published monthly).

Department of Employment (1986) *New Earnings Survey*. London: HMSO.

Home Affairs Committee (1981) *Report on the Commission for Racial Equality*. Session 1981–2, Vols I and II, House of Commons 46. London: HMSO.

Department of the Environment (1985) *Competition in the Provision of Local Authority Services* (green paper). London: HMSO.

Home Office (1975) *Sex Discrimination: A Guide to the Sex Discrimination Act 1975*.

Home Office (1977) *Racial Discrimination: A Guide to the Race Relations Act 1976*.

Joint Review Group on Employment Opportunities for Women in the Civil Service (1982) *Equal Opportunities for Women in the Civil Service*. London: HMSO.

Office of Population Census and Surveys (1985) *General Household Survey 1983*. London: HMSO.

Parliamentary Debates (Hansard) *House of Commons*. London: HMSO.

Parliamentary Debates (Hansard) *House of Lords*. London: HMSO.

Royal Commission on Equal Pay 1944–6. (1946) Report. Cmd 6937, London: HMSO.

White papers

Equality for Women (1974) Cmnd 5724, London: HMSO.

Racial Discrimination (1975) Cmnd 6234, London: HMSO.

Lifting the Burden (1981) Cmnd 9571, London: HMSO.

Building Businesses . . . not Barriers (1986) Cmnd 9794, London: HMSO.

Commission for Racial Equality publications

CRE *Annual Reports*, 1977–85 inclusive.

CRE (July 1983) *Code of Practice: for the Elimination of Racial Discrimination and the Promotion of Equality of Opportunity in Employment*.

CRE (July 1983) *The Race Relations Act 1976 — Time for a Change?*

CRE (January 1984) *Hackney Housing Investigated*.

CRE (June 1984) *A Study of Employment in the Metropolitan Borough of Kirklees*.

CRE (June 1984) *St Chad's Hospital, Birmingham: Report of a Formal Investigation*.

CRE (February 1985) *Immigration Control Procedures: Report of a Formal Investigation*.

CRE (June 1985) *Positive Action and Equal Opportunities in Employment*.

CRE (July 1985) *From Words to Action: Progress on the Code of Practice*.

CRE (July 1985) *Review of the Race Relations Act 1976: Proposals for Change.*
CRE (November 1985) *The National Bus Company.*

Equal Opportunities Commission publications

EOC *Annual Reports*, 1976–85 inclusive.
EOC (August 1977) *Guidance on Advertising Practice* (1st edn).
EOC (December 1977) *Formal Investigation Report: Tameside.*
EOC (October 1978) *Equality between the Sexes in Industry.*
EOC (March 1979) *Health and Safety Legislation: Should we Distinguish between Men and Women?*
EOC (December 1980) *Formal Investigation Report: Electrolux.*
EOC (January 1981) *Proposed Amendments to the Sex Discrimination Act 1975 and the Equal Pay Act 1970.*
EOC (November 1981) *Formal Investigation Report: British Steel Corporation.*
EOC (July 1983) *Formal Investigation Report: Sidney Stringer School and Community College, Coventry.*
EOC (October 1984) *Formal Investigation Report: Ebbw Vale College of Further Education.*
EOC (February 1985) *Formal Investigation Report: Leeds Permanent Building Society.*
EOC (March 1985) *Code of Practice: for the Elimination of Discrimination on the Grounds of Sex and Marriage and the Promotion of Equality of Opportunity in Employment.*
EOC (May 1985) *Submission to the Department of Employment on the Amended Proposals for a Directive on Parental Leave and Leave for Family Reasons.*
EOC (July 1986) *Women and Men in Britain: a Statistical Profile.* London: HMSO.
EOC (October 1986) *Legislating for Change? Review of the Sex Discrimination Legislation, a Consultative Document.*

Equal Opportunities Commission, Northern Ireland publications

EOC Northern Ireland (June 1982) *Equal Pay Act (NI) 1970 — Proposals for Amendment.*
EOC Northern Ireland (March 1983) *Sex Discrimination Act (NI) Order 1976 — Proposals for Amendment.*

Books and articles

Ades, R. and Stephens, E. (1977) 'Mice in Manchester', *Spare Rib*, July: 10–13.
Alexander, S. (1976) 'Women's Work in Nineteenth Century London', pp. 59–111 in J. Mitchell and A. Oakley (eds), *The Rights and Wrongs of Women.* Harmondsworth: Penguin.
Applebey, G. and Ellis, E. (1984) 'Formal Investigations: The CRE and the EOC as Law Enforcement Agencies', *Public Law*, Summer: 236–76.
Ashdown-Sharp, P. (1977) 'Women's Rights: the Missed Opportunity', *Sunday Times*, 20 February.
Banking, Insurance and Finance Union (1984) *Jobs for the Girls? The Impact of Automation in Women's Jobs in the Finance Industry.* London: BIFU.
Barker, A. (1982a) 'Governmental Bodies and the Networks of Mutual Accountability', pp. 3–33 in A. Barker (ed.), *Quangos in Britain.* Basingstoke: Macmillan.
Barker, A. (1982b) 'Quango: A Word and a Campaign', pp. 219–31 in A. Barker (ed.), *Quangos in Britain.* Basingstoke: Macmillan.

Barrett, M. and McIntosh, M. (1980) 'The Family Wage: Some Problems for Socialists and Feminists', *Capital and Class*, 11: 51–72.

Becker, H.S. (1967) 'Whose Side Are We On?', *Social Problems*, 14: 239–47.

Bindman, G. (1976) 'The Law and Racial Discrimination: Third Thoughts', *British Journal of Law and Society*, 3(1): 110–14.

Bindman, G. (1985) 'Reforming the Race Relations Act', *New Law Journal*, 135: 1136–8, 1167–9.

Blackstone, I.W. (1765–9) *Commentaries on the Laws of England*. Oxford: Clarendon.

Blumrosen, A.W. (1977) 'Toward Effective Administration of New Regulatory Statutes — Part 2', *Administrative Law Review*, Spring: 209–37.

Brophy, J. (1984) 'The Backlash in Family Law: The Matrimonial and Family Proceedings Bill', *Critical Social Policy*, 10: 114–20.

Brown, C. (1984) *Black and White Britain: the Third PSI Survey*. London: Heinemann.

Brown, C. and Gay, P. (1985) *Racial Discrimination: 17 Years after the Act*. London: Policy Studies Institute.

Browne-Wilkinson, The Hon Mr Justice (1982) 'The Role of the Employment Appeal Tribunal in the 1980s', *Industrial Law Journal*, 11: 69–77.

Byrne, D. (1982) 'A Critical Assessment of the ACAS Role in Individual Conciliation', MSc dissertation, London School of Economics and Political Science, University of London.

Byrne, P. and Lovenduski, J. (1978) 'The Equal Opportunities Commission', *Women's Studies International Quarterly*, 1(2): 131–47.

Cameron, S. (1977) 'A "Creature of Government" ', *Financial Times*, 19 September.

Cawson, A. (1982) *Corporation and Welfare*. London: Heinemann.

Cockburn, C. (1977) *The Local State*. London: Pluto.

Community Development Project (1977) *Gilding the Ghetto*. London: CDP Inter-Project Editorial Team.

Conroy, D. (1971) 'Do Applicants Need Advice or Representation?', pp. 2–11 in *The Future of Administrative Tribunals*. Birmingham: Institute of Judicial Administration, University of Birmingham.

Coote, A. (1978) 'Equality and the Curse of the Quango', *New Statesman*, 1 December: 734–7.

Coote, A. and Campbell, B. (1982) *Sweet Freedom: The Struggle for Women's Liberation*. London: Picador.

Coote, A. and Phillips, M. (1979) 'The Quango as Referee', *New Statesman*, 13 July: 50–53.

Corcoran, J. and Donnelly, E. (1984) *Report of a Comparative Analysis of the Provision for Legal Redress in Member States of the European Community*. Luxembourg: Commission of the European Communities.

Corrigan, P. (1977) 'The Welfare State as an Arena for Class Struggle', *Marxism Today*, March: 87–93.

Coussins, J. (1976) *The Equality Report*. London: National Council for Civil Liberties.

Dam, K.W. (1975) 'Class Actions: Efficiency, Compensation, Deterrence and Conflict of Interest', *Journal of Legal Studies*, 4: 47–73.

Davies, A. (1982) 'Patronage and Quasi-government: Some Proposals for Reform', pp. 167–80 in A. Barker (ed.), *Quangos in Britain*. Basingstoke: Macmillan.

DeCrow, K. (1974) *Sexist Justice*. New York: Random House.

Denning, Lord (1980) *Misuse of Power (The Richard Dimbleby Lecture)*. London: British Broadcasting Corporation.

de Smith, S.A. (1974) *Constitutional and Administrative Law*. Harmondsworth: Penguin.

Dickens, L. (1983) 'Tribunals in the Firing Line', *Employee Relations*, 5(1): 27–31.

Dickens, L. (1985) 'Industrial Tribunals — The People's Courts?', *Employee Relations*, 7(1): 27–32.

Dickens, L., Hart, M., Jones, M. and Weekes, B. (1981) 'Re-employment of Unfairly Dismissed Workers: The Lost Remedy', *Industrial Law Journal*, 10(3): 160–75.

Dickens, L., Jones, M., Weekes, B. and Hart, M. (1985) *Dismissed: A Study of Unfair Dismissal and the Industrial Tribunal System*. Oxford: Blackwell.

Draper, H. and Lipow, A.G. (1976) 'Marxist Women versus Bourgeois Feminism', pp. 179–226 in R. Miliband and J. Saville (eds.), *The Socialist Register*. London: Merlin Press.

Dworkin, R. (1977) *Taking Rights Seriously*. London: Duckworth.

Eastwood, M. (1971) 'The Double Standard of Justice: Women's Rights under the Constitution', *Valparaiso University Law Review*, 5(2): 281–317.

Frankel, L.J. (1973) 'Sex Discrimination in the Criminal Law: the Effect of the Equal Rights Amendment', *American Criminal Law Review*, 11(2): 469–510.

Friedan, B. (1977) *It Changed my Life*. New York: Dell.

General, Municipal, Boilermakers and Allied Trades Union (1986) *Fair Laws and Rights in Employment Campaign (FLARE)*. London: GMBATU.

Gifford, T. (1986) *Where's the Justice?* Harmondsworth: Penguin.

Gordon, P. (1983) *White Law: Racism in the Police, Courts and Prisons*. London: Pluto.

Graham, C. and Lewis, N. (1985) *The Role of ACAS Conciliation in Equal Pay and Sex Discrimination Cases*. Manchester: Equal Opportunities Commission.

Greater London Council (1985) *Equality Moves Forward: GLC Equal Opportunities Second Annual Monitoring Report*. London: GLC.

Gregory, J. (1982) 'Equal Pay and Sex Discrimination: Why Women are Giving Up the Fight', *Feminist Review*, (10): 75–89.

Gregory, J. (1984) 'Discrimination, Employment and the Law', PhD dissertation, London School of Economics and Political Science, University of London.

Gregory, J. (1986) 'Conciliating Individual Employment Disputes: A Shabby Compromise?', *Employee Relations*, 8(1): 27–31.

Gregory, J. and Stoddart, J. (1987) 'Equal Pay: Out of the Ghetto?' *International Labour Report*, 23.

Griffith, J.A.G. (1977) *The Politics of the Judiciary*. London: Fontana.

Habermas, J. (1976) *Legitimation Crisis*. London: Heinemann.

Halsaa, B. (1986) 'Socialist-Feminists in Norway', paper presented to the Socialist-Feminist conference in Hamburg, November.

Harvard Civil Rights — Civil Liberties Law Review, (1971) 'Equal Rights for Women: a Symposium on the Proposed Constitutional Amendment', 6(2): 215–87.

Hepple, B.A. (1983) 'Judging Equal Rights', *Current Legal Problems*, 36: 71–90.

Hill, H. (1977) 'The Equal Employment Opportunity Acts of 1964 and 1972', *Industrial Relations Law Journal*, 2(1): 1–96.

Hitner, T., Knights, D., Green, E. and Torrington, D. (1982) *Racial Minority Employment: Equal Opportunities Policy and Practice*. Research Paper No 35. London: Department of Employment.

Hoskyns, C. (1985) 'Women's Equality and the European Community', *Feminist Review*, 20: 71–88.

Hoskyns, C. (1986) 'Women, European Law and Transnational Politics', *International Journal of the Sociology of Law*, 14: 299–315.

Hutton, J. (1984) 'How the SDA has Failed', *Legal Action*, April: 10–11.
Jackson, C. (1984) 'Policies and Implementation of Anti-discrimination Strategies', pp. 191–201 in G. Schmid and R. Weitzel (eds), *Sex Discrimination and Equal Opportunity*. Aldershot: Gower.
Jowell, J. (1975) *Law and Bureaucracy*. New York: Dunellen.
Kingman, M. (1978) 'The Equal Pay Act: A Study of the Experiences of Women who have Made Applications to Industrial Tribunals for Equal Pay', MA dissertation, Warwick: University of Warwick.
Knights, D. and Hitner, T. (1982) 'Race Relations in Industry: Problems and Prospects for Equal Opportunity', *Employee Relations*, 4(5): 12–16.
Krause, K. (1974) 'Denial of Work Release Programs to Women: A Violation of Equal Protection', *Southern Californian Law Review*, 47(4): 1453–90.
Kumar, V. (1986) *Industrial Tribunal Applicants under the Race Relations Act 1976*. London: Commission for Racial Equality.
Labour Party (1986) *Labour's Ministry for Women: Statement by the National Executive Committee*. London: The Labour Party.
Labour Research (1983) 'Race at Work', July: 182–3.
Labour Research (1986) 'Women in Unions — A Long Way to Go', April: 13–15.
Labour Research (1986) 'How Well are Councils tackling Jobs Race Bias?', May: 11–14.
Labour Research Department (1985) *Black Workers, Trade Unions and the Law*. London: LRD Publications.
Labour Research Department (1986) *Women's Pay: Claiming Equal Value*. London: LRD Publications.
Lancashire Association of Trades Councils (1985) *Trade Union Structure and Black Workers' Participation*. London: Commission for Racial Equality.
Land, H. and Ward, S. (1986) *Women Won't Benefit*. London: National Council for Civil Liberties.
Law Reform Commission of Canada (1985) *Independent Administrative Agencies*. Ottawa: LRC, Canada.
Lea, J. (1980) 'The Contradictions of the Sixties Race Relations Legislation', pp. 122–48 in National Deviancy Conference (eds), *Permissiveness and Control*. Basingstoke: Macmillan.
Legum, M. (1977) 'Race Relations: Another Expensive Blueprint for Failure?', *The Times*, 17 August.
Leonard, A.M. (1987a) *Judging Inequality: The Effectiveness of the Tribunal System in Sex Discrimination and Equal Pay Cases*. London: Cobden Trust.
Leonard, A.M. (1987b) *Pyrrhic Victories: Winning Sex Discrimination and Equal Pay Cases in the Industrial Tribunals, 1980–84*. London: HMSO.
Lester, A. and Bindman, G. (1972) *Race and Law*. Harmondsworth: Penguin.
Lewis, P. (1982) 'The Role of ACAS Conciliators in Unfair Dismissal Cases', *Industrial Relations Journal*, 13(3): 50–6.
London Association of Community Relations Councils (1985) *In a Critical Condition: a Survey of Equal Opportunities in London's Health Authorities*. London: LACRC.
Lonsdale, S. and Walker, A. (1984) *A Right to Work: Disability and Employment*. London: Disability Alliance and Low Pay Unit.
Lustgarten, L. (1980) *Legal Control of Racial Discrimination*. London: Macmillan.
Lustgarten, L. (1986) 'Racial Inequality and the Limits of the Law', *Modern Law Review*, 49: 68–85.
Maclennan, E. (1984) 'Why are Women Low Paid?', *Low Pay Review*, 21: 3–11.

Martin, J. and Roberts, C. (1984) *Women and Employment, a Lifetime Perspective*. London: HMSO.

Marx, K. (1974) *Capital, Vol. I*. London: Lawrence and Wishart.

Mayhew, L.H. (1968) *Law and Equal Opportunity: a Study of the MCAD*. Cambridge, Massachusetts: Harvard University Press.

Meehan, E.M. (1985) *Women's Rights at Work*. Harmondsworth: Penguin.

Miller, S.M. (1974) 'A Critique of the US Experience', pp. 29–40 in H. Glennerster and S. Hatch (eds), *Positive Discrimination and Inequality*. Fabian Research series No 314. London: Fabian Society.

Moore, R. and Wybrow, P. (1984) *Women in the North Sea Oil Industry*. Manchester: Equal Opportunities Commission.

Napier, B.W. (1979) 'The French Labour Courts', *Modern Law Review*, 42: 270–84.

New Law Journal (1979) 'Class Actions and Access to Justice', 6 September: 870.

New Law Journal (1982) 'A Matter of Principle', 1 July: 622.

Novarra, V. (1980) *Women's Work, Men's Work*. London: Marion Boyars.

Pannick, D. (1985) *Sex Discrimination Law*. Oxford: Clarendon Press.

Pattullo, P. (1983) *Judging Women*. London: National Council for Civil Liberties.

Phillips, The Hon Mr Justice (1978) 'Some Notes on the Employment Appeal Tribunal', *Industrial Law Journal*, 7(3): 137–42.

Rights of Women Europe (1983) *Women's Rights and the EEC*. London: ROW Europe.

Riley, D. (1979) 'War in the Nursery', *Feminist Review*, 2: 82–108.

Robarts, S. (1981) 'Account of the Thames Television Positive Action Project, 1980–1' (mimeographed).

Robbins, D. (1986) *Wanted: Railman: Report of an Investigation into Equal Opportunities for Women in British Rail*. London: HMSO.

Rubenstein, M. (1983) 'The Law of Sexual Harassment at Work', *Industrial Law Journal*, 12(1): 1–16.

Sachs, A. and Wilson, J.H. (1978) *Sexism and the Law*. Oxford: Martin Robertson.

Sacks, V. (1986) 'The Equal Opportunities Commission — Ten Years On', *Modern Law Review*, 49(5): 560–92.

Scheingold, S.A. (1974) *The Politics of Right*. New Haven: Yale University Press.

Sedley, A. and Benn, M. (1984) *Sexual Harassment at Work*. London: National Council for Civil Liberties.

Singer, L.R. (1973) 'Women and the Correctional Process', *American Criminal Law Review*, 11(2): 295–308.

Smart, C. (1984) *The Ties that Bind*. London: Routledge & Kegan Paul.

Snell, M. (1979) 'The Equal Pay and Sex Discrimination Acts: their Impact in the Workplace', *Feminist Review*, 1: 37–57.

Snell, M., Glucklich, P. and Povall, M. (1981) 'Equal Pay and Opportunities', Research Paper No 20. London: Department of Employment.

Social Democratic Party (1986) *Citizen's Rights: Policy Document No. 10*. London: SDP.

Stamp, P. and Robarts, S. (1986) *Positive Action: Changing the Workplace for Women*. London: National Council for Civil Liberties.

Taylor, B. (1979) 'The Men are as Bad as their Masters . . .: Socialism, Feminism and Sexual Antagonism in the London Tailoring Trade in the Early 1830s', *Feminist Studies*, 5(1): 7–40.

Temin, C.E. (1973) 'Discriminatory Sentencing of Women Offenders', *American Criminal Law Review*, 11(2): 355–72.

Thompson, D. (1976) 'Women and Nineteenth Century Radical Politics', pp. 112–38 in J. Mitchell and A. Oakley (eds), *The Rights and Wrongs of Women*. Harmondsworth, Penguin.

TUC–Labour Party Liaison Committee (1986) *People at Work: New Rights, New Responsibilities*.

United States Commission on Civil Rights (1970) *The Federal Civil Rights Enforcement Effort*. Washington DC.

Van Bueren, G. (1983) 'Statutory Class Action', *Legal Action Group Bulletin*, August: 7–11.

Wainwright, D. (1986) 'Implementing Equal Opportunity Policies', *Equal Opportunities Review*, 9: 19–22.

Wedderburn, K.W. (1986) *The Worker and the Law*. Harmondsworth: Penguin.

Wedderburn, K.W. and Davies, P.L. (1969) *Employment Grievances and Disputes Procedures in Britain*. Berkeley and Los Angeles: University of California Press.

Widdison, R. (1983) 'Class Actions: A Survey', *New Law Journal*, 2 September: 778–80.

Williams, K. and Lewis, D. (1981) 'The Aftermath of Tribunal Reinstatement and Re-engagement', Research Paper No 23. London: Department of Employment.

Wilson, E. (1980) *Only Halfway to Paradise*. London: Tavistock.

Yale Law Journal (1973) 'The Sexual Segregation of American Prisons', 82: 1229–73.

Index